Also by Steven M. Barrett

Disneyland's Hidden Mickeys:
A Field Guide to Disneyland® Resort's Best Kept
Secrets

Hidden Mickeys Go To Sea:
A Field Guide to the Disney Cruise Line®'s Best Kept
Secrets

HIDDEN MICKEYS

A Field Guide to

Walt Disney

World®'s

Best Kept Secrets

8th Edition

• • • • • • • • • • •

Steven M. Barrett

SMBBooks, Inc.

Hidden Mickeys
A Field Guide to Walt Disney World®'s Best Kept Secrets, 8th edition

by Steven M. Barrett

Published by
SMBBooks
7025 CR 46A, Suite 1071
Lake Mary, FL 32746
http://www.HiddenMickeyGuy.com

Copyright ©2017 by Steven M. Barrett
Eighth Edition
Printed in the U.S.A.
Cover design by Foster & Foster
Interior Design by Starving Artist Design Studio
Maps by Evora Taylor, revised by SMBBooks, Inc.
Library of Congress Control Number: 2017950356
ISBN-13: 978-0-615-27451-5

All rights reserved. No part of this book may be reproduced or transmitted in any form or by any means, electronic or mechanical, including photocopying, recording, or by any information storage and retrieval system, without the express written permission of the publisher, except for the inclusion of brief quotations in a review.

Trademarks, Etc. . . . . .

This book makes reference to various Disney copyrighted characters, trademarks, marks and registered marks owned by The Walt Disney Company and Disney Enterprises, Inc.

All references to these properties, and to The Twilight Zone®, a registered trademark of CBS, Inc., are made solely for editorial purposes. Neither the author nor the publisher makes any commercial claim to their use, and neither is affiliated with either The Walt Disney Company or CBS, Inc. in any way.

About the Author . . . . .

Author Steven M. Barrett paid his first visit
to Walt Disney World in the late 1980s
after attending a conference in Orlando.
He immediately fell under its spell, visiting it
twice yearly with family and friends for the
next several years, offering touring advice
to the less initiated, and reading almost
everything written about the WDW theme
parks. Barrett relocated to the Orlando
area from Houston, Texas and began
visiting the WDW parks every chance he
got to enjoy the attractions, sample the
restaurants, escort visiting friends and
relatives, and find Hidden Mickeys! Over
the years, he accumulated an extensive
file of Hidden Mickey sightings which he
organized into the Hidden Mickeys Field
Guides to Walt Disney World, Disneyland,
and the Disney Cruise Line. The books are
organized as Hidden Mickey scavenger
hunts arranged to help you spend the least
possible time waiting in line as you hunt for
the elusive Mouse.

Note: Since Mickey reserves the right to
come and go as he—and Disney—pleases,
these guides require periodic updates.
You hold in your hand the Eighth Edition
of *Hidden Mickeys: A Field Guide to
Walt Disney World®'s Best Kept Secrets,*
updated to include all the latest Mickey
sightings all over Walt Disney World. Enjoy
your hunts!

Dedication . . . .

I dedicate this book to my wife Vickie and our son Steven, who willingly accompanied me on countless research visits to Walt Disney World and added invaluable insight to this book. Furthermore, updating this book would not be possible without the many wonderful Hidden Mickey fans I've met through my website and in the Disney parks.

Thank You, My Fellow
Hidden Mickey Hunters

Scores of dedicated Mickey sleuths have helped me find the elusive Mouse in WDW. Thanks to each and every one of you. You'll find your names in the Acknowledgements, beginning on page 318.

★　　★　　★　　★

Finding Mickey
Without Scavenger Hunting

Want to look for Hidden Mickeys in an attraction, restaurant, shop, or resort without scavenger hunting? Turn to the Index on page 332. If Mickey is hiding there, the Index will direct you to the page(s) with the appropriate Clues. If the venue isn't listed, Mickey isn't hiding there. Or if he is, I haven't yet found him.

★　　★　　★　　★

Hidden Mickeys Are Elusive

New Hidden Mickeys appear from time to time and old ones may disappear (see page 19, the paragraph above "My Selection Process"). When that happens—and it will—I will let you know on my website:

www.HiddenMickeyGuy.com

So if you can't find a Mickey—or if you're looking for just a few more—be sure to check out the website.

– Steve Barrett

Table of Contents . . . . . .

Maps

Tip: To find a specific attraction, restaurant, shop, or resort, turn to the Index, page 332.

Read This First!

My guess is that you have visited Disney World before, perhaps many times. But if I've guessed wrong, and this is your first visit, then this note is for you.

Searching for Hidden Mickeys is lots of fun. But it's not a substitute for letting the magic of Disney sweep over you as you experience Walt Disney World (WDW) for the first time. For one thing, the scavenger hunts I present in this book do not include all the attractions in WDW. That's because some of them don't have Hidden Mickeys! For another, this book doesn't cover many things the first-time visitor should know and do to make that first trip to Disney World as magical as possible.

That doesn't mean you can't search for Hidden Mickeys, too. Just follow the suggestions in Chapter One of this book for "Finding Hidden Mickeys Without Scavenger Hunting."

Chapter 1

Hidden Mickey Mania

• • • • • • • • • • • •

Have you ever marveled at a "Hidden Mickey"? People in the know often shout with glee when they recognize one. Some folks are so involved with discovering them that Hidden Mickeys can be visualized where none actually exist. These outbreaks of Hidden Mickey mania are confusing to the unenlightened. So let's get enlightened!

Here's the definition of an official Hidden Mickey: a partial or complete image of Mickey Mouse that has been hidden by Disney's Imagineers and artists in the designs of Disney attractions, hotels, restaurants, and other areas. These images are designed to blend into their surroundings. Sharp-eyed visitors have the fun of finding them.

The practice probably started as an inside joke among the Imagineers (the designers and builders of Disney attractions). According to Disney guru Jim Hill (JimHillMedia.com), Hidden Mickeys originated in the late 1970s or early 1980s, when Disney management wanted to restrict Disney characters like Mickey and Minnie to the Magic Kingdom. The Imagineers designing Epcot couldn't resist slipping Mickey into the new park, and thus "Hidden Mickeys" were born. Guests and "Cast Members" (Disney employees) started spotting them and the concept took on a life of its own. Today, Hidden Mickeys are anticipated in any new construction at Walt Disney World, and Hidden Mickey fans can't wait to find them.

Walt Disney World's Hidden Mickeys

Hidden Mickeys come in all sizes and many forms. The most common is an outline of Mickey's head formed by three intersecting circles, one for Mickey's round head and two for his round ears. Among Hidden Mickey fans, this image is known as the "classic" Hidden Mickey, a term I will adopt in this book. Other Hidden Mickeys include a side or oblique (usually three-quarter) profile of Mickey's face and head, a side profile of his entire body, a full-length silhouette of his body seen from the front, a detailed picture of his face or body, or a three-dimensional Mickey Mouse. Sometimes just his gloves, handprints, shoes, or ears appear. Even his name or initials in unusual places may qualify as a Hidden Mickey.

And it's not just Mickeys that are hidden. The term "Hidden Mickey" also applies to hidden images of other popular characters. There are Hidden Minnies, Hidden Donald Ducks, Hidden Goofys, and other Hidden Characters in Disney World, and I include many of them in this book.

The sport of finding Hidden Mickeys has caught on and adds even more interest to an already fun-filled Walt Disney World vacation. This book is your "field guide" to more than 1,100 Hidden Mickeys in WDW. To add to the fun, instead of just describing them, I've organized them into six scavenger hunts, one for each of the major theme parks, one for the Walt Disney World Resort hotels, and one for all the rest of WDW: the water parks, Disney Springs, and beyond. The hunts are designed for maximum efficiency so that you can spend your time looking for Mickeys rather than cooling your heels in lines. Follow the Clues and you will find the best Hidden Mickeys WDW has to offer. If you have trouble spotting a particular Hidden Mickey (some are extraordinarily well-camouflaged!) you can turn to the Hints at the end of each scavenger hunt for

12

Chapter 1: Hidden Mickey Mania

a fuller description.

Scavenger Hunting
for Hidden Mickeys

To have the most fun and find the most Mickeys, follow these tips:

★ *Reserve FastPass+ attractions before your visit* to Walt Disney World to speed your hunts in the parks. Keep in mind, however, that many great Hidden Mickeys can only be seen from the Standby (regular) queue. You'll miss them if you take the FastPass+ route. Therefore, I recommend reserving FastPass+ for the following:

• At Magic Kingdom: *Buzz Lightyear's Space Ranger Spin, Peter Pan's Flight,* and the *Tomorrowland Speedway*.

• At Epcot: *Mission: SPACE* (choose orange level for more intense, or green level for less intense), *Spaceship Earth,* and *Living with the Land*.

• At Disney's Hollywood Studios: *The Twilight Zone Tower of Terror, Voyage of The Little Mermaid,* and *Fantasmic!*.

• At Disney's Animal Kingdom: *Kilimanjaro Safaris, Festival of the Lion King,* and *Finding Nemo—The Musical*.

★ *Arrive early* for the theme park hunts, say 30 minutes before opening time (either opening time for Extra Magic Hour - if you qualify - or "official" opening time. If you don't qualify for Extra Magic Hours, don't visit a park on an Extra Magic Hour day). Pick up a Guidemap and a Times Guide and plot your course. Then look for Hidden Mickeys in the waiting area while you wait for the rope to drop. You'll find the Clues for those areas by checking the *Index to Mickey's Hiding Places* in the back of this book. Look under "Entrance areas." If you arrive later in the day, skip down a few

Walt Disney World's Hidden Mickeys
Clues to try to stay ahead of the crowds.

★ "Clues" and "Hints"
Clues under each attraction will guide
you to the Hidden Mickey(s). If you have
trouble spotting them, you can turn to the
Hints at the end of the hunt for a fuller
description. The Clues and Hints are
numbered consecutively, that is, Hint 1
goes with Clue 1, so it's easy to find the
right Hint if you need it. In some cases (*The
Great Movie Ride* in Disney's Hollywood
Studios is a good example), you may have
to ride the attraction more than once to
find all the Hidden Mickeys.

★ Scoring
All Hidden Mickeys are fun to find, but
all Hidden Mickeys aren't the same.
Some are easier to spot than others. I
assign point values to Hidden Mickeys,
identifying them as easy to find (a value of
1 point) to difficult to find the first time (5
points). I also consider the complexity and
uniqueness of the image: the more complex
or unique the Hidden Mickey, the higher
the point value. For example, the brilliantly
camouflaged Mickey hiding in The Garden
Grill Restaurant mural in Epcot is a five-
pointer.

★ Playing the game
You can hunt solo or with others;
competitively or just for fun. There's room
to tally your score in the guide. Families
with young children may want to focus on
one- and two-point Mickeys that the little
ones will have no trouble spotting. (Of
course, little ones tend to be sharp-eyed, so
they may spot familiar shapes before you
do in some of the more complex patterns.)
Or you may want to split your party into
teams and see who can rack up the most
points (in which case, you'll probably want
to have a guide for each team).

Of course, you don't have to play the
game at all. You can simply look for

Hidden Mickeys in attractions as you come to them (see "Finding Hidden Mickeys Without Scavenger Hunting," below).

★ *Following the Clues*

The hunts often call for crisscrossing the parks. This may seem illogical at first, but trust me, it will tend to keep you ahead of the crowds. Besides, it adds to the fun of the hunt and, if you're playing competitively, keeps everyone on their toes. Warning: Many Hidden Mickeys are waiting to be found in the Disney Parks, and depending on the crowds and the park hours when you visit, you may not be able to complete the Scavenger Hunt in one day!

★ *Waiting in line*

Don't waste time in lines. If the wait is longer than 15 minutes, get a FastPass+ (if available and you're eligible) and move on to the next attraction. The lines at popular attractions should not be too long if you start your scavenger hunt when the park opens and follow the hunt Clues as given. If you do encounter long lines, come back later during a parade or in the hour before the park closes. Alternatively, if you need to board an attraction with a long wait without a FastPass+, use the Single Rider queue if available (check your Guidemap for a big "S" symbol next to the attraction).

★ *Playing fair*

Be considerate of other guests. Many Hidden Mickeys are in restaurants and shops. Ask a Cast Member's permission before searching inside sit-down restaurants, and avoid the busy mealtime hours unless you are one of the diners. Tell the Cast Members and other guests who see you looking around what you're up to, so they can share in the fun. (Note: Some restaurants, such as the Coral Reef, do not welcome drop-in Hidden Mickey Hunters. I don't include these restaurants in the Hunts, but I do post their Hidden Mickeys on my website, www.HiddenMickeyGuy.com, so you can search inside if you have dining reservations.)

Finding Hidden Mickeys
Without Scavenger Hunting

If scavenger hunts don't appeal to you, you don't have to use them. You can find Hidden Mickeys in the specific rides and other attractions you visit by using the *Index to Mickey's Hiding Places* in the back of this book. For easy lookup, in addition to being listed alphabetically, attractions in Magic Kingdom, Epcot, and Disney's Animal Kingdom are listed under their appropriate "lands" or "areas" (for example, Fantasyland in Magic Kingdom, Future World East in Epcot, and Asia in Animal Kingdom). In Epcot, attractions are also listed by pavilion. To find Hidden Mickeys in the attraction, restaurant, hotel or shop you are visiting, simply turn to the *Index*, locate the appropriate page, and follow the Clue(s) to find the Hidden Mickey(s).

Caution: You won't find every WDW attraction, restaurant, hotel or shop in the Index. Only those with confirmed Hidden Mickeys are included in this guide.

Hidden Mickeys, "Gray Zone" Mickeys,
Wishful Thinking

The classic (three-circle) Mickeys are the most controversial, for good reason. Much debate surrounds the gathering of circular forms throughout Walt Disney World. The sideways classic Mickey made of blue bubbles on the *Living with the Land* entrance-queue wall mural (Clue 89 in the Epcot Scavenger Hunt) is surely the work of a clever artist. However, three-circle configurations occur spontaneously in art and nature, as in collections of grapes, tomatoes, pumpkins, bubbles, oranges, cannonballs, and the like. Unlike the bubbles Hidden Mickey in Epcot, it may be difficult to attribute a random "classic Mickey" configuration of circles to a deliberate Imagineer design.

So which groupings of three circles qualify as Hidden Mickeys as opposed to wishful thinking? (Keep in mind that no master list of actual or "Imagineer-approved" Hidden Mickeys exists). Purists demand that a true classic Hidden Mickey should have proper proportions and positioning. The round head must be larger than the ear circles (so that three equal circles in the proper alignment would not qualify as a Hidden Mickey). The head and ears must be touching and in perfect position for Mickey's head and ears.

On the other hand, Disney's recent mantra is: "If the guest thinks it's a Hidden Mickey, then by golly it is one!" Of course, I appreciate Disney's respect for their guests' opinions. However, when the subject is Hidden Mickeys, let's apply some guidelines. My own criteria are looser than the purists' but stricter than the "anything goes" Disney approach. I prefer to use a few sensible guidelines.

To be classified as a real classic Hidden Mickey, the three circles should satisfy the following criteria:

1. Purposeful (sometimes you can sense that the circles were placed on purpose).

2. Proportionate sizes (head larger than the ears and somewhat proportionate to the ears).

3. Round or at least "roundish."

4. The ears don't touch each other, and the ears are above the head (not beside the head).

5. The head and ears touch or are close to touching.

17

6. The grouping of circles is exceptional or unique in appearance.

7. The circles are hidden or somewhat hidden and not obviously intended to be part of the décor.

Having spelled out some ground rules, allow me to now bend the rules in one instance. Some Hidden Mickeys are sentimental favorites with Disney fans, even though they may actually represent "wishful thinking." (My neighbor, Lew Brooks, calls them "two-beer Mickeys.") Who am I to defy tradition? For example, the small circles in the tile floor at the entrance of *Rock 'n' Roller Coaster* are all the same size. Nevertheless, although the image doesn't meet our classic Mickey criteria, many guests and Cast Members call the tile image a Hidden Mickey. So, I include the tile floor Mickey in the Disney's Hollywood Studios Scavenger Hunt in Chapter 4 (Clue 9).

Hidden Mickeys vs. Decorative Mickeys

Some Mickeys are truly hidden, not visible to the tourist. They may be located behind the scenes, accessible only to Cast Members. You won't find them in this field guide, as I only include Hidden Mickeys that are accessible to the guest. Other Mickeys are decorative; they were placed in plain sight to enhance the décor. For example, in a restaurant, I consider a pat of butter shaped like Mickey Mouse to be a decorative (aka décor) Mickey. Disney World is loaded with decorative Mickeys. You'll find obvious images of Mickey Mouse on items such as manhole covers, displays in shop windows, and restaurant menus. I do not include these ubiquitous and sometimes changing images in this book unless they are unique or hard to spot.

Hidden Mickeys Can Change with Time

Hidden Mickeys can change or be accidentally removed over time, by the process of nature or by the continual cleaning and refurbishing that goes on at Disney World. For example, the "Steamboat Willie" Hidden Mickey in the star map in Mickey's Star Traders shop in Tomorrowland disappeared when the shop was remodeled. Moreover, Cast Members themselves sometimes create or remove Hidden Mickeys.

My Selection Process

I trust you've concluded by now that Hidden Mickey Science is a dynamic and ever-changing specialty. Which raises the question, how did I choose the Hidden Mickeys in the scavenger hunts in this guide?

I compiled my list of Hidden Mickeys from all resources to which I had access: my own sightings, friends, family, Cast Members, websites, and books. (Cast Members in each specific area usually—but not always!—know where some Hidden Mickeys are located.) Then I embarked on my own hunts, and I took along friends or family to verify my sightings. I have included only those Hidden Mickeys I could verify.

Furthermore, some Hidden Mickeys are visible only intermittently or only from certain vantage points in ride vehicles. I don't generally include these Mickeys, unless I feel that adequate descriptions will allow anyone to find them. So the scavenger hunts include only those images I believe to be recognizable as Hidden Mickeys and visible to the general touring guest. It is likely, though, that one or more of the Hidden Mickeys described in this book will disappear over time.

Walt Disney World's Hidden Mickeys

I'll try to let you know when I discover that a Hidden Mickey has disappeared for good by posting the information on my website:

www.HiddenMickeyGuy.com

If you find one missing before I do, please email me care of my website to let me know.

I have enjoyed finding each and every Hidden Mickey in this book. I'm certain I'll find more as time goes by, and I hope you can spot new Hidden Mickeys during your visit.

So put on some comfortable walking shoes and experience Walt Disney World like you never have before!

Happy Hunting!

— *Steve Barrett*

Chapter 2

Magic Kingdom Scavenger Hunt

• • • • • • • • • • • •

Before You Start

• *Prior to your visit, try for Advance Lunch Reservations at* **Be Our Guest Restaurant**. *Otherwise, try to line up for lunch there as covered later in the Scavenger Hunt.*

• *Many great Hidden Mickeys are in Standby queues, and you might miss them if you take the FastPass+ queues. So, for optimal Hidden Mickey hunting, I recommend reserving FastPass+ for the following rides:* **Buzz Lightyear's Space Ranger Spin, Peter Pan's Flight,** *and* **Tomorrowland Speedway.**

Be sure to keep track of your three FastPass+ windows and return to those attractions at the appropriate times. In the Scavenger Hunt below, if you come to your FastPass+ attraction and it's not time for it yet, you can skip to the next stop in the Hunt and return to the FastPass+ attraction during your time window.

• *Some of the Hidden Mickeys in this park are in restaurants and shops. Be considerate of fellow guests and Cast Members as you search. Tell them what you're looking for, so they can share in the fun.*

★ Ride the *ferryboat* to and/or from the Magic Kingdom to the Transportation and Ticket Center (TTC).

Clue 1: As you walk onto or off of the ferry, look around for a classic Mickey. 4 points for one or more

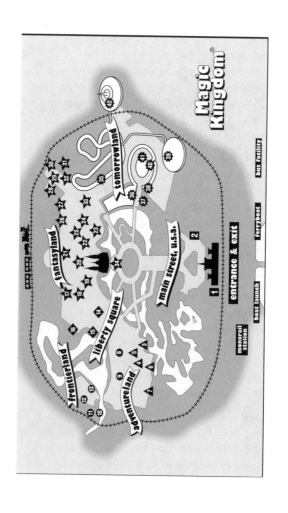

Chapter 2: Magic Kingdom Scavenger Hunt

main street, u.s.a

1. WDW Railroad
2. Mickey's Meet 'N Greet in Town Square Theater

adventureland

3. Swiss Family Treehouse
4. Walt Disney's Enchanted Tiki Room
5. The Magic Carpets of Aladdin
6. Jungle Cruise
7. Pirates of the Caribbean

frontierland

8. Frontierland Shootin' Arcade
9. Country Bear Jamboree
10. Splash Mountain
11. WDW Railroad
12. Big Thunder Mountain Railroad
13. Raft to Tom Sawyer Island

liberty square

14. The Hall of Presidents
15. Liberty Square Riverboat
16. Haunted Mansion

fantasyland

17. "it's a small world"
18. Peter Pan's Flight
19. Mickey's PhilharMagic
20. Prince Charming Regal Carrousel
21. Enchanted Tales with Belle
22. Princess Fairytale Hall
23. Fairytale Garden
24. The Many Adventures of Winnie the Pooh
25. Seven Dwarfs Mine Train
26. Under the Sea ~ Journey of The Little Mermaid
27. Ariel's Grotto
28. Pete's Silly Sideshow
29. Casey Jr. Splash 'N' Soak Station
30. WDW Railroad
31. The Barnstormer
32. Dumbo the Flying Elephant
33. Mad Tea Party
34. Castle Forecourt Stage

tomorrowland

35. Tomorrowland Speedway
36. Stitch's Great Escape!
37. Monsters, Inc. Laugh Floor
38. Buzz Lightyear's Space Ranger Spin
39. Walt Disney's Carousel of Progress
40. Tomorrowland Transit Authority PeopleMover
41. Astro Orbiter
42. Space Mountain

23

Walt Disney World's Hidden Mickeys

Clue 2: If you happen to ride the General Joe Potter ferryboat to or from the Magic Kingdom, study the inside walls for a Hidden Mickey.
5 bonus points

Clue 3: As you approach the entrance gates, look down for Mickey under your feet.
3 points

★ Check your Times Guide for any morning, afternoon, and evening parades, shows, and fireworks. There are generally both decorative and Hidden Mickeys in the shows and on the floats, vehicles, and banners.

Tip: For Hidden Mickeys in the current parades and shows, click to the "General Magic Kingdom" section from the Catalog page of www.HiddenMickeyGuy.com

Clue 4: Once you are in the park, examine the scrollwork of the roof of the Main Street Train Station.
2 points

★ If the rest of the park is not open yet, you may want to hunt for Hidden Mickeys on *Main Street, U.S.A.* (See Clues 187 to 202.)

★ Head for Fantasyland and *Seven Dwarfs Mine Train*.

Clue 5: Stay alert for a smiling Hidden Mickey above you in the first part of the outside Standby queue. (Tip: he's above a lantern).
5 points

Clue 6: Study the gems along the Standby entrance queue.
4 points for one or more images

Clue 7: On the ride, check out a Hidden Mickey next to Dopey.

Chapter 2: Magic Kingdom Scavenger Hunt

5 points

Clue 8: Watch for Grumpy on your right side. Do you see a Hidden Mickey near him?
5 points

Clue 9: Don't miss Oswald the Lucky Rabbit on your left side. He's etched in wood on a beam.
5 points

★ Line up for *The Many Adventures of Winnie the Pooh*. Study Mr. Sanders' big tree.

Clue 10: Search for a Mickey made of rocks embedded inside the tree.
3 points

Clue 11: Look for a submarine image in the wood of the tree. (Note: This is a Hidden Tribute rather than a Hidden Mickey.)
4 points

Clue 12: Find a side profile of Mickey in the bark outside.
4 points

Clue 13: Locate Mickey on a wooden post by a window outside.
5 points

Clue 14: Next check out two Hidden Mickeys inside the entryway play area.
4 points for both

★ Now hop in your honey pot and find five Hidden Characters.

Clue 15: Examine a flower-pot marker in Rabbit's Garden.
4 points

Clue 16: In Owl's house, find the picture of Mr. Toad and Owl.
3 points

Clue 17: Near the end of Owl's house,

locate a picture of Mole with Winnie the Pooh.
3 points

★ Walk to Tomorrowland

Clue 18: Look for a shadow on the pavement near the *Tomorrowland Speedway* that's shaped like a classic Mickey.
3 points

★ Now queue up for *Space Mountain*. (You can enjoy the ride after walking through the entrance queue, or exit the attraction just before boarding.)

Clue 19: In the interactive games on the left wall of the entrance queue, pay attention to the space construction objects that guests can move around and interconnect.
5 points

Clue 20: In another interactive game along the queue, be alert for a floating Hidden Mickey.
3 points

Clue 21: Watch the instructional video near the loading dock for two Hidden Mickeys and another Hidden Character.
3 points for each (9 possible points)

★ If you don't have Advance Reservations, amble over to the entrance area for *Be Our Guest Restaurant* at or after 10:30 a.m. and line up for lunch. Otherwise, go at your Reservations time.

Clue 22: As you enter Be Our Guest Restaurant, study the walls behind the suits of armor for some Hidden Mickeys.
3 points for one or more

Clue 23: Search the room to the right for a Hidden Mickey on a suit of armor.
5 points

Clue 24: In the food order room, spot two

Hidden Mickeys on books.
4 points for both

Clue 25: Look for Mickey bubbles on a wall in the Rose Gallery seating area to the right (as you enter the restaurant) of the restaurant's Ballroom.
5 points

Clue 26: Find Mickey in fabric hanging in the West Wing seating area, located to the left of the Ballroom.
5 points

Clue 27: Pay attention as you exit the restaurant and walk along the bridge toward the rest of Fantasyland. Glance to your right before you reach the end of the bridge.
4 points

Clue 28: At the entrance walkway to Be Our Guest Restaurant, examine a short rock wall for a classic Mickey at the side of the check-in station
5 points

★ Return to Tomorrowland.

★ Go to *Buzz Lightyear's Space Ranger Spin* at your allotted FastPass+ time and be on the lookout for ten Hidden Mickeys.

Note: Some of the planets with Hidden Mickeys appear in several places along the entrance queue and on the ride.

Clue 29: Inside the building on the right wall, find the planet with a continent shaped like the side profile of Mickey Mouse.
3 points

Clue 30: On this same poster, spot classic Mickey craters.
3 points

Clue 31: Look for the side-profile Mickey

continent further along the entrance queue to the left.
2 points

Clue 32: Search for a Hidden Mickey in Sector 2 nearby.
3 points

Clue 33: Pay attention to the right wall in the very first interactive room on the ride for two tiny classic Mickeys in the stars. (They're close to one another but tough to spot!)
5 points for each

Clue 34: During the first part of the ride, spot another side profile of Mickey. Look to the left of your vehicle in the room with batteries.
3 points

Clue 35: Also in the battery room, to the right of your vehicle, stare at the star field to the right of the cone over Zurg to find a blue classic Mickey star.
5 points

Clue 36: Catch another view of the planet with a side-profile Mickey in the space video room.
3 points

Clue 37: Just past the space video room, look straight ahead to spot that side-profile Mickey planet one more time.
2 points

★ Cross over to Frontierland and ride *Splash Mountain*.

★ Hop in line and keep your eyes peeled for seven Hidden Mickeys on the ride and at least four more after you exit.

Clue 38: Soon after you start the ride, search for barrels that form a classic Mickey.
3 points

28

Chapter 2: Magic Kingdom Scavenger Hunt

Clue 39: Just as your boat goes outside, spot a tiny classic Mickey on a "moonshine" barrel!
5 points

Clue 40: Look for a rabbit with a broom and then try to catch a moving Hidden Mickey silhouette on a wall nearby.
5 points

Clue 41: Just past Brer Frog, find the fishing bobbers that form a Hidden Mickey.
4 points

Clue 42: In the room with jumping water, spot the hanging rope classic Mickey.
4 points

Clue 43: As your boat ascends toward the big drop, look toward the opening for a side profile of Mickey's face.
3 points

Clue 44: In the riverboat scene after the big drop, admire the full-body Hidden Mickey in the clouds.
5 points

Clue 45: Along the exit walkway, look for the birdhouse with at least two acorn classic Mickeys.
3 points for two or more

Clue 46: Do you see a Hidden Mickey in the children's play area along the exit?
3 points

Clue 47: After the ride, take another look at the mountain from the outside viewing area to spot that Clue 50 side profile (again).
3 points

★ Now get in line to ride *Big Thunder Mountain Railroad*.

Clue 48: During the first climb, search the cavern floor to the right of the coaster.

Walt Disney World's Hidden Mickeys
4 points

Clue 49: Study the reddish rock along the exit walkway for a Hidden Tinker Bell.
4 points

★ Go to *Peter Pan's Flight* at your FastPass+ time.

Clue 50: Study the overhead attraction sign at the entrance for two decent Mickey images.
5 points for spotting both

★ Clue 51: If you're lucky, you may spot Mickey on the rotating moon and earn yourself some bonus points.
5 bonus points

Clue 52: Search for a classic Mickey near mermaids.
3 points

Clue 53: Squint your eyes for two shadow Hidden Mickeys near two different sets of cannonballs.
5 points for each one

★ From near *Big Thunder Mountain Railroad*, float on the *raft* over *to Tom Sawyer Island*.

Clue 54: Look across the river for a classic Mickey rock formation at the right end of the bridge in Frontierland. (Note: This Hidden Mickey is also visible from the *Liberty Square Riverboat*.)
4 points

Clue 55: Search one of the caves for Goofy.
3 points

Clue 56: In Fort Langhorn, look around in the rear right Rifle Roost for a Mickey in wood.
4 points

Clue 57: Also inside the Fort, admire the

display inside the Blacksmith's shop for a
Hidden Mickey.
3 points

★ Now hop on *Jungle Cruise* and search
for four Hidden Mickeys, two Hidden
Donalds, and a Hidden Minnie.

Clue 58: Study the sign outside for a
Hidden Mickey.
2 points

Clue 59: Along the Standby entrance
queue, look for a map with a Hidden
Mickey.
4 points

Clue 60: Study a tree across the river from
the loading dock for a small white classic
Mickey.
4 points

Clue 61: Watch for Donald Duck's face on
a canoe.
4 points

Clue 62: Stay alert for a Hidden Mickey on
an airplane.
4 points

Clue 63: Search the riverbanks for Donald
Duck's face on a native.
4 points

Clue 64: Coming out of the temple, look
hard at the first undecorated column on the
left for a chipped area of brick that forms
part of a profile of Minnie Mouse's head
and face. (This is a tough one!)
5 points

★ Walk to *Pirates of the Caribbean* and
find three Hidden Mickeys along the
left entrance queue. Then find six classic
Hidden Mickeys on the ride and four more
after the ride.

Clue 65: Look near a faux fireplace along

the queue for a Hidden Mickey. (This image is fading with time).
5 points

Clue 66: Now search for two classic Mickey locks in the left queue.
4 points for spotting both

Clue 67: If Davy Jones appears in the mist on the ride, look up for a classic Mickey. (Note: you may see Blackbeard instead.)
5 bonus points

Clue 68: Watch for a Hidden Mickey in front of a window to your left.
5 points

Clue 69: Try to spot the classic Mickey shadow above the drunken pirate's cat.
4 points

Clue 70: Near the end of the ride, look left at the recessed doors in the wall.
4 points

Clue 71: Don't miss an image to the right of the treasure room.
4 points

Clue 72: Now glance at the wall behind Jack Sparrow.
4 points

Clue 73: As you exit the ride, search for some coins and jewels.
5 points for both

Clue 74: In the gift shop, spot a classic Mickey in a painting.
3 points

Clue 75: Outside the attraction entrance, look around for a Hidden Mickey on a cart.
3 points

★ Stop by the *Frontierland Shootin' Arcade*.

Chapter 2: Magic Kingdom Scavenger Hunt

Clue 76: Find a classic Mickey in front of the target area.
1 point

★ Then turn right to *Liberty Square* and cross the street.

Clue 77: Find the classic Mickey near the *Liberty Square Riverboat* entrance.
1 point

★ Head for *Haunted Mansion* in Liberty Square. Find six classic Mickeys, two Donald Ducks, and a Mr. Toad!

Clue 78: Along the interactive "Scenic" left-side entrance queue, search for a Mickey made of barnacles.
4 points

Clue 79: In the first room inside the entrance, look for some classic Mickeys in the border design around a portrait.
3 points

Clue 80: During the ride, be alert for Donald Duck on two different chairs.
4 points each

Clue 81: Find the Mickey on the ghostly banquet table.
2 points

Clue 82: Spot plates on the floor in the attic.
4 points

Clue 83: Look closely to your far right at the "Grim Reaper" by the opera-singing lady.
5 points

Clue 84: Outside, as you exit, look for a classic Mickey next to a gate.
3 points

Clue 85: Find Mr. Toad along the exit walkway.

Walt Disney World's Hidden Mickeys
3 points

★ Enter *Columbia Harbour House* restaurant and look for a classic Hidden Mickey. (Be considerate of the diners.)

Clue 86: Check the art on the downstairs walls.
2 points

★ At your FastPass+ Time, cross over to Tomorrowland and go to the *Tomorrowland Speedway*. (Exit before boarding the ride after you find the FastPass+ Hidden Mickeys.)

Clue 87: Spot two classic Hidden Mickeys on a wall in the FastPass+ queue.
5 points for both

★ At a FastPass+ kiosk, or on your mobile device "My Disney Experience" app, try for a FastPass+ for either *Princess Fairytale Hall* or *Ariel's Grotto*. Keep in mind that now, after you use any new FastPass+, you can then try to get another one.

★ Walk to *Under the Sea ~ Journey of The Little Mermaid*. Spend some time in the Standby entrance queue to find all the great Hidden Mickeys here (let people walk by you in line if you need to).

Note: Many collections of circular rock impressions in both the entrance and exit areas and inside this attraction suggest classic Hidden Mickeys. I include below my favorite images, which seem intentional.

Clue 88: Spot a Hidden Mickey on a rock just outside the Standby entrance queue.
4 points

Clue 89: In the outside Standby queue, be alert for another Hidden Mickey on a rock in the lagoon near a waterfall.
5 points

Clue 90: Gaze way above and to the right of the rock in the lagoon to find another classic Hidden Mickey on the rock wall.
5 points

Clue 91: Look down over the right side of a bridge railing for a classic Hidden Mickey.
5 points

Clue 92: Now stare high above this railing for a small classic Hidden Mickey in the rock.
5 points

Clue 93: Also in the outside Standby queue, study the rock walls for a submarine image. (Not a Hidden Mickey, but an awesome Hidden Image!)
5 points

Clue 94: Just before you enter the inside portion of the queue, stop and look above and behind you for a three-circle Hidden Mickey impressed in the rock.
5 points

Clue 95: In the inside Standby entrance queue, at a large opening in the rock ceiling on your right and just past a carved wooden figure, stay alert for a classic Mickey in light on the lower wall to your left. This Hidden Mickey is designed to appear only on November 18 (Mickey's birthday) around noon, but it just might appear other times of the year!
10 bonus points

Clue 96: Along the inside Standby entrance queue, find a Hidden Mickey in the rock wall above some bottles on your left.
5 points

Clue 97: Search for Mickey on the ceiling just as you enter the room with Scuttle, the talking seagull.
5 points

Clue 98: On the ride, look for a purple-coral classic Mickey on your right.
5 points

Clue 99: Keep your eyes peeled and gaze to the left side to spot a green fish with a Hidden Mickey.
4 points

Clue 100: Don't miss the frogs with Hidden Mickeys!
4 points for one or more

Clue 101: Along the inside exit walkway, study the wall near the floor to your left for Mickey.
4 points for one or more

Clue 102: Look through the large opening in the exit walkway's left wall for another classic Hidden Mickey.
4 points

Clue 103: Outside the cave exit, look around for Steamboat Willie!
5 points

★ Go to *"it's a small world"* and try to spot two classic Hidden Mickeys.

Clue 104: In the Africa room, look up at the vine with purple leaves.
3 points

Clue 105: In the South Pacific Room, search for an animal classic Mickey.
3 points

★ Walk over to the *"Tangled" Tower restroom area*.

Clue 106: Spot a Hidden Mickey on a wall poster.
3 points

Clue 107: Check out a wall of the women's restroom for a Hidden Mickey. (You can see this wall from outside the restroom).

Chapter 2: Magic Kingdom Scavenger Hunt
4 points

★ Head *toward Peter Pan's Flight*.

Clue 108: Find grapes arranged like a classic Mickey.
2 points

★ Enter *Pinocchio Village Haus* restaurant.

Clue 109: Look for a tiny, dark classic Mickey on the wall near the exit to the restrooms.
4 points

Clue 110: Locate a minuscule, white classic Mickey near the word "All."
4 points

Clue 111: Keep searching this wall for another tiny, white classic Mickey at the other side of the same mural.
5 points

★ Walk to *Sir Mickey's Store*.

Clue 112: Observe a classic Mickey outside the store.
1 point

Clue 113: Gaze inside a display window of the store to find more classic Mickeys.
4 points for two or more

★ Enter the *Castle Couture* shop.

Clue 114: Search high on a wall for a bronze frieze with a tiny classic Mickey on a bush.
5 points

★ Go to *The Hall of Presidents* in Liberty Square. (After spotting the Hidden Mickey, you can exit before the show.)

Clue 115: In the waiting room for the show, study the paintings for a tiny classic Mickey.

Walt Disney World's Hidden Mickeys
4 points

★ Check the shields on the *Adventureland bridge to the Hub*. (The Hub is in front of Cinderella Castle.)

Clue 116: Find two Hidden Mickeys.
3 points for both

★ Enjoy *Walt Disney's Enchanted Tiki Room*.

Clue 117: Find classic Mickeys at the bottom of two bird perches. One is in the left corner as you enter, and you'll find the other in the right corner as you exit.
3 points each

Clue 118: Near the entrance to *Walt Disney's Enchanted Tiki Room*, look around for a Hidden Mickey on a statue.
3 points

Clue 119: Study the cement for a tiny classic Mickey between the Agrabah Bazaar shop and *The Magic Carpets of Aladdin* ride.
4 points

★ Walk to Fantasyland to see *Mickey's PhilharMagic*.

Clue 120: In the first waiting area inside, squint at the wall mural.
4 points for two or more

Clue 121: Inside the main theater, examine the border of the video screen.
2 points

Clue 122: In the show, look for a shadow Mickey on a table.
4 points

Clue 123: Stare at Ariel's jewels for a classic Mickey in a ring.
5 points

Clue 124: In "The Lion King" segment,

38

watch for orange treetops that form classic Mickeys at times.
5 points

Clue 125: Keep alert for a classic Mickey during the magic carpet ride.
5 points

Clue 126: Stop in the gift shop at the exit and find a classic Mickey.
2 points

★ Go to *Ariel's Grotto* or *Princess Fairytale Hall.* at your FastPass+ time (if you have one). Choose the left queue - usually Rapunzel - at *Princess Fairytale Hall*. If you don't have a FastPass+, try to get one. After you go FastPass+ for one of them, then get a FastPass+ for the other one. You can see the Hidden Mickey from the Standby queue at *Princess Fairytale Hall*, but you need to be in the FastPass+ queue in *Ariel's Grotto* to find the Hidden Mickey there.

Clue 127: At *Ariel's Grotto*, examine the short rock wall along the FastPass+ entrance queue for a Hidden Mickey.
4 points

Clue 128: At *Princess Fairytale Hall*, keep your eyes peeled for a painting on a wall with a Hidden Mickey.
5 points

★ Now cross the park to Tomorrowland and go to *Tomorrowland Transit Authority PeopleMover*. Find a Hidden Mickey as you ride.

Clue 129: In the last part of the ride, observe the accessories of the woman getting her hair done.
3 points

★ Scan the wall mural inside *Mickey's Star Traders* shop.

Clue 130: Look for the train on the mural.
2 points

Clue 131: Find the Hidden Stitch.
3 points

Clue 132: Spot Mickey hats on a building.
2 points

Clue 133: Look up higher at the satellite dishes.
2 points

Clue 134: Scan the road layout.
3 points

Clue 135: Find three clear domes.
2 points

Clue 136: Follow the mural around to another classic Mickey on a building.
1 point

★ Stroll toward *Space Mountain* and into the *Tomorrowland "Cool Scanner" Station*.

Clue 137: Look up for tiny Hidden Mickeys.
3 points for one or more

★ Go to *Walt Disney's Carousel of Progress*. Check the first scene for Clue 138, the third scene for Clue 139, the last scene for Clues 140 to 146, and the exit for Clue 147.

Clue 138: Admire a classic Mickey on a mirror.
3 points

Clue 139: Search for Mickey's blue hat.
4 points

Clue 140: Observe a painting on the rear wall.
4 points

Clue 141: Find a Mickey nutcracker.
2 points

Clue 142: Spot a Mickey Mouse doll.
2 points

Clue 143: Search around for green Mickey ears.
3 points

Clue 144: Look fast for a classic Mickey on a spaceship.
5 points

Clue 145: View objects with Mickey ears in the kitchen.
3 points

Clue 146: Squint for a tiny classic Mickey in a basket.
5 points

Clue 147: Don't miss Hidden Mickeys along the exit walkway.
2 points

★ Walk to the far side of *Astro Orbiter* and search carefully for a small classic Mickey traced in the cement nearby.

Clue 148: Check the side facing *Space Mountain*.
5 points

★ Go to the outside of the *Monsters, Inc. Laugh Floor*.

Clue 149: Find the moon with classic Mickey craters.
1 point

Clue 150: Spot the asteroid shaped like a classic Mickey.
1 point

★ Get in line for *Monsters, Inc. Laugh Floor*. (After finding the Hidden Mickey, you can exit before the show or stick around and enjoy the jokes.)

Clue 151: As you enter the waiting area,

search for a classic Mickey in a window display.
4 points

★ Eat dinner - one option: The Columbia Harbour House.

★ Head for Fantasyland and join the Standby queue for *Enchanted Tales with Belle*.

Clue 152: In Maurice's cottage, study the window glass to the left. Can you see a Disney Character?
5 points

Clue 153: Look near the fireplace in the first room for two Hidden Mickeys.
5 points for both

Clue 154: Search below your feet in the Wardrobe Room for a Hidden Mickey.
3 points for one or more

Clue 155: Spot Hidden Mickeys on a book near the back wall of the Library.
5 points for both

★ Stroll over to Town Square Theater on Main Street, U.S.A. and visit *Mickey's Meet 'N' Greet*. (Hidden Mickeys in here change at times).

Clue 156: In the queue, look for some special mail.
2 points

Clue 157: In Mickey's Room, find a Hidden Mickey made of rings.
2 points

Clue 158: Spot another classic Mickey in Mickey's magic chest. (It's sometimes covered by a scarf.)
2 points

Clue 159: Don't miss Oswald the Lucky Rabbit!

Chapter 2: Magic Kingdom Scavenger Hunt
4 points

Clue 160: Look around for Sorcerer
Mickey.
4 points

Clue 161: In the gift shop at the exit, find
Mickey hanging on a table and on a
nearby tall display case.
3 points for both

Clue 162: In the gift shop, search for
Mickey on a house.
3 points

★ Check out *Fairytale Garden*.

Clue 163: Find a classic Mickey on a light
pole.
3 points

Clue 164: Search for a Hidden Character
on a wall.
4 points

★ Now walk to the *exit area* of the
Fantasyland Train Station in Storybook
Circus.

Clue 165: Check the walkway that stretches
from near the train station exit to *Dumbo
the Flying Elephant* for at least two Hidden
Mickeys.
5 points for two or more

★ Stand outside *Casey Jr. Splash 'N' Soak
Station*.

Clue 166: Look over the boxcars in *Casey
Jr. Splash 'N' Soak* for a classic Mickey.
5 points

★ Cruise over to *The Barnstormer*.

Clue 167: Find a classic Mickey near a
picture of Goofy outside *The Barnstormer*.
3 points

Walt Disney World's Hidden Mickeys

Clue 168: Study a large billboard outside *The Barnstormer* for a Hidden Mickey.
5 points

★ Walk back to *Pete's Silly Sideshow*.

Clue 169: Search for a classic Mickey on a poster outside *Pete's Silly Sideshow*.
5 points

★ Check out the large tent next to *Pete's Silly Sideshow*.

Clue 170: Locate tiny Mickey balloons.
5 points for finding eight balloons

★ Explore inside the *Big Top Souvenirs* store.

Clue 171: Spot Mickey on an animal on the wall.
5 points

★ Return to the *area near Dumbo the Flying Elephant*.

Clue 172: Look for a classic Mickey near the entrance to the *Dumbo* FastPass+ queue.
3 points

★ Now, over by *Ariel's Grotto* . . .

Clue 173: Find a Hidden Mickey at the Disney Vacation Club kiosk.
2 points

Clue 174: Search for a Hidden Mickey in the walkway near the Disney Vacation Club kiosk.
5 points

★ Locate *Gaston's Statue*.

Clue 175: Study the statue for a Hidden Mickey.
5 points

★ Gaze around inside the *Bonjour Village*

Gifts shop.

Clue 176: Find a Hidden Mickey on a wall.
2 points

Clue 177: Donald Duck is in the shop, too!
3 points

★ Walk toward *Enchanted Tales with Belle*.

Clue 178: Before you reach the entrance walkway to Be Our Guest Restaurant, keep your eyes down for a horseshoe Hidden Mickey.
4 points

Clue 179: In the main walkway, not far from the entrance sign for *Enchanted Tales with Belle*, search for a pebble image of Oswald the Lucky Rabbit. (Psst: it's not in the side walkway to *Enchanted Tales with Belle*!)
5 points

★ Now look inside *Ye Olde Christmas Shoppe* in Liberty Square.

Clue 180: Spot a stack of logs with a Hidden Mickey.
2 points

★ Walk into the *Liberty Tree Tavern*.

Clue 181: Search for a classic Mickey in the waiting area.
3 points

Clue 182: Now look for a classic Mickey in a painting in one of the seating areas to the left of the waiting area. (Psst! You'll have to climb some stairs to find this Hidden Mickey.)
4 points

★ Enter the *Frontier Trading Post* in Frontierland.

Clue 183: Look for two rope classic

Mickeys.
3 points for spotting both

Clue 184: Spot a cowboy with a Hidden Mickey.
3 points

★ Check out the inside of *Pecos Bill Tall Tale Inn and Cafe*.

Clue 185: Squint for a classic Mickey on a plate that's sitting on a ledge.
4 points

★ Head for Adventureland and stop inside *Tortuga Tavern*.

Clue 186: Search for a candle image.
3 points

★ Cross the nearest bridge to *Main Street, U.S.A.* and search for 14 or more classic Mickeys as you stroll toward the park entrance.

Clue 187: Look around the outside of The Crystal Palace restaurant.
3 points

Clue 188: As you enter the short side street off of Main Street, study the area near the bricks outside the entrance to the Crystal Arts store for a tiny classic Mickey.
5 points

Clue 189: Near the Emporium store outside, search for Hidden Mickeys on a door sign.
3 points for all

Clue 190: Find Mickey in stained-glass windows high on the Emporium exterior.
3 points

Clue 191: Study the outside display windows of the Emporium store for a Hidden Mickey in a logo.
4 points

Clue 192: Inside the Emporium store, study the merchandise stands.
2 points

Clue 193: Look for a tiny Mickey on a building in an outside display window of the Emporium store.
5 points

Clue 194: Find a Hidden Mickey made of gears or circles in a display window of the Main Street Confectionery store near Town Square.
2 points

Clue 195: Spot another classic Hidden Mickey made of something sweet in a display window of the Main Street Confectionery store.
3 points

★ Clue 196: Closely examine the *Caffe Italiano coffee cart* (present seasonally) near Tony's Town Square Restaurant to earn some bonus points.
2 bonus points

Clue 197: As you enter Tony's Town Square Restaurant dining area, study the floor near the left wall for a classic Mickey.
5 points

Clue 198: Look up for a classic Mickey as you exit the restaurant.
3 points

Clue 199: Find Hidden Mickeys on Main Street's horse-drawn trolley.
2 points for one or more

Clue 200: Stand in Town Square plaza and look for a classic Mickey on a ceiling.
2 points

Clue 201: Find a Hidden Mickey on the wall inside the Main Street Train Station.
3 points

Walt Disney World's Hidden Mickeys

★ You can often spot a classic Mickey in the sky during the evening *fireworks* show. If you see one, give yourself bonus points!
5 bonus points for spotting one or more

★ Keep your eyes peeled for another Hidden Mickey or two as you end your day in the park.

Clue 202: As you leave Main Street under the train station, search for Mickey on a gate.
2 points

★ If you go through the *Transportation and Ticket Center*, check out a cool Hidden Mickey and earn some bonus points.

Clue 203: Study the TTC ceiling skylights.
5 bonus points

Now tally your score.

Total Points for Magic Kingdom =

How'd you do?

Up to 310 points – Bronze
311 to 620 points – Silver
621 points and over – Gold
776 points – Perfect Score

If you earned bonus points in *Under the Sea ~ Journey of the Little Mermaid, Peter Pan's Flight, Pirates of the Caribbean,* on Main Street, U.S.A., at the fireworks, in the TTC, or on the ferryboat, you may have done even better.

Ferryboats

Hint 1: Ropes coiled into classic Mickeys can often be spotted at the ferry loading docks at the Magic Kingdom and at the Transportation and Ticket Center. Look next to a large post on either side as you walk onto or leave the boat at either loading dock. Cast Members usually maintain these rope images.

Hint 2: If you ride on the General Joe Potter ferryboat to or from the Magic Kingdom, look for this classic Hidden Mickey on the middle of an inside wall and below a "Life Vest Instructions" poster. It's on the port side between two doors and about 20 to 30 feet back from the front staircase (as your ferry approaches the Magic Kingdom).

49

Magic Kingdom Entrance

Hint 3: Classic Mickeys are formed in the bell clapper designs of some of the commemorative bricks in the walkways in front of the Magic Kingdom.

Main Street, U.S.A. – Train Station

Hint 4: The periphery of the Main Street Train Station roof, second level, has scrollwork that repeats a classic Mickey motif.

Fantasyland

– Seven Dwarfs Mine Train

Hint 5: Not far into the Standby entrance queue, a classic Mickey with eyes and a smile is impressed into the side of a wooden crossbar. Look above you to the part of the crossbar that holds a lantern above your walkway.

Hint 6: Bright colored gems are in the interactive games along the Standby entrance queue. At times in these games, three gems come together to form a classic Hidden Mickey. One good image, made of a green gem for the "head" and two clear gems for the "ears," is at the top of the first barrel in the "Spin the Barrels" game.

Hint 7: On the right side of your train and to the right of Dopey's ears, a classic Hidden Mickey is formed by jewels. Find the larger red jewel for Mickey's head—the left ear is a smaller red jewel and the right ear, an amber diamond.

Hint 8: Along the ride on your right side, three gems (a purple "head" and one green and one light purple "ear') are stuck in the wall behind Grumpy's head. Grumpy is pulling on a rope.

Hint 9: After passing Doc going up the second lift, Oswald the Lucky Rabbit can be seen as a 3-D image on the left hand side of the ride on a horizontal log. You can see his tiny legs, his belly pooching out, his round tan face with eyes and nose, and his right hand to the upper left of his face. His dark ears flop back from the top of his head and are less distinct. (This image is difficult to spot; you'll only get a fleeting glimpse.)

– *The Many Adventures of Winnie the Pooh*

Hint 10: Inside the big tree, a classic Mickey, tilted to the left, is formed by embedded rocks above the frame of the smaller children's entrance.

Hint 11: Above the frame of the larger entrance inside the big tree is a depression in the wood shaped like a submarine: a tribute to *20,000 Leagues Under the Sea* - the previous attraction near this location; thus, a Hidden Tribute rather than a Hidden Mickey.

Hint 12: On the outside of the big tree, in back, a side profile of Mickey is carved into the bark. It's at the upper left corner above the lower window.

Hint 13: Outside on the far side of the big tree, behind the fence, a classic Mickey is etched into the wood in the middle of a vertical brown post on the left side of a window.

Hint 14: Two Hidden Mickeys are in Rabbit's Garden along the entry area (accessed through the Standby queue):
  - A head of lettuce and two tomatoes form a classic Mickey.
  - Three watermelon drums are positioned to create a classic Mickey.

Hint 15: At the beginning of the ride, in Rabbit's Garden, the small marker with

51

radishes (in the middle pot to the left of the "Letus" sign) has one radish shaped like a classic Hidden Mickey.

Hint 16: At the beginning of the left wall of Owl's house (the second room on the ride) is a picture of Mr. Toad handing the deed to the house over to Owl (a tribute to the previous attraction in this building, *Mr. Toad's Wild Ride*).

Hint 17: Near the end of this room, on the right side of the floor, is a picture of Mole standing with Winnie the Pooh.

Tomorrowland

Hint 18: A tall lamppost casts a classic Mickey shadow on the pavement outside *Tomorrowland Speedway*. It's best seen on a sunny day in the late morning or early afternoon.

– *Space Mountain*

Hint 19: In one or more of the interactive games on the left wall of the entrance queue, guests can at times connect space construction objects together to form classic Mickeys.

Hint 20: In one of the last interactive screens along the Standby queue, one game shows random objects floating in the air. A Mickey hat with ears and "Mickey" embroidered on it is one of the objects that floats by.

Hint 21: In the instructional video near the loading area, a man with a full-face image of Mickey Mouse on the front of his T-shirt sits down in the front seat of a ride vehicle. At another time in the video, a woman removes her Mickey ears before riding. Also look for a Stitch doll being placed in the storage compartment of a rider's seat.

Fantasyland

– Be Our Guest Restaurant

Hint 22: Just inside the entrance to Be Our Guest Restaurant, in the room with the suits of armor, classic Hidden Mickeys are formed at times in the corners and intersections of the border design on the wall behind the suits of armor.

Hint 23: In the room with suits of armor, the ax blade at the end of the room on the right has a classic Hidden Mickey hole cut out of it.

Hint 24: At the right rear terminal as you enter the food order room, take a look at the stack of books. Two images form Hidden Mickeys; one is at each corner of the top book cover, and another is on the spine of the second book from the bottom.

Hint 25: On the left side of the rear wall of the Rose Gallery seating area (to the right of the restaurant's Ballroom dining room), look for a small painting of Mrs. Potts and Chip. Chip is playing in a dish filled with bubbles. Three of those bubbles form a classic Mickey.

Hint 26: Inside the Be Our Guest Restaurant, walk to the West Wing room and stand in front of the rose at the rear of the room. Now turn and look up to your right to spot a small Hidden Mickey hole in tattered fabric hanging from the ceiling.

Hint 27: Outside along the bridge, on your right as you exit toward the rest of Fantasyland, a classic Hidden Mickey is etched in stone. The Hidden Mickey, tilted left, is on the back of the partial wall behind the check-in station.

Hint 28: A faint classic Mickey in swirls is on top of a short rock wall to the left of the check-in station (as you face the station) at the beginning of the entrance walkway to Be Our Guest Restaurant. It's on top of the last flat rectangular stone before the wall ends.

Tomorrowland

– *Buzz Lightyear's Space Ranger Spin*

Hint 29: Just inside the building, in the entrance queue, the second poster on the right wall is called "Planets of the Galactic Alliance." In Sector 1, the central continent on the planet "Pollost Prime" is shaped like a side profile of Mickey Mouse's head.

Hint 30: At the right lower corner of this poster, a purple planet ("Planet Z") has three craters that form a sideways classic Mickey with "ears" to the left. (Planet Z with its Mickey craters appears in several posters along the queue.)

Hint 31: The side-profile Mickey continent appears in the top left of a recessed wall farther along the entrance queue, just before the last right turn in the queue.

Hint 32: Sector 2 in this same mural contains a planet made of many spheres, some of which form classic Mickeys. One of them is at the outer edge of the planet at about the "ten o'clock" location.

Hint 33: On the ride, in the very first interactive room with targets, scan for two Hidden Mickeys. You have to rotate back and to the right in your vehicle to see them. First, a tiny classic Mickey with a green head and blue ears is on the first part of the lower right wall. This Hidden Mickey is below and between two five-point green stars. Another classic Mickey is a few inches to the left and below the first one. It's made of dark markings on a round white star.

Hint 34: You go through three different

rooms during the first part of this ride. When you enter the room with lots of batteries, look to the left of the ride vehicle. You'll see a side profile of Mickey's head in the rear left under the words, "Initiate Battery Unload."

Hint 35: Also in the battery room, look to the right of your vehicle and high over Zurg's left (your right) shoulder to spot a tiny blue classic Mickey star, tilted to the left. It's in the star field to the right of the large blue and yellow cone suspended over Zurg.

Hint 36: As the ride vehicle moves through the space video room, planet "Pollost Prime," with continent Mickey, flies by on the right wall.

Hint 37: Just past the space video room, in the final battle scene on the ride, "Pollost Prime" shows up yet again on a wall straight ahead and to the upper left.

Frontierland

– Splash Mountain

Hint 38: As you ride halfway up the second crankhill, on the right side, three barrels in the lower right corner of a stack of barrels form a classic Mickey.

Hint 39: During the first part of the ride, when your boat is outside, look to your right for a barrel with "Muskrat Moonshine" painted on the side. A classic Mickey is formed by holes in the paint, above the "s" in "Muskrat."

Hint 40: On the right side of your boat and to the left of the rabbit sweeping a porch, small animal silhouettes run right to left along the top of a hill on the rear wall. Just before the last animal disappears, its head becomes a classic Mickey silhouette. These moving animal silhouettes repeat at regular

55

intervals.

Hint 41: Look for a picnic basket up on a small ledge. You'll spot it just past Brer Frog, who is sitting on an alligator and fishing with his toe. Near the basket are three red-and-white-striped fishing bobbers in the shape of a classic Hidden Mickey.

Hint 42: On the right side of your boat, in the room with jumping water, a classic Mickey design in a rope is hanging halfway down from the ceiling. It's in the shadows behind a lantern and just past a turtle lying on a geyser.

Hint 43: The hole in the mountain at the top of the big drop is sculpted to form a side profile of Mickey's face. As you approach the big drop in your boat, Mickey's nose juts out from the left side of the hole. (You can also see this one from the outside viewing area; see Hint 53.)

Hint 44: Near the end of the ride, the upper outline of one of the white clouds on the right side of the riverboat scene is shaped like Mickey Mouse lying on his back, with his head to the right. (This Hidden Mickey is also visible from the *Walt Disney World Railroad* train as it passes through *Splash Mountain* just before the Frontierland Train Station stop).

Hint 45: As you pass the photo viewing area on your way out, look over to the entrance queue to spot two classic Mickeys formed by acorns on a birdhouse with a rope ladder. One classic Mickey formation is above a door and below blue roof slats. The other is on the right side of the birdhouse and near the peanut-shell chimney, above the curve of the red rail. (Other classic Mickey images are simulated elsewhere in the acorns).

Hint 46: Along the exit walkway, at the Laughin' Place children's play area, a classic Mickey is formed by the ends of three logs stuck to the wall to the right of the "Laughin' Place" sign.

Hint 47: Walk in front of *Splash Mountain* after your ride. The hole in the mountain for the big drop forms a side profile of Mickey's face. From the outside, Mickey's nose juts out from the right side of the hole.

– Big Thunder Mountain Railroad

Hint 48: Three stalagmites in the cavern to your right at the beginning of the ride form a classic Mickey. Look down at the left side of the floor of the cavern to spot it.

Hint 49: On the left side as you exit the ride (in the exit closest to the Standby line entrance), a cutout in the reddish rock resembles a side profile of Tinker Bell. She's behind the fence and between two metal carts, and she faces to your left.

Fantasyland

– Peter Pan's Flight

Hint 50: At the lower right of the entrance-sign cloud formation is an incomplete classic cloud Mickey. It's just to the right of the "t" in "Flight." Peter Pan is standing between the ears of another Hidden Mickey in the sign; you can see just the top of Mickey's head and his ears.

Hint 51: Bonus Points Hint - When the rotating moon is in just the right position, you can see a faint dark classic Mickey on the moon, above the silhouettes of the flying Peter Pan and his entourage. Unfortunately, since the moon rotates, you can't spot this Hidden Mickey on every ride through the attraction.

Hint 52: On the rocky edge of the mermaid lagoon, three flowers on the grass form a classic Mickey; the "head" is yellow and

57

the "ears" are light orange.

Hint 53: As you fly over one side of the
ship with the fallen pirates and then back
over the other, look down for two sets
of cannonballs, one on each side of the
ship. Shadows directly below the first
pile of cannonballs form a classic Hidden
Mickey. A more pronounced "shadow"
classic Mickey is next to and apart from
the second pile of cannonballs; this Hidden
Mickey appears to be painted on the deck
of the ship.

Frontierland

– *Tom Sawyer Island*

Hint 54: Across the river from the island
docks, look at the right end of the bridge
in Frontierland for three rocks that form a
classic Mickey. They're located halfway
between the last two vertical posts that
support the handrail, about one foot down
from the top of the rocks. The Hidden
Mickey is in the second row of rocks from
the top. (Note: This Hidden Mickey is also
visible from the *Liberty Square Riverboat*.)

Hint 55: Halfway through Old Scratch's
Mystery Mine, bright shining gems
embedded in the wall form a side profile of
Goofy. He's looking to your right.

Hint 56: In Fort Langhorn, enter the Rifle
Roost at the far right corner. To get there,
climb up the stairs to your immediate right
after you enter the fort and walk across the
right upper walkway to the far right Rifle
Roost. On top of the right handrail, about
halfway up the steps to the top of the Rifle
Roost, there is a Hidden Mickey created
by: a wood knot, an additional mark, and
an indentation in the wood.

Hint 57: Inside the Blacksmith's shop,
an upside-down classic Mickey (slightly
distorted) is impressed on the side of horse

bridle gear, which is hanging about six feet high on a post to the right of a man standing with his back to us.

Adventureland

– Jungle Cruise

Hint 58: Check the big sign outside. On the side of the sign that faces the attraction, three barnacles under the "J" in "Jungle Cruise" form a classic Mickey.

Hint 59: About halfway along the Standby entrance queue, a classic Hidden Mickey made of dark round circles and tilted to the right is at the lower left of a map of Africa in a display cabinet on a wall. The display cabinet is to the right of several masks on the wall.

Hint 60: Across the river from the loading dock, look for a hut with a tall tree behind it that leans to the right. There's a white classic Mickey marking on the tree bark above the hut. To spot it, follow the right-leaning tree trunk high up to the Mickey marking. It's about two-thirds of the distance up the trunk, where the trunk angles slightly more to the right.

Hint 61: Along the right side of the boat, watch for the Pygmy War Canoes sitting on a beach. The bow of the middle canoe resembles Donald Duck.

Hint 62: After the waterfall, a wrecked silver plane sits to the right of the boat. Look back to spot three circles etched in the metal at the lower right of the visible section of fuselage. The circles are all the same size, but many folks and Cast Members consider them a Hidden Mickey.

Hint 63: Along the left side of the boat, be alert for menacing natives with spears. The last isolated native of the group wears a Donald mask.

Hint 64: The first undecorated column on the left wall (the third column from the end as you come out of the temple) has a chipped area of brick on the third block from the top. The chipped area forms part of a profile view of Minnie Mouse's head and face. Don't get discouraged if you have trouble spotting it; this one is tough to find—especially the first time.

– Pirates of the Caribbean

Hint 65: Along the left entrance queue is a room with a faux fireplace on the right side. A classic Mickey is in the plaster on the sloping area to the right and above the fireplace mantle. It's about seven feet up from the floor. (This image is fading with time.)

Hint 66: Tall gun cabinets stand on both sides of the left entrance queue. On two of the cabinets are classic Mickey-shaped locks (one on each side).

Hint 67: At the beginning of the ride, Davy Jones's image is sometimes projected on a wall of mist in front of the boat. Look up at the left side of his hat (his right side, viewers' left). Below and to the left of the bottom of the "V" at the front of his hat, three tiny gold balls form a classic Mickey.

Hint 68: In the room with women chasing men in circles to the left of your boat, a black classic Mickey is suspended in front of the left side of an upper-story window.

Hint 69: About halfway through the ride and past the red-haired lady, a cat behind an intoxicated pirate casts a classic Hidden Mickey moving shadow on the corner of the wall above and behind it.

Hint 70: As your boat approaches the last scene (the treasure room), a classic Mickey lock hangs on large wooden recessed doors to the left.

Hint 71: As the treasure room comes into view, a classic Mickey lock hangs on a wooden door on the right. A long key with a cord hanging from it juts out of the keyhole of the lock.

Hint 72: Classic Mickey locks hang on the cabinets behind Captain Jack Sparrow in the treasure room.

Hint 73: Just as you enter the gift shop after exiting your boat, several classic Mickeys are formed by coins and jewels in two hanging plates near the right wall. Look along the edges of the plates for some of the best images.

Hint 74: Inside the gift shop, turn left and find a painting at the lower right of a wall map on the shop's rear wall. In the painting, a lady in a multicolored gown has a classic Mickey on her left shoulder.

Hint 75: Along a side pathway outside the entrance to the *Pirates of the Caribbean* attraction, the wheel of a cart forms a classic Mickey with two barrels above it. To spot it, walk to the side of the cart away from the main Adventureland path.

Frontierland

– Frontierland Shootin' Arcade

Hint 76: In the front center of the target area is a group of cactus plants. One near the middle, just below the gray tombstone, has three lobes forming a classic Hidden Mickey.

Liberty Square

– Stocks near the Liberty Square Riverboat entrance

Hint 77: Padlocks on the stocks near the entrance are shaped to resemble classic

Hidden Mickeys (even though the "ears" are a bit small).

– Haunted Mansion

Hint 78: Along the interactive "Scenic Route," a classic Mickey made of barnacles is on a huge bathtub with the words "Here Floats Captain Culpepper Clyne." The classic Mickey is tilted right and is below and between the letters "R" and "C" in the name.

Hint 79: Just inside the entrance to the first room, you'll find some small classic Mickeys in the oval border design around the portrait of the dressed-up aging man above the fireplace.

Hint 80: As you pass by the library room (at the beginning of the ride) and then the "endless hallway" on your right, check out the backs of two purple chairs for an abstract Donald Duck. Near the top of the chairs, you can see his cap, which sits above his distorted eyes, face, and bill. (Note that the chairs may change locations at times.)

Hint 81: A plate and two saucers on the ghostly banquet table are arranged to form a classic Mickey. They're usually at the bottom left corner of the table.

Hint 82: In the first part of the attic area, on the floor to your left under a small table with shelves, plates form a classic Mickey. A large lower plate serves as the "head," and two smaller plates or dishes are the "ears."

Hint 83: To the right of the opera-singing lady (her left) is a ghost resembling the Grim Reaper. He is holding up his left arm. Hanging from his left hand is a cloth with dark markings at the top that form a classic Hidden Mickey.

Hint 84: Outside, at the left end of the covered walkway, a classic Mickey metal latch holds a wrought-iron gate open.

Hint 85: In the pet cemetery on the left side of the outside exit walkway, a Mr. Toad tombstone stands at the rear left corner.

– Columbia Harbour House restaurant

Hint 86: In the downstairs table area, a wall across from the food-order counters is decorated with three small circular maps covered by a single piece of glass. (The central map is labeled "Charles V.") The three circles form a classic Mickey.

Tomorrowland

– Tomorrowland Speedway

Hint 87: Find a *Tomorrowland Speedway* map to your left on the purple wall at the end of the FastPass+ queue. Look for two small classic Hidden Mickeys formed of blue "heads" with two faint white "ears." One is at the right middle of the map (a red object points to this Hidden Mickey). The second Hidden Mickey is in the right lower corner of the map, next to an angle in the blue field.

Fantasyland

– Under the Sea ~ Journey of The Little Mermaid

Hint 88: A classic Hidden Mickey made of three circular impressions in the rock is to the upper right of the sign at the Standby entrance to the attraction.

Hint 89: On the right side along the outside Standby entrance queue, a classic Mickey made of impressions is at the top right side of a rock that sits in the middle of the small lagoon in front of the waterfall.

Hint 90: Above the lagoon rock with the Hidden Mickey is another small classic Mickey made of impressions in the rock wall. Look for it on a flat sloping wall face just below the very top of the rock wall. The Hidden Mickey is above the right edge of the large opening in the wall; the waterfall spills over the left side of this opening.

Hint 91: Directly below the right side of a bridge with a rope-covered side rail is a classic Hidden Mickey made of impressions in the rock. You're facing a rock arch with a waterfall, and the Hidden Mickey is at the right side of the rock base of the stream below you. Water streaming over the Mickey blurs the image.

Hint 92: Now stare up at the higher part of the rock arch. To the right of the small waterfall, a tiny classic Mickey impression is in the rock in the upper middle of the arch.

Hint 93: At the left side of the outside Standby entrance queue, a Nautilus submarine impression is in a rock wall behind a small pond. When you reach a fence on your left strewn with ropes and nets, look back to your left and study the rear rock wall near the waterline. First spot the round porthole that resembles an eye; the nose of the submarine points to the left.

Note: "Nautilus" is the submarine, commanded by Captain Nemo, in Jules Verne's novel *Twenty Thousand Leagues Under the Sea*. It was the ride vehicle in the WDW ride of the same name, which closed in 1994.

Hint 94: Just before you enter the inside portion of the queue, look up high above and behind you for three circle depressions on a rock that is jutting out. The circle Hidden Mickey is tilted slightly to the left.

Hint 95: Each year on Mickey Mouse's birthday (November 18) the noontime sun shines through holes carved in the rockwork above you at just the right angle to form a classic Mickey on the wall of the inside entrance queue. The Mickey-shaped light lasts for several minutes. The top of Mickey's head is formed by the carving in the highest rock, and the lower part of his head is formed by the carving in the rock closer to you. Stay alert, because the sunlight just might shine through both rock openings at other times of the year to form Mickey!

Hint 96: Along the left side of the inside Standby entrance queue, a classic Mickey tilted to the left is formed by holes in the rock above some bottles on a table.

Hint 97: A side profile of Mickey Mouse, looking left, is etched in the ceiling. He's at the beginning of the room with the talking Scuttle, high to your left as you enter and near a cubed light cover.

Hint 98: In the first part of the room where the song "Under the Sea" is playing, three oval purple corals clinging to a rock to the right of your ride vehicle form a classic Mickey. They're just past and behind the singing chorus line of fish that are standing on their tails.

Hint 99: Just past Ariel in the "Under the Sea" room, a green fish with a purple seashell hat has a classic Hidden Mickey at the top of her earring. For the best vantage point, look back to the earring after you pass by the fish.

Hint 100: Toward the end of the ride, check the pond (to your right) for frogs with dark green spots on their backs that form sideways classic Mickeys. The frogs are perched on lily pads to the left of a boat with Ariel and Eric.

Walt Disney World's Hidden Mickeys

Hint 101: Along the left side of the exit walkway inside the cave, spot a classic Hidden Mickey made of a large depression for the "head" and two smaller depressions for the "ears." This upright Hidden Mickey is just inches up from the floor and below a large opening in the left wall that looks into the exit path from *Ariel's Grotto*.

Hint 102: Through the large opening mentioned above, you can see another Hidden Mickey: a classic Mickey formed of three impressions in the rock wall along the left side of the exit from *Ariel's Grotto*. This image is tilted to the left and it's about halfway up the wall and below a ceiling light. (Note: You'll probably find other rock impressions along the exit that resemble classic Mickeys.)

Hint 103: At the end of the exit walkway from *Under the Sea*, turn to your right to spot an amazing Hidden "Steamboat Willie" Mickey Mouse. The Imagineers sculpted this image on a series of rocks. His left leg and shoe are closest to you, then his right leg and shoe are on the next rock. Two holes in the rocks represent the buttons on his shorts. His whitish face is on a flat rock, and he's looking left. His tall hat is the last rock above his head. There's even a ship's wheel in the rock to the left of his face!

– *"it's a small world"*

Hint 104: Toward the end of the Africa room, vines on the right above the giraffes and to the left of your boat have purple leaves shaped like classic Mickey heads.

Hint 105: Near the end of the South Pacific room, several koala bears hang on a tree. As you approach the bears on your left, the back of the blue bear's head forms a classic Mickey.

– *"Tangled" Restroom area*

Chapter 2: Magic Kingdom Scavenger Hunt

Hint 106: On a wall poster outside the Ladies' Restroom near the "Tangled" Tower, a classic Hidden Mickey is on a Mime's lips. Smaller round, solid black circles form the "ears" just above the upper lip.

Hint 107: In the Tangled area women's restroom, three purple spots - a classic Mickey - are at the lower right corner of a mural painted on the left wall as you enter the restroom. (You can spot this wall from outside the restroom, but I recommend that guys not stand and stare!)

– Near Peter Pan's Flight

Hint 108: Between the entrance to *Peter Pan's Flight* and Columbia Harbour House, you'll find paintings of grape clusters on the walls. Three grapes at the lower right of the upper left cluster of grapes form a classic Mickey.

– Pinocchio Village Haus restaurant

Hint 109: As you head from the dining area to the restrooms, a tiny dark classic Mickey appears above the word "dreams" on the "When You Wish Upon A Star" mural. You'll find it on the left wall near the exit to the restrooms.

Hint 110: A tiny white classic Mickey is in this same area of the mural, below and left of the word "All."

Hint 111: On the left side of the same mural, a tiny white classic Mickey hides near a sparkling star. It's to the left of the Fairy - at her mid-thigh level - and her right thumb points to it.

– Sir Mickey's Store

Hint 112: You'll find a classic Mickey toward the top of the store's sign-shield. The shield is hanging under a vine, across from Castle Couture shop.

Hint 113: In a display window to the right of the main entrance to the store, classic Mickeys are along the border of the archer's collar in a painting on the rear wall of the display. You can also usually find classic Mickeys made by arrangements of buttons on the floor of the display.

– Castle Couture shop

Hint 114: To find a tiny classic Mickey on the wall, walk through the entrance doors to the right of the Cinderella fountain. Then turn right and look up at the bronze horizontal frieze near the ceiling. You'll spot a series of arches over bushes with flowers. Walk forward to the far end of the frieze and count back six arches to a bush with three flowers at its upper left that form a classic Mickey. If you have trouble spotting it, ask a Cast Member to point it out for you. (You can also see this image repeated elsewhere in the frieze).

Liberty Square

– The Hall of Presidents

Hint 115: On a wall painting in the waiting room for the show, a tiny classic Mickey is at the end of the object George Washington holds in his left hand.

Adventureland

– Adventureland bridge to the Hub

Hint 116: Shields are propped at the sides of the bridge connecting Adventureland with the Hub in front of Cinderella Castle. Two classic Mickeys with smiley faces for "ears" appear on separate shields. One with white ears is at the bottom of one shield, while the other, an upside-down classic Mickey with blue ears, is at the top of a second shield.

– *Walt Disney's Enchanted Tiki Room*

Hint 117: Upside-down classic Mickeys are camouflaged in the designs at the bottom of two bird perches. One perch is in the left corner as you enter the theater. The other is to the right of the exit door.

Hint 118: To the right of the entrance to *Walt Disney's Enchanted Tiki Room*, a statue with several faces has classic Mickeys formed by beads in the middle of the forehead, above the nose.

– *Near The Magic Carpets of Aladdin*

Hint 119: A charm embedded in the cement between *The Magic Carpets of Aladdin* exit and the Agrabah Bazaar shop contains a tiny classic Mickey. It's near a shop pole that has blue paint above its base.

Fantasyland

– *Mickey's PhilharMagic*

Hint 120: In the first waiting area inside, the wall mural with musical instruments has several small white classic Mickeys.

Hint 121: On the right vertical border of the video screen in the main theater, a classic Mickey hides inside a French horn.

Hint 122: In the "Be Our Guest" portion of the movie, there is a point where you are watching Lumiere dancing on the table with other characters. The view goes to an overhead shot and there are shadows cast on the table from the candle hands of Lumiere. These shadows come together at times to form what appear to be Hidden Mickeys.

Hint 123: In "The Little Mermaid" segment, Ariel throws jewels out into the water in front of her. Stay focused on the right side of the screen (your right), to spot a ring as it rotates slowly from a side position to an open circle. A dark classic Mickey image is visible just as you first spot the open center of the ring. The image disappears as the ring completes its rotation.

Hint 124: Stay alert for the orange dancing trees in "The Lion King" segment. At times, a blue zebra's tail is over the left (the viewer's right) ear of a classic Mickey made of the circular tops of orange trees.

Hint 125: Watch closely as Aladdin and Jasmine ride their magic carpet in the sky. Stare at the bottom left of the screen for a quick glimpse of three round buildings on the ground. They're clustered to form a classic Mickey.

Hint 126: Music stands shaped like classic Mickeys are on shelves high up above the merchandise in Fantasy Faire at the exit of *Mickey's PhilharMagic*.

– Ariel's Grotto

Hint 127: As you make the first left turn in the FastPass+ queue of *Ariel's Grotto*, three round impressions at the top of the short rock wall to your left come together as a classic Mickey. The Hidden Mickey is near a group of tall, vertical green leaves.

– Princess Fairytale Hall

Hint 128: Mickey's profile is in a painting in *Princess Fairytale Hall*, left-side queue. The side view of Mickey's ghostly face looking in a window is in this painting of a cottage with a water wheel in front. Find the painting on the right wall at the end of the FastPass+ queue. You can also spot this painting from the end of the Standby queue, just before entering to meet the Princesses.

Tomorrowland

– Tomorrowland Transit Authority PeopleMover

Hint 129: The woman getting her hair done sports a belt buckle with a classic Hidden Mickey.

– Mickey's Star Traders shop

Hint 130: On the mural, the headlights of a train form a classic Mickey.

Hint 131: Stitch races beside a train in the mural.

Hint 132: Mickey hats sit atop windows halfway up the sides of a building.

Hint 133: Satellite dishes form a classic Mickey on top of this building.

Hint 134: Across the room on another mural, the middle circle of freeway loops forms a classic Mickey.

Hint 135: Over one of the entrance doors, clear domes form a classic Mickey.

Hint 136: The blue glass dome covering one building is a classic Mickey with ears.

– Tomorrowland "Cool Scanner" Station

Hint 137: Several tiny, dark classic Mickeys are formed by holes underneath the overhead dome of the station.

– Walt Disney's Carousel of Progress

Hint 138: In the first scene, on the right side of the stage, where the daughter is getting ready for the evening (on Valentine's Day), a classic Mickey made of cloth decorates the top of her mirror.

Hint 139: In the third scene, Mickey's

71

Sorcerer's Hat sits at the right side of the room, next to the girl in the shaker machine.

Hint 140: In the last scene, an abstract Mickey Mouse as the Sorcerer's apprentice from the film *Fantasia* is in a painting on the dining room wall. To spot it, look immediately to the left rear of the scene as it rotates into view. The painting is on the dining room's right rear wall.

Hint 141: On the left side of the room, a nutcracker shaped like Mickey Mouse stands on the left side of the mantelpiece.

Hint 142: Under the Christmas tree, a plush Mickey Mouse is behind the wrapped boxes.

Hint 143: On the last stage, one of the Christmas presents under the tree (near Grandfather's chair) is decorated with a large classic Mickey head cut out of green paper and glued to the side of the gift, which is sometimes partially hidden by another present, so you may only see the ears and part of the top of Mickey's head. The green Mickey ears are to the right of Grandpa's lower leg.

Hint 144: A classic Mickey appears (just for a few seconds) on the top of a spaceship in the middle of the television screen. Look for it just as the game starts on the TV, before Grandma starts playing.

Hint 145: Salt and pepper shakers on the kitchen counter have Mickey ears.

Hint 146: A small basket of fruit with a blue ribbon on top sits to Mom's right. A tiny black classic Mickey is in the basket at the left side.

Hint 147: Along the exit ramps, classic Mickeys are on the backs of the round signs for the attraction.

Chapter 2: Magic Kingdom Scavenger Hunt

– Astro Orbiter

Hint 148: A small classic Mickey is traced in the cement close to a *Tomorrowland Transit Authority PeopleMover* support beam near *Astro Orbiter* on the side toward *Space Mountain*, between Cool Ship and The Lunching Pad.

– Monsters, Inc. Laugh Floor

Hint 149: On the outside wall, a picture advertising a Recreational Rocket has a moon with craters shaped like an upside-down classic Mickey.

Hint 150: Also on the outside wall, a sign advertising a Space Collectibles Convention includes an asteroid shaped like a classic Mickey.

Hint 151: As you enter the attraction, look for a window display of a city on the rear of the right-hand wall just past the entrance doors to the second room. A classic Mickey is under the apex of the triangular roof segment on the building in the front center of the window display.

Fantasyland

– Enchanted Tales with Belle

Hint 152: Along the Standby entrance queue, in the window to your left as you enter the first room of Maurice's cottage, look at the lower left pane. An image of Donald Duck is in the glass swirls at the middle right side of the pane.

Hint 153: Inside the first room of Maurice's cottage, a stack of firewood stands to the left of the fireplace. An upright classic Mickey made of three logs is at the lower middle of the stack, and a sideways classic Mickey is at the upper middle left of the stack. Other combinations of logs also resemble classic Mickeys.

Hint 154: The red carpet in the Wardrobe Room has a number of small Hidden Mickeys. A pseudo-triangle looks like a hat on each Mickey head.

Hint 155: In the Library where you meet Belle, a book with Mickey-shaped bookmarks on its spine is at the right rear corner of the room. It's the fifth book from the right, above a blue and gold horizontal frieze midway up the wall.

Main Street, U.S.A.

– Town Square Theater

Hint 156: In the last room in the queue just before you enter Mickey's Dressing Room for *Mickey's Meet 'n' Greet*, there are mail slots for the theater cast. Mickey has his own personal mail slot.

Hint 157: A classic Mickey made of metal rings lies in an upper compartment of Mickey's open magic chest in the Greeting Room.

Hint 158: Inside Mickey's magic chest, on the right, there's a classic Mickey lock on a chain. (It's sometimes covered by a scarf.) Additional Mickey-shaped locks can often be spotted in various locations in the Greeting Room.

Hint 159: Oswald the Lucky Rabbit is drawn on a piece of paper at the upper part of a bulletin board at the back of the room. He's next to a drawing of Mickey Mouse.

Hint 160: Just before the exit door from the Greeting Room, three large Mickey Mouse playing cards are held upright by a long clip on the floor. In the middle of the clip, a classic Mickey wearing a triangular "hat" resembles a Sorcerer Mickey.

Hint 161: Classic Mickey locks hang from

the side of several metal display tables in the gift shop, and more classic Mickey locks hang high on the front of the "Tank of Terror" display case.

Hint 162: A birdhouse from the now-closed Mickey's Toontown Fair sits on a tall merchandise cabinet at the left side of the shop (as you enter from outside). The front door of the birdhouse is shaped like a classic Mickey.

Fantasyland

– Fairytale Garden

Hint 163: At the base of the first light pole on the right as you enter, a classic Mickey that looks like a piece of different-colored stucco is in the cement on the side next to the fence.

Hint 164: A side profile of Pluto's head is on the wall, upper left of the stage. It's left of the brick circle and above the stairs.

– Storybook Circus area

Hint 165: Between the exit of the Fantasyland Train Station and *Dumbo the Flying Elephant* is a trail of large and small (mother and baby) elephant tracks. These prints in the pavement come together at times to form classic Mickeys.

Hint 166: On the "Giraffes" boxcar in *Casey Jr. Splash 'N' Soak Station*, a classic Mickey is hidden in the clouds behind a giraffe in a painting on the side of the boxcar that faces the restrooms. This cloud Hidden Mickey is behind the lower part of the neck of the tall giraffe, and it's tilted to the right.

Hint 167: Under the entrance sign to *The Barnstormer*, two classic Mickeys are in the scrollwork below Goofy's picture. The images are at the top corners on each side of the faux ticket booth window.

Hint 168: On the huge billboard on the right side of *The Barnstormer* (the billboard the ride train hurtles through), a tiny gray classic Mickey hides in the middle of the propeller of the lower plane on the far right side of the billboard.

Hint 169: A poster of Daisy Duck ("Madame Daisy Fortuna") is outside to the left of the entrance to *Pete's Silly Sideshow*. A faint classic Mickey is traced on the upper part of her light green blouse, just to the right of her right index finger.

Hint 170: Eight tiny Mickey balloons are scattered around the large "Storybook Circus" painting at the rear of a tent next to *Pete's Silly Sideshow*.

Hint 171: A classic Hidden Mickey is on a sleeping cheetah inside Big Top Souvenirs. The cheetah is on a wall painting behind a register counter and its leg hangs down from a tree branch. The reddish-brown Mickey spot is on the hanging left lower leg, just above the ankle area.

Hint 172: A classic Mickey is formed by a manhole cover (the "head") and two elephant tracks (the "ears") near the entrance to the FastPass+ queue for *Dumbo the Flying Elephant*.

Hint 173: A classic three-circle Mickey metal design sits atop the Disney Vacation Club sign.

Hint 174: Embedded in the cement walkway in front of the Disney Vacation Club kiosk and across from *Ariel's Grotto* is a classic Hidden Mickey formed of a survey marker and two adjacent pebbles. It's near a cart track indented in the cement.

– *Gaston's Tavern area*

Hint 175: A tiny classic Mickey made of dark impressions hides on the rock that forms the base of Gaston's Statue, which stands in front of Gaston's Tavern. The Hidden Mickey is near the waterline below the back of Gaston's left leg.

Hint 176: Groups of circles in several antique maps on the wall inside the Bonjour Village Gifts shop resemble classic Mickeys. The most convincing image is on the "Terrestrial Globe" map on the left wall, on which a globe forms the head of an upside-down classic Mickey.

Hint 177: A Hidden Donald Duck is at the upper left corner of a portrait in the Bonjour Village Gifts shop. The portrait is centered on the wall at the rear of the store and hangs near the ceiling.

Hint 178: A classic Hidden Mickey is formed by horseshoe prints in the sidewalk. Find it as you walk from Gaston's Tavern toward Be Our Guest Restaurant; it's near the end of the short rock wall on your right and close to a pole with lanterns. Two horseshoe prints form the "head" and two other prints form the "ears."

– *Near Enchanted Tales with Belle*

Hint 179: An image that resembles Oswald the Lucky Rabbit is formed by three embedded pebbles in the middle of a walkway. To find the image, stop across from the *Enchanted Tales with Belle* entrance (and waiting time) sign and look down in the middle of the main walkway to Be Our Guest Restaurant.

Liberty Square

– *Ye Olde Christmas Shoppe*

Hint 180: In the framed log collage under a register in the middle of the store, a classic Hidden Mickey formed by three logs hides in the upper left corner of a stack of logs.

– Liberty Tree Tavern

Hint 181: Look for a spice rack to the right of the fireplace on the rear wall of the waiting area. Three grapes in a small still-life painting on the spice rack form a classic Mickey.

Hint 182: Turn left from the waiting area and go up the stairs. Then turn right and enter a brown room with a fireplace on the inside. Go up to the fireplace (you'll have to climb a few more steps) and look for a classic Mickey in the clouds. You'll find it on the left side of the upper part of the painting that's hanging to the left of George Washington's portrait.

Frontierland

– Frontier Trading Post store

Hint 183: A "How to Pin Trade" sign, behind a register inside the store to the right, sports a rope classic Mickey. Another rope classic Mickey is attached to a pole. It stands above the merchandise and near the middle entrance to the store, but it may be moved around inside the store.

Hint 184: In the "How to Pin Trade" wall posters, a cowboy's lanyard has a black classic Mickey.

– Pecos Bill Tall Tale Inn and Cafe

Hint 185: Inside the cafe, find the plates sitting upright along a ledge near the ceiling behind the middle of the serving counter. On the third plate from the left, at the upper left and near the inside circle of the plate, three red spots behind the white bird form a classic Mickey.

Adventureland

Hint 186: In a window display about pirates inside the Tortuga Tavern restaurant, three candles stuck in a bowl form a classic Hidden Mickey.

Main Street, U.S.A.

Hint 187: On the roof of The Crystal Palace restaurant, the circles in the middle row of the tower above the main entrance resemble Mickey ears.

Hint 188: A tiny classic Mickey is impressed in the cement outside the Crystal Arts store entrance. It's on a gray flagstone between the red cement and the bricks of the side street off of Main Street. Find a long crack (between red cement sections) that's parallel to Main Street and starts in front of the entrance pillars at the store entrance. The gray flagstone is at the end of this crack, and the Hidden Mickey is at the lower right corner of the flagstone as you face the store.

Hint 189: Outside along Main Street, just to the right of the Emporium shop and near the Athletic Club, a sign on a door has two classic Mickeys, at the top and bottom along the border.

Hint 190: The cupola above the Emporium, in the middle recessed area of the store, has stained-glass windows just below the highest eaves. The central flower circle in each window is joined with two frosted "ear" panels to form classic Mickeys.

Hint 191: In an outside display window in the middle recessed area of the Emporium store, a classic Mickey image hides on a piano above the words "Steinmouse & Sons." The display window is under a sign that says "Collectibles."

Hint 192: In the Emporium store, metal

poles that hold up merchandise shelves sport classic Mickey holes. (You can also spot Mickey holes on merchandise poles in other Disney stores.)

Hint 193: In the outside Aladdin display window of the Emporium store, you'll find a small classic Mickey window in a building wall.

Hint 194: At the Main Street Confectionery store, classic Hidden Mickeys made of circular objects, such as gears, are often present in an outside display window facing Main Street.

Hint 195: An upside-down classic Hidden Mickey made of three colorful lollipops hides in a framed poster in a Confectionery shop window display facing Main Street. You can find the same image inside the store. It is just to the right of the entrance door as you enter from Town Square through the door at the corner of the store. Is the image an upside-down Minnie Mouse because of the bow?

Hint 196: The sign on the Caffe Italiano cart, which appears seasonally in front of Tony's Town Square Restaurant, includes a classic Mickey
in its design.

Hint 197: When you enter Tony's Town Square Restaurant inside dining area, look left to the corner and find the second floor tile to the right of the corner. There's a classic Mickey impression at the center right side of this black tile. If you view the Hidden Mickey from the seating area, it will appear upside-down.

Hint 198: A small classic Hidden Mickey is on the middle back of the overhanging entrance sign to Tony's Town Square Restaurant. Look up as you exit the restaurant.

Hint 199: Several classic Mickeys adorn the gear on the horse pulling the Main Street Trolley.

Hint 200: In Town Square plaza, walk about seven or eight steps away from the island curb toward the train station. As you approach the station, a classic Mickey is formed by circles on the train station ceiling. You might call this a "positional" classic Mickey because you have to be in just the right position to see it.

Hint 201: A classic Mickey-shaped lock can be found inside the Main Street Station's faux ticket office upstairs. Look for the lock hanging on the right wall behind the windows. (Walk up the outside stairs to the office window, which faces Main Street.)

– Train Station Exit from Main Street

Hint 202: Classic Mickeys are repeated atop a tall gate, which is usually folded inside a recess beside the entrance and exit tunnel walkway under the Main Street Train Station.

Transportation and Ticket Center

Hint 203: An imprint of Mickey's face, full frontal image, has remained over the years. It looks as though it was made by a balloon that melted against the glass. This Hidden Mickey is in the second overhead glass bubble from the tram, in the first row of bubble skylights to the right as you walk from the trams toward the monorail entrance ramps. The image is fading with time, so try different viewing angles to spot it. However, bright sunlight may block it from view.

Chapter 3

Epcot
Scavenger Hunt

• • • • • • • • • •

Before You Start

• *Many great Hidden Mickeys are in Standby queues, and you might miss them if you take the FastPass+ queues. So, for optimal Hidden Mickey hunting, I recommend reserving FastPass+ for the following rides:* **Mission: SPACE** *(choose either Orange level—more intense, or Green level—less intense),* **Spaceship Earth,** *and* **Living with the Land.**

Be sure to keep track of your three FastPass+ windows and return to those attractions at the appropriate times. In the Scavenger Hunt below, if you come to your FastPass+ attraction and it's not time for it yet, you can skip to the next stop in the Hunt and return to the FastPass+ attraction during your time window.

• *Some of the Hidden Mickeys in this park are in restaurants and shops. Be considerate of fellow guests and Cast Members as you search. Tell them what you're looking for, so they can share in the fun. Avoid searching restaurants at busy meal times unless you are one of the diners.*

★ Make a beeline for *Frozen Ever After.*

Clue 1: When you reach the inside Standby queue, look high for a Hidden Mickey.
4 points

★ Cross Future World to The Land pavilion and get in line for *Soarin'.*

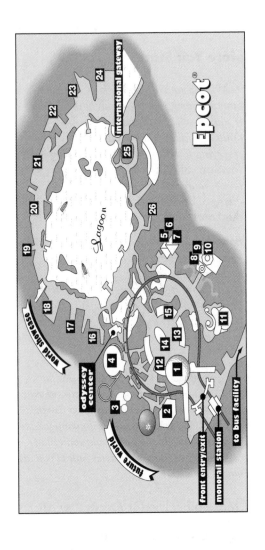

WORLD SHOWCASE

16 Mexico:
   Gran Fiesta Tour
17 Norway:
   Frozen *Ever After*
18 China:
   Reflections of China
19 Germany
20 Italy
21 The American Adventure:
   The American Adventure show
22 Japan
23 Morocco
24 France:
   Impressions de France
25 United Kingdom
26 Canada:
   O Canada!

FUTURE WORLD

1 Spaceship Earth Pavilion
2 Universe of Energy Pavilion
   Ellen's Energy Adventure
3 Mission: SPACE Pavilion
4 Test Track Pavilion
   Imagination! Pavilion
5 Disney & Pixar Short Film
   Festival
6 Journey Into Imagination
   With Figment
7 ImageWorks

The Land Pavilion
8 Living with the Land
9 The Circle of Life
10 Soarin'

11 The Seas with Nemo &
   Friends Pavilion
   Turtle Talk with Crush
12 Innoventions East
13 Innoventions West
14 Innoventions Plaza
15 Epcot Character Spot

85

Walt Disney World's Hidden Mickeys

Clue 2: In the pre-show video, spot the Mickey ears.
2 points

Clue 3: In the pre-show video, stay alert for Hidden Character clothing logos.
4 points for spotting two

Clue 4: During the ride, focus on the sky for a floating Hidden Mickey.
4 points

Clue 5: Look for some floating Mickeys below you near the end of the ride.
3 points

Clue 6: A huge classic Mickey in the sky greets you at the end of your *Soarin'* ride.
3 points

★ Walk to *Test Track*. Let folks pass by you in line while you search for three Hidden Mickeys in the Standby queue.

Clue 7: In the Standby entrance queue, look for a classic Mickey traced on the wall.
5 points

Clue 8: Now spot a white classic Mickey on the wall.
4 points

Clue 9: Watch for an interactive touch screen on the right wall of the Standby entrance queue. Make your own classic Mickey on top of the car!
5 points

Clue 10: On the ride, watch for a road sign on your right to spot a Hidden Mickey.
5 points

Clue 11: Look for a small, red Hidden Mickey to your left before the fast drive outside.
5 points

Clue 12: Keep your eyes left for a small, purple Hidden Mickey on the wall.
5 points

★ Return to *Mission: SPACE* at your FastPass+ time. Three Hidden Mickeys wait to be found along the entrance queue.

Clue 13: Search for a Hidden Mickey on a planet.
4 points

Clue 14: Spot a Hidden Mickey in "status lights" on a monitor.
4 points

Clue 15: Look for waveform images on a monitor that form a Hidden Mickey.
4 points

Clue 16: Just before launch, keep your eyes open for two identical Hidden Mickeys.
4 points

Clue 17: As you land on Mars, glance around for a Hidden Mickey on a building.
4 points

Clue 18: After the ride, look for a Hidden Mickey on a video console in the exhibit area.
2 points

Clue 19: Spot a Hidden Mickey on the ceiling of the gift shop at the attraction exit.
4 points

Clue 20: Search for Donald and Pluto on the ceiling.
4 points for spotting both

Clue 21: Study the spaceship in a mural in the gift shop.
3 points

Clue 22: Now squint for a small black Hidden Mickey in the same mural.
3 points

Walt Disney World's Hidden Mickeys

Clue 23: While you're at it, examine the mural for an upside-down classic Mickey.
3 points

Clue 24: Now glance low for classic Mickeys near the floor.
2 points

Clue 25: Find two classic Mickeys and a side-profile Mickey on the wall of the gift shop.
2 points for spotting all three

Clue 26: Outside in the front plaza, search for a classic Mickey on the moon.
3 points

Clue 27: Look down for a classic Mickey in the blue tile area out front.
5 points

Clue 28: In a blue tile stripe out front, spot a white classic Mickey near a bluish and salmon-colored disk.
4 points

Clue 29: Find two more classic tile Mickeys near a drain cover.
4 points for spotting both

★ Walk across Future World to The Seas with Nemo & Friends pavilion. Check out *Turtle Talk With Crush*. In the waiting area, search for two Hidden Mickeys.

Clue 30: Spot a tiny Mickey in the coral on the wall.
5 points

Clue 31: Admire a Hidden Mickey on a starfish.
4 points

Clue 32: During the show, study the undersea images on the show screen for a classic Mickey.
3 points

Chapter 3: Epcot Scavenger Hunt

★ Line up for the *Epcot Character Spot*.

Clue 33: When you go inside to meet the characters, spot Mickey listening to music.
1 point

Clue 34: Do you see a Mickey video camera?
2 points

Clue 35: Now notice a Mickey above Mickey.
2 points

Clue 36: Outside the *Character Spot*, look around for a Mickey hat.
3 points

★ After World Showcase opens at 11:00 a.m., head toward the Mexico Pavilion. Take the path behind MouseGear shop for a hard-to-find Hidden Mickey. (This path is between MouseGear and Test Track, and it connects to the main walkway to World Showcase.)

Clue 37: As you walk, stare at the cement until you discover a Hidden Mickey.
5 points

★ Eat an early lunch to avoid the crowds. The San Angel Inn Restaurante in the Mexico pavilion is an ideal choice if you have 11:30 a.m. or so reservations. If not, try fast food at Mexico's La Cantina de San Angel or the Kringla Bakeri Og Kafe in Norway. Ride *Gran Fiesta Tour Starring the Three Caballeros* before or after lunch.

★ If you eat in the San Angel Inn, look for classic Mickeys in the smoke rising from the volcano (see Clue 46).

★ Go to *Gran Fiesta Tour Starring the Three Caballeros* in Mexico and keep your eyes peeled for Hidden Mickeys.

Clue 38:Squint for a classic Mickey in the

water to the right of your boat.
5 points

Clue 39: At the beginning of the ride, take a close look at the smoke rising from the volcano.
4 points

Clue 40: In the first tunnel, search for Mickey on a necklace.
5 points

Clue 41: Glance in the water to the right of your boat for a classic Mickey.
4 points

Clue 42: Find Mickey on a video screen on the wall.
5 points

Clue 43: Spot classic Mickeys in a small blue pond to the left of the boat.
4 points

Clue 44: Don't miss Mickey in a barge!
3 points

Clue 45: In the final scene, turn on a light (your camera, phone, etc.) and highlight a Hidden Mickey under the platform to the left of your boat. (Psst! There are three of them. You might get lucky and see all three!)
5 points for one or more

★ After exiting the ride, walk to the outside of the San Angel Inn Restaurante (if you haven't already been there) and look for classic Mickeys that appear and disappear.

Clue 46: Observe the smoke rising from the volcano.
4 points

★ Stroll over to *China*.

Clue 47: Search for Hidden Mickeys on posts in the courtyard.

4 points

★ Now study the water for possible bonus points.
2 bonus points for one or more Hidden Mickeys

★ Cross over the bridge to the *Outpost*.

Clue 48: Check out the wooden poles.
3 points

Clue 49: Locate Mickey's name (twice) hidden high inside the *Village Traders Shop*.
5 points for both

★ Walk left to *Germany* to find five classic Hidden Mickeys.

Clue 50: As you walk into the plaza, look for the classic Mickey on a suit of armor on the building to your right.
3 points

Clue 51: Spot Mickey behind a large bell.
3 points

Clue 52: Search for Mickey near a lion.
3 points

Clue 53: Admire the outside display windows of the Karamell-Küche shop to find a small Hidden Mickey.
5 points

Clue 54: Study the woodwork inside Karamell-Küche for a Hidden Mickey.
5 points

★ Check out the landscaping around the train attraction to earn yourself some possible bonus points. (Note: These Hidden Mickeys come and go.)
1 bonus point for each one you spot.

★ Stop at *Italy* to inspect the shops, statues, and restaurants.

Clue 55: A classic Mickey is near the wine!
2 points

Clue 56: Look for Mickey behind a statue.
3 points

★ Go to *The American Adventure* pavilion.

Clue 57: Admire the banner over the entrance to the rotunda to locate a Hidden Mickey.
5 points

Clue 58: Search the walls inside for a classic Mickey in roses.
4 points

★ Now inspect the rear wall of the rotunda, upstairs and down, for classic Hidden Mickeys.

Clue 59: Study a picture in the rotunda for Hidden Mickeys on two metal beams.
3 points for spotting both

Clue 60: Take a good look at the bronze eagle reliefs in the rotunda.
2 points for each floor; 4 points total

★ Watch *The American Adventure show* and keep an eye out for four hard-to-spot classic Hidden Mickeys. (Tip: Try to sit on the right side of the theater for the best view of the Hidden Mickeys.)

Clue 61: At the beginning of the film, look at the rocks behind a kneeling female pilgrim.
4 points

Clue 62: Stay alert for a Mickey image on a stockade.
3 points

Clue 63: Study some fruit at the gas station.
3 points

Clue 64: At the end, watch the fireworks' explosions behind the Statue of Liberty Torch.
4 points

Clue 65: At a time between stage performances, wander over to America Gardens Theatre and find a Hidden Mickey near the stage.
2 points

★ Stroll over to *Japan*.

Clue 66: Search for a classic Mickey in the koi fish pond.
2 points

Clue 67: Check out the grates at the bases of the trees in the courtyard.
2 points

Clue 68: Study the pond by Katsura Grill.
4 bonus points

Clue 69: Locate a classic Mickey in the Kawaii exhibit at the rear of the pavilion.
3 points

Clue 70: In the Mitsukoshi store, admire the oyster exhibit for a Hidden Mickey!
3 points

Clue 71: Look around for Mickey in the bushes by the lagoon.
3 points

★ Meander to *Morocco*.

Clue 72: Gaze at the front of the shop on the promenade for Hidden Mickeys.
2 points for one or more

Clue 73: Find a Mickey made of basket lids on the wall of a shop.
4 points

Clue 74: Study a mural at the rear of the pavilion for three Hidden Mickeys.

93

Walt Disney World's Hidden Mickeys

5 points for spotting all three

★ Go to *France*.

Clue 75: Examine the grates at the bases of the trees in the courtyard.
2 points

Clue 76: Find the classic Mickey bush on the right side of the ornamental garden.
3 points

Clue 77: Look high for classic Mickeys on the outside of a shop.
2 points

Clue 78: Search for Remy the rat inside a shop in the pavilion.
4 points

Clue 79: In the movie *Impressions de France*, spot Mickey's head and ears in the background of the wedding scene.
4 points

★ Enter the *United Kingdom*.

Clue 80: Check out a classic sports Mickey from the street.
2 points

★ Now walk over to *Canada* to find more classic Mickeys.

Clue 81: Examine the totem pole on the left near the steps into the pavilion.
3 points

Clue 82: Inside a store, search for a classic Mickey on an animal.
4 points

Clue 83: Study the front of the stone steps near the theater for a classic Mickey.
4 points

Clue 84: Step inside Le Cellier Steakhouse to find a Mickey made of wine.

3 points

★ Return to Future World and walk to *Club Cool* at the end of Innoventions West. Enjoy free exotic and refreshing soft drinks from foreign countries.

Clue 85: At the front entrance, look near the outside sign for Mickey.
3 points

Clue 86: Search inside Club Cool for a classic Mickey in the interior design.
3 points

Clue 87: Find a Hidden Mickey on the rear doors.
3 points

Clue 88: Spot Mickey outside above the rear entrance.
3 points

★ Go to the *Living with the Land* ride in The Land pavilion at your FastPass+ time. Study the wall murals to find three classic Hidden Mickeys and a Hidden Surprise.

Clue 89: Take a good look at the bubbles in the mural at the rear of the entrance queue.
3 points

Clue 90: Don't miss a Hidden Surprise image on the far right wall that you pass by just before reaching the loading dock. Scan this wall for an outline of a Prince and Princess!
5 points

Clue 91: Examine the mural behind the loading area near the farmer's hat.
3 points

Clue 92: Now check the lower part of the mural behind the loading area (You can spot this image from the boat).
3 points

Clue 93: On the ride, keep alert for a Cast Member with a Hidden Mickey on a video screen.
4 points

Clue 94: Search for a garden hose classic Mickey.
4 points

Clue 95: Spot Mickey in a horizontal water tube. (Minnie may be in there, too!)
4 points for Mickey and 4 bonus points for Minnie

Clue 96: Don't miss a Mickey-shaped wire frame! You'll often see vines growing over it.
2 points

Clue 97: Look for plants arranged to form a Hidden Mickey.
4 points

Clue 98: Along the ride, stay alert for one or more plastic gourds shaped like Mickey.
3 bonus points

Clue 99: In the last room, scan inside a fish tank for a Hidden Mickey.
5 points

Clue 100: Toward the end of the ride, find the green Hidden Mickey in the round test tube holder in a lab room.
3 points

Clue 101: Spot Mickey's name in this same lab room.
2 points

★ Go to the outside railing of *The Garden Grill* restaurant upstairs and take a good look at the back wall.

Clue 102: Find and then marvel at the green face of Mickey Mouse on the left side of the large mural of vegetation. He's in three-quarter profile on the right side of

a single fern and he's well camouflaged by the fern's leaves. (He's easier to spot from inside the restaurant.)
5 points

★ Go to the *interior railing* to the left of the pavilion's main entrance.

Clue 103: Focus on the side of one of the globes hanging over the lobby to spot another Mickey.
3 points

★ Now walk *outside* under the overhang *and face the entrance doors*.

Clue 104: Study the mosaic mural on the wall to your right for a classic Mickey in jewels.
4 points

Clue 105: Search the same mosaic mural for a classic Mickey in grapes.
4 points

★ Walk down the sloping walkway (from the pavilion) until you come to *"The Land" sign* out front.

Clue 106: Search for a classic Mickey in the stones embedded in a support for "The Land" sign. (Tip: The support is covered with tiles and stone designs.)
4 points

★ Head over to *The Seas with Nemo & Friends* pavilion to find twelve or more Hidden Mickeys.

Clue 107: Look up along the entrance queue for the ride for a Hidden Mickey.
3 bonus points (This image is not always present.)

Clue 108: On the ride, keep alert for a Mickey in the rock. Look below the fifth video screen to spot it.
5 points

Clue 109: Walk upstairs and search for one or more Hidden Mickeys on the aquarium floor.
5 points for one or more

Clue 110: Stroll to the upper level of the manatee viewing area and look for Hidden Mickeys on the wall. (These Hidden Mickeys come and go.)
3 bonus points

Clue 111: Cross to the upper display room above *Turtle Talk with Crush* to find two Hidden Mickeys on the wall in a lower panel.
5 points for both

Clue 112: Study an upper panel in this same display window for another Hidden Mickey.
5 points

Clue 113: Downstairs, find two Hidden Mickeys in bubbles on the wall near the manatees.
5 points for spotting both

Clue 114: In Bruce's room downstairs, look around for classic Mickeys in two different windows.
4 points for spotting both

Clue 115: Now search for Mickey near the exit gift shop.
3 points

★ Go to the Imagination! pavilion and ride *Journey Into Imagination with Figment*.

Clue 116: At the beginning of the queue, pore over the reception desk for a Hidden Mickey.
3 points

Clue 117: Locate a small Buzz Lightyear figure along the entrance queue.
5 points

Clue 118: Find a tiny Tinker Bell near Buzz.
5 points

Clue 119: On the ride, find a Hidden Mickey on a greaseboard. (Note: It's not always there.)
5 bonus points

Clue 120: Squint for a black pair of Mickey ears in the Sight Room.
4 points

Clue 121: Look up at Figment's bathtub for a classic Mickey.
3 points

Clue 122: Now look up again in Figment's bathroom for another classic Mickey near the bathtub.
3 points

Clue 123: Find a classic Mickey on a cloud in the rainbow room.
3 points

Clue 124: Search for a Mickey in snow.
5 points

Clue 125: Look for a classic Mickey on the wall along the exit hallway.
3 points

★ When you reach *ImageWorks* . . .

Clue 126: Locate a Hidden Mickey in big bubbles that rotate on a wall.
3 points

Clue 127: Gaze down inside *ImageWorks* for a classic Mickey.
4 points

Clue 128: Now scan upwards inside near the ceiling for Figment.
5 points

★ Stroll inside Innoventions East to the *Colortopia* exhibit.

Clue 129: Look for classic Mickeys inside the exhibit.
2 points

★ Check out the Universe of Energy. Find a Hidden Mickey as you take in the show and ride.

Clue 130: After the dinosaur section of the ride, watch the movie and look for the shadow of Disney's Hollywood Studios' "Earful" Tower (the tower with Mickey ears) in the door of a church in the background.
5 points

★ Head for *Spaceship Earth* at your FastPass+ time. Line up for the ride.

Clue 131: During the ride, keep alert for classic Mickey light patterns on the floor to your right.
5 points

Clue 132: Now look quickly to your left for a Hidden Mickey in scrolls.
5 points

Clue 133: During the ride, notice the Hidden Mickey on the document in front of the sleeping monk.
4 points

Clue 134: In the Renaissance section, look quickly to your left to spot the classic Mickey formed by paint circles on a tabletop near a painter.
4 points

Clue 135: Watch for a chalkboard with the name of a famous Mickey Mouse cartoon.
4 points

Clue 136: After you exit the ride vehicle, look up for Mickey in the "Project Tomorrow" area.
3 points

Chapter 3: Epcot Scavenger Hunt

★ Go to the *MouseGear* shop, where you'll find a number of Hidden Mickeys and décor Mickeys.

Clue 137: Before you enter MouseGear, find the classic Mickey in the sign above the shop entrance.
1 point

Clue 138: At one of the store entrances, admire huge Mickeys on the outside walls.
2 points for both

★ Now step inside, and keep your eyes peeled.

Clue 139: Examine the nuts on the display racks' bolts.
1 point

Clue 140: Observe the gauges on the wall.
1 point

Clue 141: Search for Donald's shadow.
3 points

Clue 142: Spot a set of Hidden Mickey gears.
2 points

Clue 143: Can you find an image of Donald Duck with a classic Mickey on him?
2 points

★ Keep your reservations for dinner. If you don't have reservations, eat at the Food Court in The Land.

Time now to tally your score.

Walt Disney World's Hidden Mickeys

Total Points for Epcot =

```
┌─────────────────────┐
│                     │
│                     │
│                     │
└─────────────────────┘
```

How'd you do?
Up to 196 points – Bronze
197 to 392 points – Silver
393 points and over – Gold
491 points – Perfect Score

If you earned bonus points in China,
Germany, Japan, *Living with the Land, The
Seas with Nemo & Friends,* **and/or** *Journey
Into Imagination with Figment,* **you may have
done even better!**

- Frozen Ever After

Hint 1: Along the inside entrance queue, three plates on the wall come together to form a classic Hidden Mickey. To find the image, after you walk into the room to the left (the "Ice Master & Deliverer of Arendelle" room) just inside the building, turn around back toward the entrance door and look above you. The three-plate Mickey is in the middle of a group of plates high up on the wall.

The Land

– Soarin'

Hint 2: In the pre-show video, a man who is wearing Mickey Mouse ears is asked to take them off.

Hint 3: In the pre-show video, a boy sitting

in his ride seat is wearing a red shirt with a Grumpy logo and shorts sporting Mickey Mouse.

Hint 4: In the scene with hot air balloons floating above the desert, three colorful balloons in the distance merge together as a classic Hidden Mickey. The image is visible for only a few seconds.

Hint 5: As you approach Spaceship Earth near the end of the ride, some people walking below you are carrying Mickey balloons.

Hint 6: The last big image is a classic Mickey made of bursts of fireworks (Mickey's "ears") over Spaceship Earth (his "head").

Test Track

Hint 7: On the wall, along the right side of the Standby entrance queue is a photo collage of artists and designers. A classic Mickey is traced on a transparent drawing board, just above the right hand of a man wearing glasses and drawing with a Magic Marker.

Hint 8: In the middle of the photo collage of artists and designers, a tiny white classic Mickey lies above a white vertical dashed line. This Hidden Mickey is above the left forearm of a girl who is drawing on white paper.

Hint 9: A bit further along on the right wall of the Standby queue, look for an interactive screen with design criteria (efficiency, etc.) listed above a car. Touch the area along the top of the car and circles will appear. You can arrange these circles with your finger to form a classic Mickey.

Hint 10: On the ride, about halfway along the inside track, a classic Mickey hides on
104

the first road sign on your right.

Hint 11: Before the long fast drive outside, look for the words "Scan Complete" on the wall to the left of the vehicle. A small, red classic Mickey is on the wall under the "C" in "Complete."

Hint 12: Keep your eyes left just before you burst onto the outside track. A small, purple classic Mickey is on the wall, above eye level.

Mission: SPACE

Hint 13: On the far right and left (outer) video monitors in the Mission Control room, classic Mickey circles appear on the lower part of the surface of Mars.

Hint 14: Continue to watch the video loops as three "status lights" form a classic Mickey at the lower right side of the rightmost monitor screen.

Hint 15: During the video loop on either of the middle monitors, three small waveform images merge into a classic Mickey on the lower left of the screen.

Hint 16: You'll see identical faint classic Hidden Mickeys above a horizontal bar on both sides of the launch door before it opens and before you see the sky.

Hint 17: As your spacecraft is landing on Mars, look sharp for a classic Mickey made of satellite dishes on top of the second building from the end, on the right side of the landing strip.

Hint 18: In the Expedition Mars section of the exit exhibit area, you'll find small classic Mickeys in the design of the video-game joystick consoles at the upper left and upper right corners.

Hint 19: In the center of the gift shop

near the exit doors, a large side profile of Mickey Mouse is painted on the ceiling in the middle square.

Hint 20: On either side of Mickey's side profile on the ceiling are reddish side profiles of Donald Duck and Pluto (or is it Goofy?).

Hint 21: On the right side of the mural behind the gift shop's cash register, the three round thrusters behind the blue X-2 spaceship form an upside-down classic Mickey.

Hint 22: Look for Minnie Mouse in the same mural. There's a small black classic Mickey in the dirt under her left foot.

Hint 23: On the left side of the mural behind the gift shop's cash register, you'll find an upside-down classic Mickey on the lower part of the moon.

Hint 24: The bases of some of the merchandise stands near the gift shop exit contain "support arches" in the shape of Mickey.

Hint 25: You can spot Hidden Mickeys in the electrical tubing on the wall on both sides of the exit door from the gift shop. There's a classic Mickey on one side and both a classic Mickey and a side-profile Mickey on the other.

– In the entrance plaza

Hint 26: Spot three craters that approximate a classic Mickey at the upper left of the Luna 8 landing site on the back side of the moon.

Hint 27: In the middle of a blue tile area, very near and to the left of a gold strip (as you face the attraction), you'll find a tiny tile classic Mickey (black head and blue ears).

106

Hint 28: A small classic Mickey formed of white tiles is toward the bottom of a blue tile stripe. Look for a bluish and salmon-colored disc in the cement, near the lowest part of the stripe. Mickey is hiding about four feet from the disc as you go toward the Mars planet.

Hint 29: Two more tile or stone classic Mickeys (black head and white ears) lie next to a drain cover. Look for the cover in a circle of tiles to the left of the *Mission: SPACE* sign.

The Seas with Nemo & Friends

– Turtle Talk With Crush

Hint 30: In the waiting room, a tiny classic Mickey hides in the pink and brown coral in the first window painting to the right as you enter the room. At the lower part of the painting, the Mickey is left of the third tallest (leftmost) blue tube, about one quarter of the distance up the side of the tube. He's reclining to the right.

Hint 31: Also in the *Turtle Talk With Crush* waiting room, look at the upper left of the second window to the right (as you enter the room) to spot "Peach" the starfish. An upside-down classic Mickey lies above the left side of Peach's "eyebrow" (Peach's left, our right).

Hint 32: During the show, look closely at the middle left side of the rear screen, near the edge, to spot a classic Mickey made of coral circles on the rock. Mickey's ears are angled to the left.

Epcot Character Spot

Hint 33: At the left side of the first greeting bay, Mickey wears earphones.

Hint 34: At the right side of the first greeting bay, a white Mickeyesque movie/video camera is on a blue and white monitor screen.

Hint 35: A white classic Mickey on a flag is partially hidden near the ceiling on the left side of the first greeting bay.

Hint 36: On an outside wall of Innoventions West, a Mickey Mouse hat appears in a mural of silhouettes. The wall faces The Land pavilion and borders the walkway from Innoventions Plaza to Future World West.

Behind MouseGear store

Hint 37: Outside and behind MouseGear is a classic Mickey in the walkway cement. Exit the shop at the rear heading toward Test Track; then take the first right onto a walkway (heading toward World Showcase). Just before the path changes to an octagonal shape, look down near the left railing to find a small classic Mickey indented in the concrete.

Mexico

– Gran Fiesta Tour
Starring the Three Caballeros

Hint 38: During the boat ride, you will pass two sets of lily pads that form classic Hidden Mickeys. The first set is to the right of your boat as you float through the small lagoon in front of the San Angel Inn Restaurante, before you pass in front of the volcano. These lily pads are in the shadows, but you can usually spot them from the boat.

Hint 39: While you're in the lagoon at the beginning of the boat ride, turn to your left and watch smoke rise from the volcano. Every half minute or so, holes in the smoke form classic Mickeys that quickly disappear.

Hint 40: Along the left wall inside the first tunnel, look at the fifth man from the far end. He is wearing green shorts and has a partially covered blue classic Mickey on the front of his necklace.

Hint 41: The second set of lily pads is easier to see; you'll find this Hidden Mickey to the right of your boat just past the first tunnel with the wall murals.

Hint 42: Watch for a video screen to the right of your boat that shows a broad expanse of water in the foreground and, in the background, a shoreline edged with modern buildings set against the backdrop of a mountain. Donald Duck is parasailing over the water, but you want to focus on the buildings on the shoreline. One building on the right side of the scene has a dark classic Mickey tree in front of it.

Hint 43: About halfway through the ride, in the small blue pond to the left of the boat, classic Mickeys appear in the bubbles after Donald is taken away. Look above and also to the lower left of the octopus.

Hint 44: Toward the end of the ride, as you enter the fireworks room, three drums form a classic Hidden Mickey at the lower right of the "Viva Donald" barge to the left of your boat.

Hint 45: These Hidden Mickeys can only be seen with a light from your camera, cell phone, etc. As your boat floats by the last scene of the ride with the map of Mexico on the wall, look down at tiles that line the base of the platform to your left. The tiles are just above the side of your boat. You can spot three Mickey stickers on the tiles! They're located about one-third of the distance along the row of tiles as you float along. The first one is a full-body Mickey on tile #17 (counting from the start). Several tiles further along, on tile #20, are Mickey's face and ears. Finally, another full-body Mickey sticker is on tile #25, which is halfway along the 50 tiles on the platform.

– San Angel Inn Restaurante

Hint 46: Smoke rising from the volcano by the river forms classic Mickeys that quickly disappear.

China

Hint 47: Classic Mickey-shaped flowers are sculpted on the bases of several decorative light posts on the outside front of the pavilion.

Bonus Points Hint: In the ponds, the floating lily pads sometimes come together to form recognizable classic Mickeys.

Outpost
between China and Germany

Hint 48: At the Outpost, three of the short wooden posts at the corner closest to the bridge form a classic Mickey when viewed from above.

Hint 49: At the Outpost, a piece of brown luggage is perched high on a rear wall in the left room inside the Village Traders shop. The luggage tag is signed "M. Mouse," and a red sticker on the bottom of the luggage says "Mickey Mouse" and "Disney Magic."

Germany

Hint 50: On the second floor of the building to your right, to the right of the glockenspiel clock, are three suits of armor. The one closest to the glockenspiel has a classic Mickey on its crown.

Hint 51: In the rear of the courtyard, a three-circle classic Mickey formation is in the ironwork support behind the bell on the front of the clock tower. It's formed by the circular metal support (not by holes in the metal) and is tilted to the left.

Hint 52: At the left of the entrance to the Biergarten Restaurant, you can see a wrought-iron lion behind a lamp on the outside wall. The lion's front and rear paws are resting on an upside-down classic Mickey.

Hint 53: At the Karamell-Küche shop, in an outside display window that faces the inner courtyard and is close to the main promenade, a caramel apple at the lower right corner of a page in an open cookbook has a small light reflection that forms a white classic Mickey.

Hint 54: Inside the Karamell-Küche shop, a small orange classic Hidden Mickey is painted on the merchandise shelf siding. The image is about halfway up on a vine on the right shelf siding closest to the door to the main World Showcase promenade.

*– Landscaping around
the miniature train exhibit*

Bonus Points Hint: Check the dirt, grass, bushes, and decorations for Hidden Mickey images that come and go during the year. The landscapers often shape one or more of the tiny bushes into classic Mickeys.

Italy

Hint 55: In the wine shop, Enoteca Castello, a classic Mickey appears in the woodwork along the relief design of the upper front counter.

Hint 56: Behind the statue on the right side

111

of the walkway in front of the restaurants, a classic Mickey impression hides on the left side of the rock wall.

The American Adventure

Hint 57: A red, white, and blue banner is on the railing over the entrance to the rotunda of The American Adventure, and a small, faint classic Mickey hides on the banner. It's in the middle of the white star next to the "A" in "Adventure."

Hint 58: A classic Mickey made of roses decorates a lady's hat in a painting on the first floor on the far left wall (as you enter). Look for the painting in which a man is speaking to a crowd in front of a hardware store. The lady with the rose-trimmed hat is at the lower middle of the painting and the Hidden Mickey is on the right side of her hat.

Hint 59: A picture on a first-floor wall at the right rear of the rotunda shows workers building a skyscraper. The tops of two vertical beams behind the workers sport classic Mickey holes.

Hint 60: On the rear wall of the rotunda, first and second floors, large bronze eagle reliefs have classic Mickeys in the corners.

– The American Adventure show

Hint 61: At the beginning of the film, an upside-down classic Mickey appears on the rock behind (and to your right of) a kneeling female pilgrim.

Hint 62: Early in the show, a classic Mickey lock hangs on the right side of a stockade in a scene of the American Revolution time period.

Hint 63: In the scene with the old gas station, a classic Mickey is formed by three red apples in a crate at the lower right of

112

the scene.

Hint 64: At the end of the show, fireworks light up the sky behind the Statue of Liberty Torch as it rises from the floor. One of the last fireworks at the upper right fizzles into a classic Mickey head (best seen from the right side of the theater).

- *America Gardens Theatre*

Hint 65: Classic Hidden Mickeys are stuck on both sides of the stage apron / forestage, near the short brick wall that borders the front of the main stage.

Japan

Hint 66: In the koi fish pond across from the Mitsukoshi store, a drain cover in the water near the bamboo fence sports a classic Mickey.

Hint 67: The trees in the courtyard are encircled by metal grates with classic Mickey designs.

Hint 68: Visit the pond next to Katsura Grill for a possible bonus Hidden Mickey. Cast Members sometimes arrange rocks in the pond to form a classic Mickey.

Hint 69: The rear exhibit area is showcasing "Kawaii - Japan's Cute Culture." In one of the displays, magnets on the upper left of a refrigerator door are arranged like a classic Mickey.

Hint 70: In the middle of the Mitsukoshi store, look for Hidden Mickeys in the oyster-pearl display. Sometimes, you can find pearls arranged as a classic three-circle Mickey, and other times Cast Members arrange the oyster shells into a classic Mickey in the water. Once, I arrived right after store opening and watched the Cast Member form the familiar image with oyster shells.

Hint 71: Out on the promenade, next to the lagoon, three round bushes to the left of the Torii Gate form a classic Mickey.

Morocco

Hint 72: Three brass plates are arranged to form a classic Mickey on the left green door at the entrance to the Souk-al-Magreb "Gifts of Morocco" shop on the promenade. (Sometimes, the plates are on the nearby red door, and you might find more than one plate classic Mickey on the doors!)

Hint 73: Basket lids usually form a sideways classic Mickey on the wall inside the Brass Bazaar shop (located at the right side of the Morocco pavilion behind the Tangierine Café). As you face the rear of the pavilion from inside the shop, look above the right side of the archway.

Hint 74: Across from Restaurant Marrakesh, three small classic Mickeys hide on a mural on the rear wall of a small room. One is at the top of a tower on the right side of the mural's street. Another is on the left side of the street, next to a double archway. The third is a tiny black Mickey in an upper doorway on the left middle part of the mural.

France

Hint 75: The trees in the courtyard are encircled by metal grates with classic Mickey patterns.

Hint 76: In the patterned hedge (parterre) garden, a bush in the middle right area (on the side nearest the canal) is trimmed to the shape of a classic Mickey.

Hint 77: Classic Mickey images are high on the outside molding of Les Vins de France shop, near the entrance to *Impressions de*

114

France.

Hint 78: Inside Les Vins de France, a small plush figure of Remy (the rat from the movie *Ratatouille*) sits in a basket on a shelf near the ceiling, behind the service counter.

– *Impressions de France*

Hint 79: In the movie's outdoor wedding scene, you can see a Mickey head and ears in a second floor window of the house in the background. It's in the center screen.

United Kingdom

Hint 80: Outside the Sportsman's Shoppe, a sign has a classic Mickey with a tennis racket head, a soccer ball for one ear, and a rugby ball for the other.

Canada

Hint 81: Past the steps into the pavilion, the left totem pole has black classic Mickeys on both sides near the top by the raven's wings.

Hint 82: A small black classic Mickey is on the side of a fish, which is hanging on the outside of a box at the left rear of the first room as you enter the Northwest Mercantile shop.

Hint 83: A classic Hidden Mickey is etched on the front facing of a stone step inside Canada, close to the theater. Start at the theater and walk up the steps. You will come to a landing with a light and a trail that branches off to the left. Continue walking up the steps. The Mickey image appears before you reach the next landing.

Hint 84: Behind the check-in desk at Le Cellier Steakhouse, three horizontal bottles at the center top of a wine display form a classic Mickey.

Future World West

– Club Cool near Innoventions West

Hint 85: Holes in the metal bracket supports behind the outdoor sign form classic Mickeys.

Hint 86: Above you, on a colorful decorative border in the middle of the club, green circles form an upside-down classic Mickey.

Hint 87: A classic Mickey is formed when the rear doors open. Stand inside and watch the door on your left. When it's fully open, circles on the door and the glass wall come together to form a Hidden Mickey in the center of the door.

Hint 88: Classic Mickeys are near the bottom of the blue banners that are located outside and above the rear entrance to Club Cool.

The Land

– Living with the Land

Hint 89: In the middle section of the giant wall mural at the rear of the queue, bubbles align to form a classic Mickey, ears angled to the left.

Hint 90: A Hidden Surprise is on the first part of the far right wall of the entrance queue - the wall you pass by right before reaching the loading dock. It's a large, indistinct, bright white outline of a Prince and Princess holding each other. The image extends from the floor to near the ceiling, and the Prince faces left and bends slightly down over the Princess.

Hint 91: A classic Mickey is formed by

shrubs (the "head" has yellow dots on it) to the right of the brim of the farmer's hat near the top of the loading dock mural.

Hint 92: In the lower right area of the mural behind the boat loading area, three circles form a small classic Mickey (a purple circle forms the head and blue circles form the ears). The head is tilted slightly to the right.

Hint 93: In the first part of the ride, a female Cast Member on the last video screen on your left has a Mickey Mouse face hiding on the upper part of her name tag.

Hint 94: A garden hose is coiled into a classic Mickey to the right of the boat about halfway through the fish farming section. (Cast Members usually check on and arrange this Mickey image every morning.)

Hint 95: A classic Mickey made of wire mesh can be found in the aquaculture section. Cast Members generally place it in one of the horizontal display shrimp tubes that are part of the landscape on either side of your boat. (A wire mesh Hidden Minnie, with her hair bow, sometimes also appears in the aquatubes, not far from Mickey.)

Hint 96: A large, classic Mickey-shaped vine frame (sometimes covered with vines, sometimes not) stands upright along the right side of your boat.

Hint 97: Plants of different colors are usually arranged in groups to form a classic Mickey in the greenhouses. Often the plants are lettuces.

Hint 98: Along the ride, you can often spot hanging plastic gourds shaped like classic Mickeys. They're used to grow fruit or vegetables into Mickey shapes.

117

Hint 99: In the last room of the ride, a fish tank - labeled "Integrated Aquaculture" - is on the left side of your boat. Vertical pipes are visible along the top section of the tank. Classic (three-circle) Hidden Mickey holes are in the pipe at the top middle of the tank. (Warning: sometimes this pipe is rotated so that the holes are harder to spot).

Hint 100: Toward the end of the ride, a large circular test-tube holder on the right side of a "Biotechnology Lab" room has a green classic Mickey in the center. Mickey is formed by the test tubes' green stoppers.

Hint 101: On one or more tables in this biotech lab, a sign advertises the plant product, "Mickey's Mini Gardens."

– The Garden Grill

Hint 102: On the left side of the large wall-mural of vegetation inside the restaurant, a Mickey is hiding behind the most prominent fern that extends all the way to the top of the mural. Counting up horizontally from the bottom of the fern, his face is mostly behind the fifth through eighth leaves on the fern's right side. He's looking slightly downward and to the right in a three-quarter profile. Two black circles that form his eyes are visible above the sixth fern leaf on the right, more than halfway to the end of the leaf. Mickey's ears jut above the seventh leaf, and his mouth and nose are below the sixth leaf. His face and ears are green, and his mouth is slightly open. This Hidden Mickey is a real classic!

– Around The Land's main entrance

Hint 103: From the upper level railing, just to the left as you walk in the main entrance, a classic Mickey is on the Earth above the lobby. It's in water swirls, to the left of the tip of South America, and it's sideways to the right.

118

Hint 104: A classic Mickey hides in the mosaic mural on the pavilion's right outside wall (as you enter). Find the word "LAND" on the mural and look slightly above and to the right about six feet or so to a reddish plateau. Just above the left side of the flat upper part of the plateau are three jewels, a green "head" and two reddish "ears."

Hint 105: In the same mosaic mural, look for a cluster of grapes to the upper left of the word "LAND." A classic Mickey, tilted to the right and almost upside down, is formed by three grapes. The grape Mickey is almost completely beneath the translucent signboard.

Hint 106: The Land sign outside the pavilion's entrance rests on two large stone- and tile-covered supports. On the end of the right-hand support, embedded stones decorate the upper portion of the green-tiled area. A small classic Mickey, formed of three stones, lies near the center of the stone decoration.

The Seas with Nemo & Friends

Hint 107: As you reach the wooden rails of the walkway along the inside entrance queue for the ride, a classic Mickey made of blue moving water circles lies above you on the right side. (Note: This image isn't always present.)

Hint 108: On the ride, a classic Mickey impression in rock lies below the fifth video screen from the start. It's slightly above and between two pink clusters of standing corals, to the right of center in the rock ledge.

Hint 109: Spot one or more classic Mickeys formed of rocks at the bottom of the aquarium. They're best seen from the upstairs viewing corridor and circular viewing area. Recently, one of the images had starfish-shaped rocks for its "ears." Note: These rock Mickeys may change locations on the aquarium floor, and some may disappear at times. You may need to look through several windows in the observation area to find them.

Hint 110: You can often see classic Mickeys on the chalkboard at the upper level of the Manatee viewing area. The board lists the names and other information about the manatees in the pool. Hidden Mickeys on this chalkboard come and go.

Hint 111: Search the room upstairs directly above *Turtle Talk with Crush*. In the far left display window (as you enter the room), look for two classic Hidden Mickeys in bubbles in the lower row of panels. You'll find them in the upper right corner of the second panel from the right side of the large window.

Hint 112: In this same display window, look high in the upper left panel under the words "Finding Solutions" for another bubble classic Hidden Mickey.

Hint 113: In the manatee viewing room, lower level, bubbles in wall displays form two classic Mickeys. One is on the left wall (as you exit), in the left middle square containing the words "Manatee Zone ... Slow Speed." Another is on the right wall (as you exit) in the lower left square with the polar bear.

Hint 114: As you enter Bruce's room on the lower level, check out the second windows on both the right (labeled "Did You Know?") and left (labeled "Bruce's Scrapbook"). In both windows, an oyster contains three pearls arranged as a classic Mickey.

Hint 115: Bubbles come together to form

several classic Mickeys on the garbage cans you see in the pavilion.

Imagination!

– Journey Into Imagination with Figment

Hint 116: On the right side at the beginning of the entrance queue, a classic Mickey is doodled in one corner of an interoffice mailing envelope, which lies at the far left end of the reception desk.

Hint 117: On the right side along the entrance queue, a small Buzz Lightyear is hiding in a display across from Professor Phillip Brainard's office door.

Hint 118: Directly above Buzz Lightyear, on the upper shelf, a tiny black silhouette of Tinker Bell can be spotted inside a pyramidal container. Look through a hole in the front of the container; Tinker Bell stands to the right of the hole.

Hint 119: As you enter the Sight Room, a tiny dark classic Mickey is hidden at the lower right of a greaseboard on a wall to your right. The greaseboard is below the words "Focus Group." (Note: This Hidden Mickey may change locations on the board or even disappear at times.)

Hint 120: In the center of the Sight Room, headphones on the left of two tables have Mickey ears on an earpiece!

Hint 121: Three bubbles make a classic Mickey near Figment's hand on the edge of his bathtub.

Hint 122: In Figment's Upside-Down House, his toilet forms a classic Mickey with two red circles on the floor.

Hint 123: When you feel a blast of air and the walls open, you'll see a rainbow and balloons. Look down and to the right to see classic Mickey circles appear on a cloud at the bottom right of the stage.

Hint 124: In this same scene at the end of the ride, find the letters that spell "Action" that stand in the middle of the scene. Snow covers the top of the letter "A," and a classic Mickey sits in the snow at the bottom left of the snow cap. The Hidden Mickey image tilts to the left.

Hint 125: On the left wall of the exit hallway, a sideways classic Mickey is behind and between the "I" and "m" of the ImageWorks sign.

– ImageWorks

Hint 126: Inside *ImageWorks*, a group of big circles (bubbles?) rotates in place on a wall. At times, three circles come together at the lower right to form a classic Hidden Mickey.

Hint 127: Behind a pillar in the middle of ImageWorks, a classic Hidden Mickey is on the floor made of tan-colored tile.

Hint 128: A tiny Figment plush is hiding above you in *ImageWorks*. He's hanging from a ceiling electrical device in Studio B of the Magic Photo Studio section. (I was told by a Cast Member that the Manager of the area moves this Figment around the ceiling from time to time.)

Innoventions East

– Colortopia

Hint 129: Stop by Spinning Spectrums, which is on a wall inside Colortopia. Several of the wall designs that spin have yellow and orange classic Mickeys.

Universe of Energy

Hint 130: After the dinosaur section of the ride, the movie shows a man driving a car out of a barn and toward a church building in the background (the fourth building from the left). A shadow of the Disney's Hollywood Studios' "Earful" Tower appears in the door of the church.

Spaceship Earth

Hint 131: After the fall of Rome, you see three Islamic scholars seated around a table on the floor. They are illuminated by lights that form patterns on the floor. The outer circles of light patterns form classic Mickeys.

Hint 132: Across from the Islamic scholars, on a wall to your left, are shelves with cubbyholes full of scrolls and books. In one of the last cubbyholes you pass before you leave the scene, the round ends of three stacked scrolls lying horizontally form a classic Mickey. It's on the second shelf up from the bottom, in the right lower corner of the second cubbyhole from the right wall.

Hint 133: During the ride, in a scene to the left, monks are writing at desks. In front of the sleeping monk is a document with a small ink blot at the upper right corner. The blot is shaped like a classic Mickey and becomes visible as your vehicle passes by.

Hint 134: Just after the Gutenberg printing press scene, in the first part of the Renaissance section, look for the first painter to the left of your ride vehicle. Three white paint circles form a classic Mickey on the top left of the table near the painter. You have to look fast for this one.

Hint 135: On the right side, as you're passing the section showing black and white movies, a chalkboard marquee on the ground lists upcoming features. One is "The Band Concert," a famous

123

MickeyMouse cartoon.

Hint 136: At the exit of *Spaceship Earth*, several classic Mickeys float along on overhead blue screens in the Project Tomorrow interactive area.

Future World East

– MouseGear

Hint 137: The signs above the shop entrances have classic Mickeys with two round ears above the letter "G" as the head.

Hint 138: Two classic Mickeys made of gears sit - partially covered - on the outside walls at both sides of the store entrance that faces World Showcase. One Mickey is right-side up and the other has its "ears" to the left.

Hint 139: The large wing nuts on the bolts of some of the display racks form Mickey ears.

Hint 140: Some of the gauges on the wall are arranged as classic Mickeys.

Hint 141: The shadows of Donald Duck and his relatives are on the upper part of a wall in the center of the store.

Hint 142: Classic Mickey gears hang above a display on a wall opposite the cash registers.

Hint 143: Look for a large Donald Duck on a wall in the part of the store near the main walkway to the east side of Future World to find a classic Mickey made of gears.

Chapter 4

Disney's
Hollywood
Studios
Scavenger Hunt

• • • • • • • • • • • •

Before You Start

• *Many great Hidden Mickeys are in Standby queues, and you might miss them if you take the FastPass+ queues. So, for optimal Hidden Mickey hunting, I recommend reserving FastPass+ for the following attractions:* **The Twilight Zone Tower of Terror, Voyage of The Little Mermaid,** *and* **Fantasmic!**

Be sure to keep track of your three FastPass+ windows and return to these attractions at the appropriate times. In the Scavenger Hunt below, if you come to your FastPass+ attraction and it's not time for it yet, skip to the next stop in the Hunt and return to the FastPass+ attraction during your time window.

• *Line up for shows 20-30 minutes ahead of start time.*

• *Many of the Hidden Mickeys in this park are in restaurants and shops. Be considerate of fellow guests and Cast Members as you search. Tell them what you are looking for, so they can share in the fun. Avoid searching restaurants at busy meal times unless you are one of the diners.*

★ Walk first to *Toy Story Mania!*

Clue 1: As you get close to loading, spot a classic Mickey on the wall.
2 points

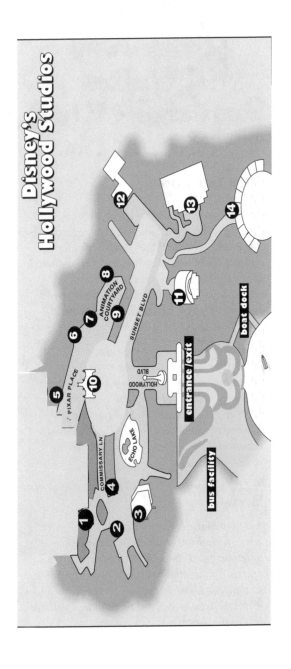

1 MuppetVision 3D

2 Star Tours® - The Adventures Continue

3 Indiana Jones™ Epic Stunt Spectacular!

4 Star Wars™: Path of the Jedi

5 Toy Story Mania!®

6 Walt Disney: One Man's Dream

7 Voyage of The Little Mermaid

8 Star Wars Launch Bay

9 Disney Junior — Live on Stage!

10 The Great Movie Ride®

11 Beauty and the Beast — Live on Stage

12 Rock 'n' Roller Coaster® Starring Aerosmith

13 The Twilight Zone Tower of Terror™

14 Fantasmic!

Clue 2: On the interactive screens, look behind the target balloons in front of the volcano to spot a classic Mickey.
5 points

Clue 3: On another screen, watch the white plates for a classic Mickey image.
3 points

Clue 4: Stay alert for a classic Mickey below an exclamation point on the wall.
5 points

Clue 5: Study a book along the exit for a tiny classic Mickey.
5 points

Clue 6: Along the exit hallway from the third (newest) ride track, check out the coloring book posters on the walls for a Hidden Mickey. (You may be able to access this exit hallway from outside the attraction).
5 points

Clue 7: Outside of the attraction, look around for popcorn Mickey.
3 points

Clue 8: Then search outside for Mickey on a plate.
2 points

★ Now go to *Rock 'n' Roller Coaster Starring Aerosmith*. (You can find the Hidden Mickeys here without riding the coaster, the first twelve by exiting before the ride, seven in—and on the way to—the gift shop by walking in through the exit from outside, and four outside in the courtyard.)

Clue 9: Study the tile floor along the entrance queue for two classic Mickeys.
5 points for both

Clue 10: Look down at the carpet along the entrance queue for Hidden Mickeys.
4 points

Clue 11: Don't miss the tiny Mickey on a wall poster just before the pre-show room.
4 points

Clue 12: Search around the pre-show room for a classic Mickey.
4 points

Clue 13: After the pre-show, locate five Hidden Characters on a big poster.
5 points for spotting all five

Clue 14: Pay attention to the instructional video overhead for a tiny classic Mickey.
4 points

Clue 15: Stare across the track for Mickey on the wall.
5 points

Clue 16: At the loading gate, look at the rear license plates of the limo ride vehicles. (Then exit if you wish.)
4 points

Clue 17: As you step out of your ride vehicle at the end, glance to your far left to spot Mickey on a wall. (If you haven't taken the ride, walk in through the gift shop to find this and the following five Mickeys.)
3 points

Clue 18: At the exit, find a box with a classic Mickey in the word "box."
4 points

Clue 19: Search for another box with a classic Mickey in a word.
4 points

Clue 20: In the gift shop, spot a Hidden Mickey on a guitar.
4 points

Clue 21: In the gift shop, look around for a Hidden Oswald the Lucky Rabbit (with long ears).

3 points

Clue 22: Also in the shop, find Mickey and Minnie made of guitar picks!
4 points for both

Clue 23: Outside in the courtyard, locate a Hidden Mickey on a food kiosk sign.
3 points

Clue 24: Also in the courtyard, search for three Hidden Mickeys on the wall of the attraction.
5 points for spotting all three

★ Walk to *The Twilight Zone Tower of Terror* at your FastPass+ time and explore the entry queue area and pre-show for three Hidden Mickeys.

Clue 25: During the pre-show film in the library, find the plush Mickey Mouse doll held by a little girl.
3 points

Clue 26: Linger in the left library to spot the words "Mickey Mouse" on sheet music on a desktop.
4 points

Clue 27: Notice a classic Mickey stain on the wall in the boiler room.
4 points

(Tip: For the best vantage point for the ride Hidden Mickeys (Clues 28 to 30), take the right queue when the line for the ride splits. Then tell the Cast Member you're hunting for Hidden Mickeys and ask to be seated in the rightmost ride vehicle.)

Clue 28: At the first stop on the ride, search for a Hidden Mickey above you.
4 points

Clue 29: Also look for a Mickey Mouse doll here.
4 points

Clue 30: Stare at the star field (the doors to the elevator shaft just before they open!) to spot a classic Hidden Mickey in the stars.
5 points

Clue 31: As you exit, spot Mickey on the floor!
4 points

★ Your next stop is *Star Tours—The Adventures Continue*.

Clue 32: Don't miss a classic Mickey on a tree along the outside queue.
5 points

Clue 33: Along the inside entrance queue, look for a Hidden Mickey near C-3PO.
3 points

Clue 34: Now wait for a shadow Hidden Mickey in a video on a wall display along the entrance queue. (Note: You may have to cool your heels awhile to spot this one!)
4 points

Clue 35: Next, study the entrance queue luggage scanner for Mickey and other Disney characters and images.
5 points total for finding Mickey and two or more other Disney images

Clue 36: Just after you're seated for the ride, watch C-3PO to your right for a tiny Hidden Mickey.
5 points

Clue 37: At the end of the ride, if you land on the Coruscant planet (as opposed to other random end destinations for the ride), look for classic Mickeys on a rear wall.
5 bonus points

Clue 38: Spot a blue-light classic Mickey on a counter in the gift shop at the exit.
4 points

131

Clue 39: Find classic Mickey on the front of another counter in the gift shop.
3 points

Clue 40: Just before you exit the gift shop, look on your left for a Hidden Mickey on the wall.
4 points

★ Stroll over to *The Great Movie Ride*. (This attraction may close). First find two classic Mickeys among the celebrity impressions in the cement in front of the Chinese Theater, then step in line and take the ride.

Clue 41: Check Harry Anderson's square.
3 points

Clue 42: Now see if you can spot a Mickey in Carol Burnett's square.
3 points

Clue 43: In the movie room of the Standby entrance queue, locate a classic Mickey on a woman in a painting.
3 points

Clue 44: In the middle of the loading dock mural, search for the Hidden Minnie above a tree stump. (Psst! It's visible at loading and unloading.)
5 points

Clue 45: On the right side of this mural, squint for a tiny black Hidden Mickey.
5 points

Clue 46: As you start down Gangster Alley, look for Mickey's brown shoes under a James Cagney poster.
4 points

Clue 47: At the end of Gangster Alley, find Mickey's shadow in a window near the top of the "Chemical Company" building.
5 points

Clue 48: In the "Western" section, spot two

references to Pocahontas.
5 points for both

Tip: To spot all of the Hidden Images in the "Raiders of the Lost Ark" room (Clues 51 to 54, below) look quickly first to your left, then to your right, then left again, and finally right again as your vehicle moves through the room.

Clue 49: Look left for R2-D2 and C-3PO on the wall!
5 points

Clue 50: Stare to the right of your vehicle for a small white classic Mickey on a tablet below the ark container.
5 points

Clue 51: Find Mickey and Donald on the left wall, at the end of the "Raiders of the Lost Ark" room. (Psst! Mickey is facing Donald.)
5 points

Clue 52: Now glance quickly to your right for a hieroglyphic Mickey.
5 points

Clue 53: In the "Tarzan" room, stare at the trees high above and to your right for a classic Mickey.
3 points

Clue 54: In the "Wizard of Oz" room, search for Mickey in the flowers.
3 points

Clue 55: Look up to spot Mickey in the trees in the "Wizard of Oz" room.
5 points

Clue 56: After you exit, study the design above the outside entrance door for a classic Mickey image.
3 points

★ Walk to *Voyage of The Little Mermaid* at

your FastPass+ time.

Clue 57: Look for a classic Mickey in the inside waiting room.
3 points
(You can stay for the show in the theater or exit out the doors you just entered to continue your Hidden Mickey search.)

★ Take a lunch break. Keep your reservations if you have them. If not, try the Backlot Express for burgers and sandwiches, the PizzeRizzo for pizza, or the ABC Commissary for salads and sandwiches.

★ Check your Times Guide for convenient show times for *Beauty and the Beast—Live on Stage*. While you're eating *scan your Studios Guidemap* for a Hidden Mickey.

Clue 58: Turn the Disney's Hollywood Studios map about 45 degrees counterclockwise (so that the right corner is at the top) and search for Mickey.
4 points

Clue 59: Now study the map for tiny classic Hidden Mickeys.
3 points

★ Go to *MuppetVision 3D* and find five Hidden Mickeys, a Hidden Pluto, and a Hidden Surprise.

Clue 60: In the waiting room for the pre-show, find bicycles that form a Hidden Mickey.
2 points

Clue 61: During the first part of the pre-show on the video monitors, observe the test pattern.
4 points

Clue 62: In the first part of the movie, keep your eyes open for shelves on a wall with trophies. Look for Mickey there!

5 points

Clue 63: After the cannon shoots holes in the theater, watch for a plush Mickey.
3 points

Clue 64: Try to spot the Mickey balloons while Kermit rides in on a fire truck.
3 points

Clue 65: Study the license plate on the fire truck for a Hidden Surprise.
4 points

Clue 66: Don't miss Pluto's appearance!
2 points

★ Cross the park to *Walt Disney: One Man's Dream.*

Clue 67: During your walk through the attraction, locate a Hidden Mickey in a painting that Walt is holding.
3 points

Clue 68: Farther along, look around for a Hidden Donald near Walt, who is holding a pointer.
3 points

Clue 69: Now find Mickey on the wall near Walt.
3 points

★ Check out the show *Disney Junior—Live on Stage!* in Animation Courtyard.

Clue 70: Watch for Mickey in the lighting and stage effects.
3 points for two or more

★ Get in line to meet BB-8 at Star Wars Launch Bay.

Clue 71: While you're waiting, scan the walls for a Hidden Mickey.
4 points

Walt Disney World's Hidden Mickeys

★ Exit Animation Courtyard through the arch and veer left to *The Hollywood Brown Derby* restaurant. Admire the mural on the wall outside, above the restaurant.

Clue 72: Look for two classic Mickeys in the mural.
5 points for spotting both

★ Now look at the pictures in the waiting area inside the restaurant.

Clue 73: Spot the man with Mickey Mouse ears.
3 points

★ Turn left as you leave and *head down Sunset Boulevard.*

Clue 74: Search for a classic Mickey in scrollwork on a blue building.
4 points

★ Walk to *Rosie's All-American Café.*

Clue 75: Look around the food order area for Mickey.
4 points

★ Catch a performance of *Beauty and the Beast—Live on Stage.*

Clue 76: Watch for Mickey on the back of one of the characters.
3 points

★ Turn left onto Hollywood Boulevard, then right to *Hollywood & Vine restaurant.*

Clue 77: Seek a Hidden Character above the restaurant's entrance.
3 points

★ Enter the restaurant and examine the left wall.

Clue 78: Find a stick-figure Mickey.
2 points

Clue 79: Search the wall for some classic Mickeys.
3 points

★ Step inside the waiting area for the *50's Prime Time Café* and look closely at the tables.

Clue 80: Check out what's holding them together.
1 point

★ Go to the *Backlot Express* restaurant.

Clue 81: Locate a Hidden Mickey on the drink station near the exit door that faces *Star Tours.*
4 points

Clue 82: Look for standing Mickeys.
4 points for finding four or more

★ Ask a restaurant Cast Member to let you check out the *Sci-Fi Dine-In Theater Restaurant* inside.

Clue 83: Look for a classic Mickey in the waiting area.
3 points

Clue 84: Find a full-body Mickey in the waiting area.
3 points

Clue 85: Study the right rear mural in the dining area. Look for two Hidden Mickeys along the treetops.
5 points for both

Clue 86: Stare at a small mosaic mural at the rear of the restaurant for a side profile of Mickey Mouse.
5 points

Clue 87: Watch the movie reel for three Hidden Characters.
8 points for spotting all three

Clue 88: Stay alert for a classic Hidden Mickey on a spacesuit.
4 points

Clue 89: When popcorn appears on the screen, search for a Hidden Mickey.
5 points

Clue 90: Find a Hidden Mickey on a dining car.
3 points

★ Wander into the *Stage 1 Company Store* and find four Hidden Mickeys.

Clue 91: Locate a classic Mickey near a bird.
2 points

Clue 92: Take a good look at the old bureau that's loaded with hats and paint cans.
3 points

Clue 93: Spot a classic Mickey on the wall.
3 points

Clue 94: Search for some famous shorts.
3 points

Clue 95: Now find several Hidden Mickeys outside the store.
5 points for four or more

★ In the waiting area for *Mama Melrose's Ristorante Italiano*, search for five classic Mickeys.

Clue 96: Check out the Dalmatian.
3 points

Clue 97: Examine the plaster on the right wall.
3 points

Clue 98: Find a classic Mickey leaf near the check-in podium. (Note: This Hidden Mickey moves around or disappears at

times!)
4 bonus points

Clue 99: Locate a small Hidden Mickey marking on the wall behind the check-in podium.
5 points

Clue 100: Now look at the plaster on the wall to the left of the check-in podium.
3 points

★ On Commissary Lane, get in line for *Mickey and Minnie Starring in Red Carpet Dreams.*

Clue 101: Don't miss a Hidden Mickey while you're smiling at Minnie!
2 points

Clue 102: In the hallway of the Meet and Greet area, pay attention to the posters on the wall.
2 points

★ Walk past *The Great Movie Ride* to the *entrance arch to Animation Courtyard.*

Clue 103: Search this area for Hidden Characters.
4 points for finding two characters

Clue 104: Find a Hidden Mickey outside above the entrance to *Voyage of The Little Mermaid.*
3 points

★ Stroll *toward Hollywood Boulevard.*

Clue 105: On the way, look for Mickey on the large plaza between *The Great Movie Ride* and Hollywood Boulevard. (Note: he's not always present.)
3 points

Clue 106: While in the plaza, look toward Min and Bill's Dockside Diner for a Hidden Mickey.

3 points

Clue 107: At the intersection of Hollywood and Sunset Boulevards, discover Mickey Mouse's previous moniker. (Psst! Read the impressions in the sidewalks, near the curb.)
5 points

Clue 108: Walk behind Keystone Clothiers and search for a classic Mickey.
2 points

★ Enter *Mickey's of Hollywood* to look for four Hidden Mickeys.

Clue 109: Check the posts holding up merchandise racks.
2 points

Clue 110: Admire the merchandise bins!
3 points for two Hidden Mickeys

Clue 111: Next find "MICKEYS" spelled out on vertical dividers.
1 point

★ Go to the *Cover Story* store and take a good look at the outside.

Clue 112: See any classic Mickeys in the design?
2 points

★ Stroll to the area just inside the *park entrance*.

Clue 113: Locate a Hidden Mickey on an animal.
4 points

★ Walk outside the park to the *charter bus area*.

Clue 114: Search the cement next to a bench.
5 points

140

★ In the evening, arrive 30 to 40 minutes before show time (even though you have FastPass+) and stay alert during the *Fantasmic!* show for two Hidden Mickeys and Tinker Bell.

Clue 115: Look for large bubbles floating up the water screen that form one or more classic Mickeys.
5 points

Clue 116: Stay alert for a classic Mickey in the water during the scene with the whale and Mickey.
5 points

Clue 117: Wave at Tinker Bell on the water screen!
3 points

It's time to tally your score.

**Total Points for
Disney's Hollywood Studios =**

How'd you do?

Up to 171 points – Bronze
172 to 342 points – Silver
343 points and over – Gold
428 points – Perfect Score

You may have done even better if you earned bonus points in *Star Tours,* and/or the check-in podium of Mama Melrose's Ristorante Italiano.

– Toy Story Mania!

Hint 1: On the wall next to the ride vehicles, a classic Mickey is formed by three ovals that outline Mr. Potato Head, Slinky Dog, and Bullseye the horse.

Hint 2: Watch for the screen with target balloons in front of the volcano spewing lava. If you pop the middle 100-point balloon on the second tier, a light classic Mickey appears on the rear surface in the lava behind the balloons.

Hint 3: Be alert for the screen with moving white plates. At one point, a large plate aligns with smaller plates behind it to form a classic Mickey.

Hint 4: Look for the words "Circus Fun!" on the wall to your right as you rotate into position for the last screen stop. The dot

143

below the exclamation point is a classic
Mickey.

Hint 5: On the upper spine of the large
"Tin Toy" book along the exit, a tiny white
classic Mickey is in a chicken's eye. It's the
fourth image from the top of the spine.

Hint 6: As you exit from the third (newest)
ride track, a faint, yellow full-body Mickey
Mouse is at the lower right of the last
coloring book poster along the right wall
of the exit hallway. At the top of the poster
are the words "It's Fun to Take a Spin with
Your Friends." (If you don't ride on the
third track, you may be able to access this
part of the exit hallway from outside the
attraction).

Hint 7: You'll find a side-profile Mickey
on a huge popcorn box that's on display
across from the *Toy Story Mania!* attraction.
Look behind the "Hey Howdy Hey!" sign.
Mickey is looking left.

Hint 8: On the left lower side of a large
"Prospector" plate, which stands on the left
side of a shelf on the rear wall of the "Hey
Howdy Hey" snack area, a horseshoe and
two circles resemble a classic Mickey.

– Rock 'n' Roller Coaster
Starring Aerosmith

Hint 9: Look down for a tiled floor just
as you step inside the building along the
Standby entrance queue. In the middle of
the walkway at the end of this tiled-floor
section, before you enter the carpeted
room, two classic Mickeys are each
formed by three tiny round tiles. The circles
are all the same size, but these images
are purposeful and they're sentimental
favorites.

Hint 10: Along the entrance queue, when
you reach the inner room past the tile floor,
distorted classic Mickeys are in the carpet.

Hint 11: On the last wall before you enter the lower level of the pre-show video room, a poster labeled "Cosmic Car Show" has a tiny classic Mickey on the bottom right under the front tire of the car. The Mickey image is at the end of the signature of "J. Mouse."

Hint 12: Cables coiled into a classic Mickey lie on the rear center of the floor in the pre-show room where Aerosmith appears.

Hint 13: You'll find five Hidden Characters (three images of Mickey Mouse and one each of Minnie and Goofy) along the right side of a framed collage. First, look for two stickers of Mickey's face, one at the upper right and one at the middle right. Just below the middle right Mickey face is a small drawing of Goofy, Minnie, and Mickey walking to the right. This large poster is on the wall to your left along the inside queue and near the boarding area.

Hint 14: Near the loading dock, an instructional safety video about the roller coaster plays continuously overhead on several screens. After a car speeds away, a tiny, black classic Mickey floats across the screen with other black smoke exhaust circles.

Hint 15: On a wall across from the front of the loading dock area, various items are hanging from a row of hooks to the left of a wall cabinet and to the right of a garage door. One of the hanging items is a pink hat with the word "Mickey" across the front. (Note: These items and/or their arrangement change from time to time.)

Hint 16: On the rear license plate of each limo ride vehicle, the year sticker at the upper right is a classic Mickey.

Hint 17: Look to your far left as you exit the ride vehicle. A black classic Mickey is on the wall where the side of a gate connects to the wall.

Hint 18: Just as people exit the ride vehicle, look for "Box #15" on the right side of the room with the guest photo screens. The "o" in "Box" is a classic Mickey.

Hint 19: On the box next to box #15, "Sash Cord" is written at the left side of a piece of tape. The "o" in "Cord" is a black classic Mickey.

Hint 20: Two guitars (one green, one blue) are stuck horizontally on the ceiling above you in the middle of the gift shop. Three tiny classic Mickeys are on a silver plate at the base of each guitar. They're formed of holes for the "ears" and screws for the "heads."

Hint 21: An image of Oswald the Lucky Rabbit's head and ears is made of wires. Find him behind the glass door of a cabinet on the right wall of the room that's at the left side of the gift shop (as you exit the ride).

Hint 22: On cashier's counters at the right rear of the gift shop, just before you reach the exit walkway, spot a Hidden Mickey and a Hidden Minnie made of guitar picks under laminated surfaces. Look for Mickey on the left counter top and Minnie (with her red bow) on the right.

Hint 23: Walk outside into the courtyard of *Rock 'n' Roller Coaster* and glance above the order windows of "The Rock Station" snack kiosk. Holes in the "R" form a distorted image that resembles a classic Hidden Mickey.

Hint 24: In the front courtyard, check the outside wall mural to your left for:
  - a boy wearing Mickey ears.
  - black classic Mickeys on a singer's light blue shirt.
  - a gold "bling" Mickey on the necklace

of the man in the black suit.

– *The Twilight Zone Tower of Terror*

Hint 25: During the pre-show film in the library, the little girl on the elevator holds a plush Mickey Mouse doll.

Hint 26: Look for sheet music on a desktop and under a trumpet to the right of the television in the left library. The words "Mickey Mouse" are part of a song title: "What! No Mickey Mouse?"

Hint 27: A black, slightly distorted classic Mickey stains the wall of the boiler room at the spot where the queue branches. He's about eight feet up from the walkway, between an "Exit" sign and a red electrical box.

Hint 28: At the first stop on the ride, a small, dark classic Mickey can be seen above the ghostly images in the lower center of the ornate design on the closest archway.

Hint 29: Also at this first stop, the little girl in the ghostly images is still holding her Mickey doll.

Hint 30: On the ride itself, you'll see a bright star field just before the doors open into the elevator shaft. Look closely as the stars you're watching converge in the middle into a small classic-Mickey shape for a split second. (Tip: You see it best from the rightmost ride vehicle.)

Hint 31: On the left side of the last room as you exit the ride (and before the gift shop), three distinct floor tiles form a classic Mickey. (It's not proportioned correctly but it is clearly purposeful.)

– *Star Tours—The Adventures Continue*

Hint 32: About halfway along the outside

147

winding queue, a white classic Mickey is high on a tree trunk, just below the walkway platform for the Ewok village above. It's on the huge central tree, directly across from the Imperial Walker.

Hint 33: Along the right side of the inside entrance queue, circles make a Mickey hat with ears on the upper part of the control panel behind C-3PO's head. It's at the lower center of the upper screen.

Hint 34: In a wall display along the entrance queue, the silhouette of R2-D2 appears several times in a continuous video loop of moving shadow figures. At one point, R2-D2 sprouts satellite ears that rotate into round "Mickey ears" for a few seconds.

Hint 35: Along the entrance queue, a robot watches a continuous scan of luggage moving along a conveyor belt. You can spot images of a plush Mickey Mouse and a plush Goofy, along with images of Buzz Lightyear, Aladdin's lamp, a Sorcerer Mickey hat, a Mr. Incredible shirt, Madame Leota's crystal ball, and some other Disney images.

Hint 36: Just after you're seated, C-3PO appears on a screen at the front right of the room. A small classic Mickey is on his right forearm near his wrist.

Hint 37: At the end of the *Star Tours* ride, there are four classic Hidden Mickeys in the Coruscant landing sequence, which is one of three different and random end destinations for the ride. After the *Star Tours* vehicle crash lands on the platform and is lowered below into the hanger, look for four recessed panels in the top half of the back wall of the hanger. A classic Mickey is in the center of each panel. To see them, focus on the background wall instead of the droid in the foreground that's flying around with the two light batons.

Hint 38: A small classic Hidden Mickey formed of blue lights is in the Tatooine Traders gift shop at the exit of *Star Tours*. As you exit the ride, turn to face the long counter to your right. The light image is at the lower right of the counter.

Hint 39: At the "Build Your Own Lightsaber" station at the other end of the long counter in the exit gift shop, a classic Mickey is on the lower right front panel. It's formed by bullet holes with surrounding black burn marks as the "ears" and a central raised circle as the "head."

Hint 40: At the left side of the exit doorway from the gift shop, a faint classic Hidden Mickey is stenciled on the wooden wall, to the left of a fire alarm box.

– The Great Movie Ride

Hint 41: Harry Anderson's celebrity impression is at the front left of the Chinese Theater (as you face the entrance). Look for a classic Mickey on Harry's tie.

Hint 42: Four squares to the right of Harry Anderson's impression, Carol Burnett's square has classic Mickey ears in the upper right side.

Hint 43: Along the Standby entrance queue, as you enter the room in which you can watch clips from movies, take note of the second painting from the far side of the rear wall (the wall opposite the movie screen). An Oriental woman is in the painting, and over the middle of her chest are three flat blue beads that come together as a classic Mickey. These beads are attached to the bottom of a larger round piece of jewelry.

Hint 44: In the loading dock area, a shadow of Minnie Mouse's head in side profile is visible on the wall mural during loading and unloading. To find it, first

149

spot the house in the middle of the mural. Then look above and to the right of the house to spot Minnie's shadow. She's looking to your left. Having trouble? Look at the stationary ride vehicles. The Minnie shadow is to the left of the front section of the second of the two vehicles.

Hint 45: On the right side of the loading dock mural, in the second to last house on the right, a tiny black classic Mickey peeks out of the bottom center of a top-floor window. It's on the side of the house and nearest the corner.

Hint 46: In the first part of Gangster Alley, Mickey Mouse's brown shoes and tail poke out at the lower left from under a James Cagney poster, "The Public Enemy," on the left side of the ride vehicle.

Hint 47: At the end of Gangster Alley, a silhouette of Mickey in side profile appears in the rightmost window, near the top of the "Chemical Company" building. It's to the rear left of your ride vehicle.

Hint 48: In the Western scene, look for two paper bulletins advertising "Pocahontas Remedies." One is on a wall to your right behind a barber pole. The other is to the left of your vehicle, just past John Wayne on a wood fence. (It's one of the lower bulletins on the fence and can generally be spotted toward the right of the collection of bulletins.) Note: The locations of the bulletins in this scene sometimes change.

Hint 49: In the "Raiders of the Lost Ark" room, R2-D2 and C-3PO are together in the hieroglyphics on the left wall. Look midway between the two huge statues. The two robots are etched on the second level of panes, to the right of a kneeling figure.

Hint 50: In the "Raiders of the Lost Ark" room, a small white classic Mickey is on a broken tablet (or flat rock) that leans against the foundation that the Ark container is sitting on. Two white men are painted on the side of the container, and the tablet with the Mickey image is below and between them.

Hint 51: At the end of the "Raiders of the Lost Ark" room, Mickey and Donald can be found in the far left corner on the left wall. They're facing one another and Mickey is to the right of Donald, on the third row of panes up from the floor.

Hint 52: At the end of the right wall in the "Raiders of the Lost Ark" room, a hieroglyphic classic Mickey is at the right lower part of the first full pane above the stones on the floor. It's to the right of the lower leg of a standing figure etched in the pane.

Hint 53: In the latter part of the "Tarzan" room, a basket high in a treehouse to the right contains three eggs that form a classic Mickey. (The eggs are all the same size, but this is a sentimental favorite Hidden Mickey among guests and Cast Members.)

Hint 54: In the "Wizard of Oz" room, several groups of flowers, among them three large blue flowers above a hut at the middle left of the room, form acceptable classic Mickeys.

Hint 55: A green classic Mickey is nestled in the top of the trees, midway along the mural above the exit from the "Wizard of Oz" room. This classic Mickey is tilted slightly to the right. It's just below and to the left of the tallest tree in the mural.

Hint 56: Near the top of the flames directly above the small gold statue that is standing over the entrance doors to the attraction, a red circle with swirls for ears resembles a classic Mickey.

– *Voyage of The Little Mermaid*

Hint 57: Opposite the entrance doors to the inside waiting room, an ornate map of the Earth's hemispheres hangs on the left side of the wall. The brass frames encircling the hemispheres form the "head" of a sideways classic Mickey, while the decorative circular elements between them form a set of "ears." (Note: There's just one set of "ears" but two possible "heads.")

– Disney's Hollywood Studios
Guidemap

Hint 58: The face of Mickey Mouse on the park map has been distorted over time, but you can still spot it. The ear on the right is formed by Echo Lake, while the buildings on the left (for The Hollywood Brown Derby and *Disney Junior—Live on Stage!*) form the distorted ear on the left. His round head is the central plaza, and his forehead "widow's peak" shows up below the word "Hollywood." Two faint gray patches in the center of the plaza form his eyes.

Hint 59: On the park map, tiny pink classic Hidden Mickeys adorn the right side of the entrance plaza.

– MuppetVision 3D

Hint 60: Near the middle of the left wall of the waiting room for the pre-show, bicycles sit on luggage, which is, in turn, on top of a wooden chest. A round black hatbox at the side of the luggage forms a classic Hidden Mickey with two bicycle wheels above it.

Hint 61: During the first part of the pre-show on the video monitors, a test pattern appears after you see the words "Video Display Test." The black lines on a white background form a classic Hidden Mickey.

Hint 62: During the first part of the movie, as Kermit walks past the long hall and toward the lab, look for shelves with trophies on the wall before he reaches the lab entrance doors. It appears that a full-body Mickey Mouse trophy is at the middle of the top left shelf.

Hint 63: After the cannon shoots holes in the theater, a person holding a plush Mickey Mouse walks left to right in front of the crowd outside.

Hint 64: After the cannon shoots holes in the theater and Kermit rides in on a fire truck, you can see that some of the observers outside are holding Mickey Mouse balloons.

Hint 65: An image of Cinderella Castle (a Hidden Surprise) is on a license plate at the right lower corner of the fire truck Kermit is riding.

Hint 66: As the fire truck backs out, Pluto shows up at the right side of the screen.

– *Walt Disney: One Man's Dream*

Hint 67: On the left side of the display aisle, in the 1940 *Fantasia* exhibit, a young Walt Disney holds a painting. Three large round bushes in the painting form an upright classic Mickey.

Hint 68: On the left side of the aisle (and before you are ushered into the theater), you see Walt Disney standing with a pointer in front of a wall map. On a desk to the left of Walt, a coffee mug near a telephone has Donald Duck on it.

Hint 69: In the same scene, you can spot a green classic Mickey tilted slightly to the right. It's on the wall to the left of Walt.

– *Disney Junior—Live on Stage!*

Hint 70: Classic Mickeys appear at times in the lighting and stage effects as well as on various stage props during the live show.

153

Look for a partial classic Mickey on the blue TV screen on the right front door after it swings open on stage.

– Meet BB-8 at Star Wars Launch Bay

Hint 71: In the second room of the queue to meet BB-8, a dark classic Mickey is on the rear wall near the ceiling, above an exit sign and behind a light fixture.

– The Hollywood Brown Derby

Hint 72: Classic Mickeys are in the clouds on the mural on the outside wall above the restaurant. One is at the far upper right of the mural, and another is at the far mid-left of the mural, above the "Stage 5" sign.

Hint 73: On a wall to the left in the waiting area, in the second row of pictures, you'll find a caricature of Jimmy Dodd (with his Mouse ears) from the 1950s "Mickey Mouse Club" TV show.

– Sunset Boulevard

Hint 74: Midway down Sunset Boulevard toward the *Tower of Terror*, the outside scrollwork about halfway to the top of a blue building on the right side of the street has a tilted upside-down classic Mickey in its design. Look inside the circular swirls.

– Rosie's All-American Café

Hint 75: Mickey's smiling face is at the right lower corner of a photo collage at the right side of Rosie's leftmost food order window.

– Beauty and the Beast—Live on Stage

Hint 76: A classic Mickey is on a wind-up device on Cogsworth's back. The device has two holes for the "ears" and a larger circle for the "head." Sometimes this image is upside down.

– Hollywood & Vine

Hint 77: Outside the restaurant, a silhouette of Roger Rabbit is in a window above and to the left of the entrance.

Hint 78: On the left wall inside, the "San Fernando Valley" mural has a stick-figure Mickey on the far right, behind a pole.

Hint 79: Bushes form several classic Mickeys to the immediate left of the stick-figure Mickey and also above him.

– 50's Prime Time Café

Hint 80: In the waiting area, washers shaped like classic Mickeys secure the white tabletops.

– Backlot Express

Hint 81: Stacks of paint cans are on top of the drink station near the exit door facing *Star Tours*. A yellow paint splotch classic Mickey is on the second can up in a stack of cans next to a pillar. The Hidden Mickey is on the side of the can facing the exit door.

Hint 82: Several full-body two-dimensional Mickeys are on the bulletin boards inside the Backlot Express restaurant. One bulletin board is near the exit door facing *Star Tours*. A second is close by at the side of the seating area across from the mural of the city park.

– Sci-Fi Dine-In Theater Restaurant

Hint 83: In the waiting area on the left wall (as you enter) is a poster for the movie *Attack of the 50 Ft. Woman*. A yellow classic Mickey is behind her right knee, just off the highway.

Hint 84: Mickey Mouse in a graduation outfit is on an "Educational Reimbursement

Program" notice on the lower middle of
a bulletin board on a wall in the waiting
area.

Hint 85: Face the kitchen, then look to
the right of it at the tall fence. You'll find
two Hidden Mickeys in the mural above
the right side of the tall fence. Look at the
treetops. A classic Mickey, tilted slightly to
the right, is above the right corner of the
tall fence. Another classic Hidden Mickey
is just to the left of the first one; this second
one appears to be waving with his left
hand.

Hint 86: In the multicolored tiles above the
kitchen door entrance (on the right as you
face the kitchen) is a side profile of Mickey.
He's outlined in yellow tiles and appears to
be looking to his left (our right). Look first
for his jaw, a curving line of yellow tiles at
the lower middle of the mosaic square.

Hint 87: Watch the movie reel for Donald
Duck, Mickey Mouse, and Tinker Bell.
Donald is in a cartoon segment about a
secretary who is kidnapped to another
planet; Donald is one of the characters
who chases her. The segment follows a clip
of Walt Disney. Mickey appears in person
later in the reel, in a "News of the Future"
segment; he wears a spacesuit and waves
to the crowd. Tinker Bell flies around above
the word "Tomorrowland."

Hint 88: Stay alert for a youngster in a
spacesuit during the movie reel, when
the words "Calling All Boys! All Girls!"
appear on the screen. A classic Mickey
formed by a circle and two knobs is on the
upper chest of the spacesuit, just below the
helmet.

Hint 89: Watch for popcorn popping all
over the movie screen. Two morsels of
popcorn, in the lower middle between the
popcorn popper and the box of popcorn,
form upside-down classic Hidden Mickeys

(actually more of a Mickey hat and ears).

Hint 90: Silver classic Mickeys are at the sides of the dining-car seats, on the running boards.

– Stage 1 Company Store

Hint 91: Blue birds are stuck high on side doors of one of the tall merchandise cabinets inside the store. Classic Mickeys decorate the ends of red scarves that are draped over the birds.

Hint 92: Look for an old bureau that's loaded with hats for sale and has paint cans at the very top. You'll find a green, painted classic Mickey near the center of the desktop.

Hint 93: In the middle of the store, across from the green-paint Hidden Mickey on the bureau, circles in the middle of a cloud at the upper left of a mural with a rainbow approximate a classic Mickey tilted slightly to the left.

Hint 94: Mickey Mouse's shorts (red with white buttons) are hanging on a line near one of the exit doors.

Hint 95: Walk around the outside of the Stage 1 Company Store and admire at least five Mickey images formed by yellow and purple paint that's spilled on the ground. One yellow classic Mickey is between a Cast Member door and a big bull's-eye on the walkway between the *Muppet-Vision 3D* building and the Stage 1 Company Store.

– Mama Melrose's Ristorante Italiano

Hint 96: Just inside the entrance, to your right, the Dalmatian has a black classic Mickey spot on its right shoulder (your left).

Hint 97: A slightly distorted classic Mickey

hides in the plaster of the right wall between the waiting room and the dining area. Look in the upper right corner, near the entrance door.

Hint 98: To the right of the check-in podium (as you face it), a green classic Mickey leaf is about one and a half feet above the bottom of the window, along the left edge. (Note: This Hidden Mickey moves around or disappears at times!)

Hint 99: Look for a red classic Mickey marking on the exposed brick wall behind the check-in podium and to the left of the hanging grapes and grape leaves. It's about six feet up from the floor and near the edge of the wall next to the opening with the hanging grapes.

Hint 100: The left wall between the waiting room and the dining area has a smaller classic Mickey plastered on the brick. You'll find it in the middle of the left wall, just above the counter.

– Mickey and Minnie Starring in Red Carpet Dreams

Hint 101: A gold classic Mickey is on the middle of the back of the chair next to Minnie.

Hint 102: In the hallway of the Meet and Greet area, you'll pass "The Sweethearts of Swing" poster on the wall to your left. In the poster, Goofy holds a classic Hidden Mickey.

– Animation Courtyard

Hint 103: Donald Duck and Goofy are etched on the ornamental arches that are adjacent to Animation Courtyard's main entrance arch.

Hint 104: On the large sign over the entrance for the *Voyage of The Little Mermaid,* a classic Mickey made of bubbles floats high above Ursula's left hand.

– *Toward Hollywood Boulevard*

Hint 105: On the plaza near *The Great Movie Ride*, a full-face Mickey Mouse formed by lights can often be spotted in the afternoon and evening.

Hint 106: Maneuver around the plaza near *The Great Movie Ride* and stare toward Min and Bill's Dockside Diner. Above the food order windows, the diner's oval sign lines up with the portholes ("ears") to produce a classic Hidden Mickey.

– *Intersection of Hollywood & Sunset Blvds.*

Hint 107: On both sides of Sunset Boulevard near its intersection with Hollywood Boulevard, you'll find small impressions in the cement sidewalks, near the curb. They read, "Mortimer & Co, 1928, Contractors." "Mortimer Mouse" was Mickey Mouse's first (and soon discarded) name; 1928 was the year he was "born." (Two more of these stamps are at the other end of Sunset Boulevard. One is near the curb just before the walkway to *Rock 'n' Roller Coaster*. The other is across the street close to the entrance walkway to the *Fantasmic!* show.)

– *Keystone Clothiers*

Hint 108: At Peevy's Polar Pipeline drink service, behind Keystone Clothiers, gauges or regulators form a classic Mickey, especially when viewed from behind.

– *Mickey's of Hollywood*

Hint 109: Classic Mickey holes are drilled in some of the store's metal support poles.

Hint 110: The round merchandise bins have classic Mickeys in the band around the top

Walt Disney World's Hidden Mickeys
and classic Mickey-shaped feet.

Hint 111: "MICKEYS" is spelled out on four vertical dividers (two on each side of the store) that separate the sections of the store.

– Cover Story

Hint 112: You'll find a design containing classic Mickeys on the outside of the store, next to The Darkroom. Look on the horizontal frieze below the second-floor windows.

– Sid Cahuenga's Antiques and Curios

Hint 113: Just inside the park entrance, a statue of a Dalmatian stands on the porch to the left of the shop's entrance doors. A black classic Mickey spot hides on the dog's left rear thigh.

– Near the charter bus area

Hint 114: Outside the park, near the charter bus area, a classic Mickey is stamped in cement. It's about nine or so benches (and three light poles) away from the main entrance promenade as you head toward the walkway to the BoardWalk Resort. Look across from the Bus Stop 25 cement marker and sign.

– Fantasmic!

Hint 115: When animated characters float up in large bubbles on the water screen, watch for Pinocchio. His bubble forms the head of a sideways classic Hidden Mickey. Two bubbles beside it form the ears. (Other bubbles on the screen also come together at times to form classic Mickeys.)

Hint 116: Watch for the scene with the whale coming after Mickey. Just after Mickey yells for help, an outline of a classic Mickey forms for a few seconds in the foam on the wall of water gushing towards you.

Hint 117: Near the end of the show, after Mickey vanquishes the villains, Tinker Bell flies across the water screen.

Chapter 5

Disney's Animal Kingdom Scavenger Hunt

• • • • • • • •

Before You Start

• *Many great Hidden Mickeys are in Standby queues, and you might miss them if you take the FastPass+ queues. So, for optimal Hidden Mickey hunting, I recommend reserving FastPass+ for the following attractions:* **Kilimanjaro Safaris, Festival of the Lion King,** *and* **Finding Nemo—The Musical.**

Be sure to keep track of your three FastPass+ windows and return to those attractions at the appropriate times. In the Scavenger Hunt below, if you come to your FastPass+ attraction and it's not time for it yet, skip to the next stop in the Hunt and return to the FastPass+ attraction during your time window.

• *Some of the Hidden Mickeys in this park are in restaurants and shops. Be considerate of fellow guests and Cast Members as you search. Tell them what you're looking for, so they can share in the fun. Avoid searching restaurants at busy meal times unless you are one of the diners.*

★ Your first stop is *Avatar Flight of Passage.*

Clue 1: Stay alert along the Standby entrance queue (and on the ride) for bioluminescent Hidden Mickeys. Look for the first one on the right side of the initial inside portion of the queue.
5 points

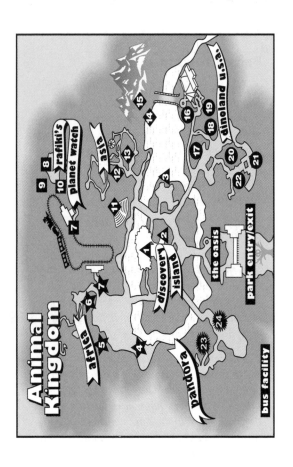

discovery island

★1 The Tree of Life
★2 It's Tough to be a Bug!
★3 Flame Tree Barbecue

africa

★4 Festival of the Lion King
★5 Kilimanjaro Safaris
★6 Gorilla Falls Exploration Trail
★7 Wildlife Express Train

rafiki's planet watch

8 Conservation Station
9 Affection Section
10 Habitat Habit!

asia

★11 Flights of Wonder
★12 Maharajah Jungle Trek
★13 Kali River Rapids
★14 Rivers of Light
★15 Expedition Everest

dinoland u.s.a.

16 Finding Nemo – The Musical
17 The Boneyard
18 TriceraTop Spin
19 Primeval Whirl
20 Cretaceous Trail
21 DINOSAUR
22 Dino-Sue T Rex

pandora – the world of avatar

✸✸ Avatar Flight of Passage
✸✸ Na'vi River Journey

165

Walt Disney World's Hidden Mickeys

Clue 2: As you continue along the queue, look high for another bioluminescent Hidden Mickey.
4 points

Clue 3: On the ride, when you stop in a cave, glance around for a classic Mickey.
4 points

Clue 4: Outside in Pandora, study the cement walkways for a classic Mickey. (Tip: it's by a seating area.)
3 points

★ Cross the park to *Expedition Everest* in Asia. One of the queue Hidden Mickeys (number 23) is only visible from the Single Rider and FastPass+ queues. Join the Standby queue to search for the Mickeys in Clues 5 through 17. After you exit the ride, you can look for Hidden Mickeys in and just outside the gift shop and then step into the Single Rider queue to look for Clue 23.

Clue 5: In the Standby queue, search for a classic Mickey in the first sunken courtyard.
3 points

Clue 6: Locate Mickey depressions on a red wall.
4 points

Clue 7: Look around for cloud Hidden Mickeys in a mural.
4 points for spotting two

Clue 8: Keep alert for pipes on a shelf that form a classic Mickey.
3 points

Clue 9: Find small Mickey ears in this room.
4 points

Clue 10: Look for a Hidden Mickey made of light-switch devices in a display.
3 points

Clue 11: Stay alert for Mickey on a book.

4 points

Clue 12: Search for Mickey on a handrail.
5 points

Clue 13: Spot a Hidden Mickey in a kettle.
4 points

Clue 14: Squint for a Hidden Mickey in an animal track.
5 points

Clue 15: Search for an animal with Mickey's ears!
3 points

Clue 16: In the last room before boarding for both the Standby and FastPass+ lines, glance around for Sorcerer Mickey near something blue.
5 points

Clue 17: In the loading area outside the Standby and FastPass+ lines, look for a classic Mickey.
3 points

Clue 18: After the ride starts, stay alert for a classic-Mickey melted spot in the snow.
5 points

Clue 19: Find a small classic Mickey made of gold balls in the gift shop at the ride exit.
3 points

Clue 20: Look around the gift shop for classic Mickey circles on a brown chest.
3 points for one or more

Clue 21: Admire a Hidden Mickey on a yellow flower near the ceiling.
4 points

Clue 22: Search outside, near the Serka Zong Bazaar shop, for a classic Mickey.
3 points

Clue 23: In either the Single Rider or the FastPass+ queue, find a Hidden Mickey on a lantern.
4 points

Clue 24: Locate a cloud Hidden Mickey outside on a truck.
4 points

Clue 25: Now walk around to spot a classic Mickey in camp supplies near a post.
3 points

★ Stroll to Africa at your FastPass+ time to enjoy riding *Kilimanjaro Safaris*.

Clue 26: Along the queue, watch a video monitor for spots on a leopard.
5 points

Clue 27: Observe the island in the flamingo pond.
4 points

Clue 28: Near the lions, watch for Donald in the rocks.
4 points

Clue 29: Locate a Hidden Mickey on a drink cart as you exit from Kilimanjaro Safaris.
4 points

★ Go to *Kali River Rapids* in Asia and find two classic Mickeys on your way to the ride. (You can exit when you get to the loading dock if you don't want to get on the raft. Ask a Cast Member to point the way out.)

Clue 30: You're getting close to the first Hidden Mickey when you see stone statues in the grass.
2 points

Clue 31: Gaze high for a classic Hidden Mickey inside the next room.

Chapter 5: Animal Kingdom Scavenger Hunt

4 points

★ Visit *DINOSAUR* next. Go back through Discovery Island and then follow the walkway into DinoLand U.S.A.

Clue 32: After the ride begins, be alert for a Hidden Mickey on a greaseboard. (Note: This Mickey image changes locations and even disappears at times.)
4 bonus points

Clue 33: Find a classic Mickey on the red dinosaur in the mural behind the counter in the ride's photo-purchase area.
4 points

★ Walk into the queue for *It's Tough to be a Bug!* on Discovery Island.

Clue 34: When you get inside *The Tree of Life*, look for Mickey above the handicapped entrance doors.
4 points

★ Stroll over to the *Maharajah Jungle Trek*. At the tiger exhibit area, find seven classic Hidden Mickeys in the building with arches.

Clue 35: Check in the water in the painting to the right of the first arch.
2 points

Clue 36: Look for the earring Mickey on the left mural inside the first arch.
2 points

Clue 37: Find a leaf Mickey on the left mural inside the first arch.
2 points

Clue 38: Search the right mural inside the first arch for a Hidden Mickey on a man.
2 points

Clue 39: Inside the building with arches, on the right wall, check the flowers on two square panels to find classic Mickeys.

Walt Disney World's Hidden Mickeys

2 points for one or more

Clue 40: Look for a classic Mickey in the mountains inside the second arch.
2 points

Clue 41: Now find a classic Mickey in the cloud formation inside the same arch.
2 points

Clue 42: After you exit the temple ruins, search for two Hidden Mickeys in the leaves to your left.
8 points for spotting both

Clue 43: Further along the trail, before you get to the aviary entrance, try to spot a classic Mickey in a man's necklace in a carving on the wall.
2 points

Clue 44: On another carving, locate a Hidden Mickey on an ear.
2 points

★ Eat lunch at a convenient time. The Rainforest Cafe at the park entrance is a good place to eat and has an interesting ambiance.

★ Before or after lunch, wander over to the *Gorilla Falls Exploration Trail* in Africa. Look for two Hidden Mickeys in the building with the Naked Mole Rat exhibit.

Clue 45: Find Mickey on a small box. (Note: At times, this box is moved around and may even disappear.)
4 bonus points

Clue 46: Spot a backpack with a Mickey emblem.
3 points

Clue 47: Past the gorilla viewing area, search for a Hidden Jafar.
5 points

★ Be aware of your FastPass+ times for *Finding Nemo – The Musical* and *Festival of the Lion King*.

★ See *Finding Nemo – The Musical* at Theater in the Wild in DinoLand.

Clue 48: Look around for a Hidden Mickey near the stage.
3 points

Clue 49: Find two Hidden Mickeys in the show-time signs outside.
4 points for spotting both

★ Go to Africa and see *Festival of the Lion King*.

Clue 50: Along the FastPass+ queue, watch for some poles near the ceiling that make a classic Hidden Mickey.
3 points

Clue 51: Be alert for an upright classic Mickey on Timon the meerkat's float.
4 points

Clue 52: Now search for an upside-down classic Mickey on Timon's float.
4 points

Clue 53: Check out a classic Mickey image on Pumbaa the warthog's float.
3 points

Clue 54: Study the center stage for a classic Mickey.
4 points

Tip: If Timon's float and the props are still there after the show has ended, you can look for the Hidden Mickeys in Clues 51 to 54 as you exit. If you need help, ask a Cast Member.

★ Take the *Wildlife Express Train* to Rafiki's Planet Watch to search *Conservation Station* for a Hidden Mickey bonanza.

Walt Disney World's Hidden Mickeys

Clue 55: Look at the mosaic in the pavement outside the main entrance to *Conservation Station* for a tiny classic Mickey.
4 points

Clue 56: Find the Hidden Mickey profile in the changing, repeating panels inside the entrance.
4 points

Clue 57: On the wall mural just to the right, spot a Mickey Mouse profile on an opossum.
4 points

Clue 58: Look for a butterfly wearing classic Mickeys.
3 points

Clue 59: Gaze closely at a spider nearby with a classic Mickey marking.
3 points

Clue 60: Spot a classic Mickey on an ostrich.
3 points

Clue 61: Look for a classic Mickey on a green snake.
3 points

Clue 62: Search for another classic Mickey on a lizard's ear.
4 points

Clue 63: Locate a side-profile Mickey on a hippo.
4 points

Clue 64: Glance at a llama for a classic Mickey.
3 points

Clue 65: A squirrel nearby sports a classic Mickey.
3 points

Clue 66: Look for a classic Mickey on an alligator.
3 points

Clue 67: Find a frog bearing a tiny image of Mickey's face.
5 points

Clue 68: Scan a walrus for a Hidden Mickey.
4 points

Clue 69: Find the Hidden Mickey on an owl.
3 points

Clue 70: Search for the amazing Mickey image on a second butterfly!
5 points

Clue 71: Look up for a classic Mickey on a frog behind a monkey.
5 points

Clue 72: Scan the mural for a fish with a partially hidden classic Mickey.
5 points

Clue 73: Locate a butterfly with two Hidden Mickeys.
4 points for both

Clue 74: Look around carefully for a frog with a side-profile Mickey.
5 points

Clue 75: Find a yellow butterfly with a classic Mickey.
3 points

Clue 76: Look lower for a chameleon with Mickey spots.
3 points

Clue 77: Admire this chameleon a bit longer so you don't overlook another Hidden Mickey!
4 points

173

Clue 78: Scan overhead for a Mickey in tree leaves.
3 points

Clue 79: Next to the "Song of the Rainforest" area, spot a fly with a tiny classic Mickey on its back.
5 points

Clue 80: Search for a tiny flower Hidden Mickey at the first entrance to the "Song of the Rainforest" area.
4 points

Clue 81: Look for a classic Mickey indentation on a tree toward the front of the Rainforest area.
3 points

Clue 82: Don't stray far for a Mickey hole in a leaf.
4 points

Clue 83: Check the trees inside the Rainforest area for a side-profile Mickey shadow.
4 points

Clue 84: Look for the classic Mickey shadow on the ceiling near door number eight in the "Song of the Rainforest" area.
4 points

Clue 85: Now find a Hidden Mickey on a tree near door number six.
3 points

Clue 86: Search for a green moss side-profile Mickey in the Rainforest area.
4 points

Clue 87: Walk out to the front of the Rainforest area and search for a side-profile Mickey.
4 points

Clue 88: Spot a classic Mickey made of short plant stalks on the Grandmother

Willow tree.
3 points

Clue 89: Also in the Rainforest area, spot a classic Mickey on a cockroach.
4 points

Clue 90: Now find a classic Mickey on a lizard on the same tree.
3 points

Clue 91: Stay with this tree and admire a berry Hidden Mickey.
4 points

Clue 92: Look for a butterfly wearing a tiny Hidden Mickey on this tree.
5 points

Clue 93: Examine the grates around the bottoms of the trees in the main lobby.
2 points

Clue 94: Locate a Hidden Mickey on a plate in a window display at the rear of the lobby.
3 points

Clue 95: Spot a reptile classic Mickey on a ledge in the rear area displays and laboratories.
3 points

★ Walk outside to *Affection Section* to spot another classic Hidden Mickey.

Clue 96: Study the animals in the petting zoo. (Note: These Hidden Mickeys come and go.)
4 bonus points

★ Wander on over to the *Wildlife Express Train station* and look for classic Mickeys.

Clue 97: Examine the rafters inside the station.
2 points

Walt Disney World's Hidden Mickeys

★ Ride the train to Africa, then check out *Harambe Fruit Market* for a cool Hidden Mickey.

Clue 98: This full-body Mickey is somewhere inside the Fruit Market.
4 points

Clue 99: Check the beginning of the cement and flagstone path at the side of the Fruit Market.
4 points

Clue 100: Turn left at the opposite end of the path and follow the cement walkway a few feet to find a large, faint classic Mickey in the cement.
5 points

Clue 101: In *Zuri's Sweets Shop*, scan high for Mickey.
3 points

★ Outside the *Mombasa Marketplace* store, look for a classic Mickey formed by a small utility cover and the pebbles adjacent to it.

Clue 102: It's near an entrance door to the store.
5 points

★ Stroll inside *Tusker House Restaurant*.

Clue 103: Locate a classic Mickey on an Assignment Board on a wall.
4 points

★ Go to the far side of *Tamu Tamu Refreshments*.

Clue 104: Find another classic Mickey formed by a small utility cover and adjacent pebbles.
5 points

Clue 105: Marvel at a Hidden Baloo the bear inside the small seating area behind Tamu Tamu Refreshments.

Chapter 5: Animal Kingdom Scavenger Hunt

5 points

Clue 106: Search for another Hidden Character here.
4 points

★ Walk a short way down the *path to Asia*.

Clue 107: Look over to *The Tree of Life* and spot the Hidden Mickey on it. (Psst! It's near the hippo.)
4 points

★ Cross the bridge from Africa to Discovery Island and amble on into *Pizzafari* restaurant to find four Hidden Mickeys.

Clue 108: Spot Mickey in the room across from the food order counters.
3 points

Clue 109: In the first dining room to the left as you walk down the hall, search for a tiny orange classic Mickey.
5 points

Clue 110: In the Nocturnal Room (the dining room directly to the left of the food counters as you face the counters), study the firefly wings.
3 points

Clue 111: In the Nocturnal Room, look around for a classic Mickey in the trees.
4 points

★ Return to DinoLand U.S.A. Enter *The Boneyard* and find two Hidden Mickeys.

Clue 112: Search upstairs at the rear for a tiny Hidden Mickey figurine.
4 points

Clue 113: Look around the children's dig area for Hidden Mickey hard hats.
2 points

Walt Disney World's Hidden Mickeys

★ Enter *Restaurantosaurus* through a rear door (from near the restrooms).

Clue 114: Locate a Hidden Mickey near the ceiling of the large dining room closest to *DINOSAUR*.
4 points

★ Walk to the *Cretaceous Trail* in the middle of DinoLand and go dino hunting.

Clue 115: Find a dark Mickey on a dinosaur's back.
3 points

★ Go to *TriceraTop Spin*.

Clue 116: Search in front of the attraction for a classic Mickey on a dinosaur with a ball.
3 points

Clue 117: Spot a classic Mickey in one of the parking spaces near the attraction.
3 points

Clue 118: Study the nearby horned dinosaur studded with gems and find a Mickey pin.
4 points

★ Check inside *Chester & Hester's Dinosaur Treasures* shop.

Clue 119: Find a marionette Mickey in the shop.
2 points

Clue 120: Scan inside the store near the rear entrance for a black classic Mickey.
5 points

Clue 121: Study the pavement outside the store entrance that faces *Primeval Whirl* for a classic Mickey.
5 points

★ Cross back to *Primeval Whirl* and look

for classic Mickeys on the outside of the attraction.

Clue 122: Check the meteors.
5 points for two or more

★ Walk along the outer walkway *behind the Fossil Fun Games area*.

Clue 123: Check out the fence signs for a classic Hidden Mickey.
3 points

★ On *Discovery Island*, enter the *Island Mercantile* shop.

Clue 124: Look for three classic Mickeys made of spots.
5 points for all three

★ Back outside the shop, find a classic Mickey made of green moss.

Clue 125: Study the front of *The Tree of Life*.
5 points

★ Step inside the *Riverside Depot* shop.

Clue 126: Scan the walls for a Hidden Mickey.
3 points

★ Wind your way over to the *Discovery Trading Company* next door.

Clue 127: Locate a Hidden Mickey in a constellation high on a wall.
5 points

Clue 128: Search outside the exit door closest to *Flame Tree Barbecue* for a tiny classic Mickey in the pavement.
4 points

★ Stroll to the *Flame Tree Barbecue Restaurant* to find two classic Mickeys.

Clue 129: Search the ground in the food

179

order area for a rock classic Mickey.
4 points

Clue 130: Now find a classic Mickey in the seating area outside.
2 points

★ Go to the *Rainforest Cafe entrance sign* inside the park.

Clue 131: Look for a Hidden Mickey on the sign.
3 points

★ Keep your eyes open *as you leave the park.*

Clue 132: Search the outside walls of the ticket booths for Hidden Mickeys.
4 points for two

Clue 133: Outside the entrance turnstiles, check the metal grates around some of the trees near the tram loading area.
2 points

**Total Points for
Disney's Animal Kingdom =**

How'd you do?

Up to 190 points – Bronze
191 to 381 points – Silver
382 points and over – Gold
477 points – Perfect Score

You may have done even better if you earned bonus points in *DINOSAUR, Gorilla Falls Exploration Trail,* **and/or** *Affection Section.*

Pandora - The World of Avatar

– Avatar Flight of Passage

Hint 1: A bioluminescent classic Mickey is on the right wall of the cave soon after you enter the inside queue. The image is at the upper part of a cluster of flower-like growths about halfway up the wall.

Hint 2: After you pass by the "Attention" message painted on the right wall, begin scanning near the ceiling for another bioluminescent Hidden Mickey. You can spot the image up high as you make a U-turn in the queue.

Hint 3: On the ride, when your banshee stops in a cave, look down over the left side to find another bioluminescent Hidden Mickey, similar to the ones along the entrance queue.

Hint 4: Outside, walk away from Pongu

Pongu refreshment stand and locate a small seating area by a lightpost. On the cement walkway by the lightpost are rust circles left by barrels that have been moved. Three of these circles come together as a classic Mickey. First spot the smaller "ears" and then the larger "head" under them. One side of the "head" has a ragged appearance.

Asia

– Expedition Everest

Note: Hints 5 through 17 apply to Hidden Mickeys you'll find in the Standby queue. The Hidden Mickey in Hint 23 can only be spotted from the Single Rider and FastPass+ queues.

Hint 5: A classic Mickey made of a central circle with swirls for ears hides in the base of a Yeti statue. You'll find it in a sunken outdoor courtyard past the first room (an office).

Hint 6: Just past the first room, a classic Mickey is formed by shallow depressions in the left wall of a small red building. The upright image is at the far left lower corner of the wall, below and to the left of a small curved drainpipe.

Hint 7: On the rear wall of the same red building just past the first room, classic Mickeys lie in the clouds on the left and right sides of a Yeti mural.

Hint 8: As you enter the second building (Tashi's Trek and Tongba Shop), an upside-down classic Mickey is formed by the highest pipes on the top shelf in the right corner.

Hint 9: Along the far wall of Tashi's Trek and Tongba Shop, a small white Yeti doll on the top right shelf inside a cupboard wears black Mickey ears.

Hint 10: In Tashi's Trek and Tongba Shop, light-switch devices in a glass case on the left side of the queue form a classic Mickey.

Hint 11: Inside the Yeti Museum, on the right side of the queue after the first left turn, look for a Yeti book at the far left of the book display. A partial image of Mickey's head and ears is imprinted in the snow on the book's front cover.

Hint 12: Just past the snow Mickey of Hint 7, a classic Mickey is etched into the top end of a wooden handrail.

Hint 13: Dents in a kettle in the Yeti Museum's second display form a classic Mickey.

Hint 14: Also in the museum a classic Mickey is hiding in an "animal track." It's at the lower left of a tall glass cabinet in a display labeled "Documenting Bio-Diversity." Look near the top of the third paper from the left, above the label "Small Mammal Tracks."

Hint 15: The next-to-last display cabinet in the museum has a photo of a bear with ears that look like Mickey's ears. The bear is on the right side of the cabinet, under the words "The Yeti, Interpreting the Findings."

Hint 16: In the last room before boarding, look for a photo of a woman in blue listening to a hand-held radio. Mickey in his Sorcerer's Hat is etched on a wall to the woman's left.

Hint 17: Outside in the loading area, look for a classic Mickey in the blue scrollwork above the first window. (You can see this Hidden Mickey from both the FastPass+ and Standby queues.)

Hint 18: In the first part of the ride, as your train is climbing the mountain, a dark, melted classic Mickey-shaped spot appears in the snow to your left. The "ear" farthest away from the train is contiguous with a larger dark spot above it.

Hint 19: Small gold balls form classic Mickeys at the bottom of both sides of a merchandise display in the middle of the gift shop at the ride exit. The display is across from the photo pickup area.

Hint 20: Brown chests sit on an upper shelf of a merchandise cabinet at the right side of the gift shop's right exit door (as you exit the ride). Circles along the front and sides of the lower chest form several classic Mickeys. One is at the middle bottom of the left front. It's tilted to the left.

Hint 21: Find a yellow flower at the top center of this same merchandise cabinet (at the right side of the right exit door). A petal at the seven o'clock position on the flower forms a classic Mickey.

Hint 22: Outside and across from the Serka Zong Bazaar gift shop, an upside-down classic Mickey is etched near the top of the second stone tablet from the edge closest to the shop.

Hint 23: In the Yeti Museum as seen from both the FastPass+ and Single Rider queues, a sideways classic Mickey is formed by three dents in a lantern in the second glassed-in display. (Note: You cannot spot this lantern image from the Standby queue.)

Hint 24: At the front of the left side of the Anandapur Ice Cream Truck, look for a painting with two towers. A classic Hidden Mickey, tilted to the left, hides in the clouds at the upper right of the painting. (Note: the images on this truck change from time to time.)

Hint 25: Outside the attraction, base camp

supplies hang in the Gupta's Gear area.
A three-circle image hangs among these
supplies, near the second post from the end
nearest the restrooms.

Africa

– Kilimanjaro Safaris

Hint 26: Near the end of the entrance
queue, just before you reach the final
loading dock, a monitor above you shows
a continuous video loop. Look for the
resting orange-and-white leopard with
black spots. Three spots on white fur form a
classic Mickey on the left side (your right)
of the leopard's neck.

Hint 27: In elephant country, and about
halfway through the ride, the island in
the flamingo pond is shaped like a classic
Hidden Mickey. It's to the left of your ride
vehicle.

Hint 28: The rocks in the lion area are
arranged to resemble Donald Duck. Spot
his cap first, then his face, eyes, and beak.
(Note: These rocks have shifted positions
slightly over time.)

Hint 29: Walk to a cashier's cart at the end
of the exit path from *Kilimanjaro Safaris* and
not far from the entrance to the *Gorilla Falls
Exploration Trail*. A Hidden Mickey is in the
tile on the top (not the side or front) of the
counter of the drink and merchandise cart.
Small ceramic circles (a white and blue
"head" and two black "ears") stuck in the
surface of the cart form a classic Hidden
Mickey.

Asia

– Kali River Rapids

Hint 30: Along the entrance queue, keep
your eyes peeled for stone statues in the

185

grass. As you approach the next room to your right, look at the lower left corner of the outer wall. Three of the plates on the wall form a classic Mickey, tilted down to the right. (Note: These images change from time to time.)

Hint 31: Inside the next room to your right - a museum - a dark classic Mickey is on the back of a light brown boot, which is high on a shelf near the ceiling in the middle of a collection of boots. To find it, walk through the first door to the museum and look up behind you to the shelf. (If the room is roped off, ask any Cast Member nearby if you can just look around in the museum for a few minutes).

DinoLand U.S.A.

– DINOSAUR

Hint 32: Just as the ride starts and before you travel back in time, a classic Mickey at the lower left corner of a white greaseboard appears to the left of your vehicle. (This Mickey image changes locations and even disappears at times.)

Hint 33: On the mural behind the counter in the ride's photo-purchase area, a large red dinosaur has a small classic Mickey on its lower neck.

Discovery Island

– It's Tough to be a Bug!

Hint 34: Inside *The Tree of Life*, look for the handicapped entrance doors to *It's Tough to be a Bug!* (You reach them before you get to the main entrance doors to the theater.) Look at the upper left area near the doors— and just to the right of the "Cast Members Only" door—to find a small dark classic Mickey.

Asia

— Maharajah Jungle Trek

Hint 35: To the right of the first arch, swirls in the water under a tiger form a classic Mickey.

Hint 36: Inside the first arch, on the left mural, the king's gold earring forms a solid upside-down classic Mickey.

Hint 37: Inside the first arch, on the left mural, three leaves under the wrist of the king's extended arm form a classic Mickey.

Hint 38: Inside the first arch, on the right mural, a man is wearing an upside-down classic Mickey gold earring.

Hint 39: On the right wall inside the building with arches, two square panels are decorated with flowers. Some of the outer flowers have circles at the bases of their petals that form classic Mickeys.

Hint 40: Inside the second arch, on the left mural, there's a small classic Mickey in a brown rock formation on the left side of the mountains.

Hint 41: Inside the second arch, on the right mural, a classic Mickey appears in the upper part of the left cloud formation.

Hint 42: As you exit the temple ruins, turn to your immediate left to a large wall mural. Among the leaves is a dark green classic Mickey. It's about nine feet above the ground and one foot from the bricks at the left side of the mural. Another even darker green classic Mickey is further to the right on this mural. It's above the tiger running toward the left, and between two large, light green fan-shaped leaves.

Hint 43: On a wall to the right, just before you reach the aviary entrance, you can

187

spot an upside-down down classic Mickey in the necklace of a man in the middle carving.

Hint 44: On the wall carving to the left of the above Hidden Mickey, an earring on a crouching man (his right ear—on the left as you face the man) forms a classic Hidden Mickey.

Africa

– Gorilla Falls Exploration Trail

Hint 45: To the left of the entrance to the building with the Naked Mole Rat Exhibit, a small box of Asepso soap on a desk near a lamp has a classic Mickey as the "o" in "Asepso." (Note: At times this box is moved around and may even disappear.)

Hint 46: In the far left corner of the room with the Naked Mole Rat Exhibit, the left side of a backpack sports a small classic Mickey emblem.

Hint 47: A three-dimensional head of Jafar is carved out of a 25- to 30-foot rock. You'll find it past the gorilla viewing area, to the right of the first section of the first suspension bridge.

DinoLand U.S.A.

– Finding Nemo–The Musical

Hint 48: Three bubbles touch to form a classic Mickey at the lower left of the stage.

Hint 49: Two sideways classic Mickeys formed by bubbles hide in each of the two outdoor signs announcing the show times for the day. One is in the bottom right corner of the signs, and the other is under the word "The" and near the bottom of the signs. These signs are posted on both the walkway from Asia and the walkway from the rest of DinoLand U.S.A.

Africa

– Festival of the Lion King

Hint 50: Near the end of the FastPass+ queue, round poles are stacked two deep in a crate on a plank near the ceiling and next to the outside main walkway. Three poles to the right of the middle of the stack form a classic Hidden Mickey tilted down to the right.

Hint 51: A white classic Mickey is painted on the lower middle front of Timon's (and the giraffe's) float. You can see it as the float enters the arena.

Hint 52: An upside-down white classic Mickey is on the lower right side of Timon's float, under the giraffe's front leg.

Hint 53: Three circles form a classic Mickey at the front left (Pumbaa's left) side, and near the top of the side, of Pumbaa's float.

Hint 54: A classic Mickey in relief is on the lower side of the movable center stage, to the right of some steps. It is usually facing the Elephant section of the audience.

Rafiki's Planet Watch

– Conservation Station

Hint 55: A classic Mickey made of circles (two dark and one light) hides in the circular mosaic in the pavement right outside the main entrance to *Conservation Station*. Mickey is above the second "T" in "Station" and below the elephant's trunk.

Hint 56: The front wall facing you as you enter the building has a section of changing, repeating panels. A small side profile of Mickey Mouse is in the center of the orange starfish.

Hint 57: Find an opossum on the right side of the mural just inside the entrance. There is a side profile of Mickey Mouse in its left eye.

Hint 58: Above the opossum, at the upper right, a butterfly has classic Mickeys on its wings.

Hint 59: About six feet up from the floor, not far from the opossum, a spider has a light pink classic Mickey marking on its thorax.

Hint 60: On the wall to the left of the restrooms, near the entrance, the pupil of an ostrich's eye is a classic Mickey.

Hint 61: Toward the middle of the mural at the front, near the entrance, a green snake sports a black classic Mickey on its upper back.

Hint 62: Near the upper right border of the changing screen, a dark classic Mickey marking is at the top of a green lizard's ear, above a deer.

Hint 63: A hippopotamus is the fifth animal from the left at the bottom of the entrance mural on the left wall. A side-profile Mickey is on its lower jaw, under the middle tooth.

Hint 64: To the immediate left of the hippopotamus, a llama sports a dark brown classic Mickey on its neck.

Hint 65: Under the hippopotamus, a squirrel's eye has a black classic Mickey pupil.

Hint 66: On the hippo's right side, an alligator has a small dark classic Mickey to the left of its green eye.

Hint 67: To the right of the alligator, Mickey Mouse's smiling face is under a frog's right eye.

Hint 68: Directly above the frog with the smiling Mickey is a walrus with a dark classic Mickey on the left side (your right) of his neck.

Hint 69: A bit farther along on this left wall mural, the pupils of an owl's eyes are classic Mickeys.

Hint 70: The entrance murals curve toward the inside of the building. On the right curving mural, look closely for the butterfly with an image of Mickey's face on its body (not on its wings!).

Hint 71: Midway along the right curving mural, high up near the ceiling, a classic Mickey-shaped marking is on the white skin of the chin under the middle of a frog's face. The frog is behind a red-faced monkey.

Hint 72: Toward the top and near the end of the left side of the entrance mural, a dark classic Mickey, partially hidden by an octopus nearby, is on the side of a fish, to the left of the fish's fin.

Hint 73: Along the bottom of the right mural as you near Rafiki's Theater, two black classic Mickeys are near the bottom of the wings of an orange butterfly under a monkey.

Hint 74: Near the bottom of the same mural, just before the theater, a side-profile Mickey is in a silver frog's left pupil.

Hint 75: Before the first entrance to the "Song of the Rainforest" area, about halfway up the wall and above a bat, a yellow butterfly has a black classic Mickey on its left wing.

Hint 76: In the same area, a tan and green chameleon has a group of spots directly behind the eye that form an upside-down classic Mickey.

Hint 77: This same chameleon sports a small dark classic Mickey behind the neck and just above the front leg. It's at about the same level as the upside-down Hidden Mickey described above.

Hint 78: A hole in the tree leaves overhead resembles a classic Mickey. It's directly above the first entrance.

Hint 79: The fly with a tiny classic Mickey on its back is on the left panel of the first entrance to the "Song of the Rainforest" area.

Hint 80: On the same panel, a tiny yellow-flower classic Mickey blooms on a green plant near the floor.

Hint 81: Turn to the right panel mural at the same entrance to the Rainforest area to see a classic Mickey indentation on a tree. It's about four feet up from the floor.

Hint 82: Look for a classic Mickey hole in a green leaf near the Mickey indentation in Hint 81.

Hint 83: Now go inside to see a side-profile Mickey shadow about seven feet up from the floor on the front of a tree inside the Rainforest area.

Hint 84: Above and in front of door number eight in the Rainforest area, you can spot a dark classic Mickey shadow on the ceiling to the right.

Hint 85: A white classic Mickey is outlined on a tree by door number six, to the left of the words "The Accidental Florist."

Hint 86: Turn around and walk out toward

the lobby to look at the right side of the tree with "The Song of the Rainforest" sign (the Grandmother Willow tree). A rear horizontal panel has a green moss side-profile Mickey about six feet up from the floor.

Hint 87: A side-profile Mickey indentation appears on the same tree under the sign and to the lower right (as you face her) of Grandmother Willow's face. (Tip: You have to walk farther into the lobby to spot it.)

Hint 88: Three plant stalks form a classic Mickey in the mural near the floor on the bottom left of the Grandmother Willow tree (as you face it from the lobby).

Hint 89: To the right of the Grandmother Willow tree, there is a cockroach display inside a tree in front of the "Song of the Rainforest" area. A cockroach inside and toward the back of the tree bears a dark, upside-down classic Mickey on its back.

Hint 90: A lizard above the "Giant Cockroach" sign on the same tree has a classic Mickey above its front leg.

Hint 91: On the right front side of this tree, locate a long strand of red berries. The three berries at the very bottom of the strand form a classic Mickey.

Hint 92: On the left front of the tree with the cockroach display, a light brown butterfly about six and a half to seven feet up from the floor has a tiny black classic Mickey on its back between the wings.

Hint 93: The grates around the bottoms of the trees in the lobby have classic Mickey patterns, as do those outside by *Affection Section*.

Hint 94: A classic Mickey on a "Microtiter Plate" is usually in the first display room to the right in the rear of the lobby. Look into the second window of the "Wildlife Tracking Center." The plate changes color from time to time.

Hint 95: A classic Mickey made of three containers with reptile skins is on a ledge in the far left window of a room with reptiles.

– Affection Section

Hint 96: One of the animals usually has a classic Mickey shaved into its coat.

– Wildlife Express Train station

Hint 97: High up in the rafters inside the train station, look for classic Mickeys where the beams intersect.

Africa

– In and around Harambe

Hint 98: At the Harambe Fruit Market in Harambe village, a tiny, colorful Mickey Mouse doll is hiding on support poles halfway to the top of the ceiling.

Hint 99: At one side of the Harambe Fruit Market, a short cement and flagstone path with benches leads through some trees. A large Mickey Mouse head in the cement marks the beginning of the path. It's several feet in diameter.

Hint 100: At the opposite end of this short path, turn left onto the cement walkway and walk a few feet. Nearby you'll find a faint depression in the cement that forms a very large classic Mickey (six feet or more in diameter). This Hidden Mickey is best seen after a rain when the pavement is wet. It is often partially covered with parked strollers.

Hint 101: A striped Mickey Mouse figurine is inside Zuri's Sweets Shop, which is across from Harambe Market. Look high to your right for this Mickey in a small display on a shelf opposite the entrance door to the shop.

Hint 102: Outside, near an entrance door to the Mombasa Marketplace store, you'll find a classic Mickey formed by a small utility cover (with the letter "D" in the middle) and the pebbles adjacent to it. The cover is on the path, on the side facing the Tusker House Restaurant.

Hint 103: In Tusker House Restaurant, walk to a small dining room on the left side of the hallway to the restrooms. A classic Mickey is formed by one of the magnets on a display Assignment Board on a wall inside the room.

Hint 104: Near Tamu Tamu Refreshments, on the walkway that connects Africa and Asia, a small utility cover and the pebbles adjacent to it form a classic Mickey. Here, the utility cover has the letter "S" in the middle.

Hint 105: Inside the small seating area behind Tamu Tamu Refreshments, a white Hidden Baloo (the bear) is on the wall nearest the path to Asia. He's often covered by a curtain.

Hint 106: Also inside the small seating area behind Tamu Tamu Refreshments, a Hidden Scar (the lion) is formed by the exposed brown brick on a corner wall and under a vase in a recessed opening.

Hint 107: On the back of *The Tree of Life*, and visible from the path between Africa and Asia, is an upside-down classic Mickey. Look above the eye of the hippopotamus to spot him.

Discovery Island

– Pizzafari restaurant

195

Hint 108: A yellow classic Mickey image is under a bat, which is on a wall in the seating area across from the food order counters. As you enter the room, turn left to face the rear wall and look for the bat on the right.

Hint 109: On the rear wall of the first dining room to the left (as you walk down the hall away from the food order area), a tiny orange classic Mickey is at the lower left of a turtle shell.

Hint 110: On the left rear wall of the Nocturnal Room (the dining room directly to the left of the food order counters as you face the counters), the wings of the lower left firefly resemble Mickey Mouse ears.

Hint 111: In the same room, a classic Mickey made of tree leaves lies above the head of a reddish raccoon. It's tilted with the "ears" to the left as you face the wall.

DinoLand U.S.A.

– The Boneyard

Hint 112: Upstairs to the rear left in a fenced-off archeology display, a small full-body Mickey figurine sits on the horizontal bar of a red bicycle. Various plastic dinosaurs perch on other parts of the bicycle.

Hint 113: On the right side of the children's dig area, in a small display, a fan and two hard hats form a classic Mickey.

– Restaurantosaurus

Hint 114: A black smudge classic Mickey is on the bottom of a boot wedged high in the rafters over the large dining room closest to *DINOSAUR*.

– Cretaceous Trail

Hint 115: At one end of this short trail in the middle of DinoLand, you'll find a large dinosaur. Three dark spots on its middle back make a classic Mickey.

– *TriceraTop Spin*

Hint 116: In front of *TriceraTop Spin*, a green dinosaur balances a red and yellow-striped ball on its horns. A classic Mickey, tilted to the right, appears in the scales on the dino's right side, under the front horn.

Hint 117: In the parking spaces across from *TriceraTop Spin*, a classic Mickey is formed by cracks in the cement at the front of the second parking space from the horned dinosaur.

Hint 118: On the right side of the horned dinosaur (as you face it), a gold "Steamboat Willie" Cast Member pin is located on a spine on the dinosaur's upper back, near a large silver medallion.

– *Chester & Hester's Dinosaur Treasures shop*

Hint 119: Inside, near the middle of the shop, look up to see a Mickey Mouse marionette.

Hint 120: Near the rear entrance, a classic Hidden Mickey is made of dark spots at the lower left of the left side of a "Cold Drinks" dispenser. It's just above the lower red horizontal band.

Hint 121: In front of the store, near the restrooms, a tiny orange image is embedded in the cement a few feet to the right of the leftmost post (as you face the store with your back to *Primeval Whirl*).

– *Primeval Whirl*

Hint 122: In the outside decorations, the sides of three meteors sport sideways classic Mickey craters:
   - One is under "Head for the Hills."

197

- Another is over the "Primeval Whirl" sign at the entrance to the attraction.

- The third *Primeval Whirl* classic Mickey craters are near the top of a meteor, on the right side of the attraction and near a dinosaur holding a sign.

– Behind Fossil Fun Games

Hint 123: Along the outer walkway behind the *Fossil Fun Games* area, look for a sign on the fence that says "Games of Chance." An upside-down classic Mickey made of gold spots lies on the upper left thigh of the blue dinosaur, on the right side of the sign.

Discovery Island

– Island Mercantile shop

Hint 124: Three classic Mickeys made of spots hide on two orange and blue bumblebee honeycombs on posts inside the shop. These posts are along a rear wall opposite the entrance doors closest to the walkway to the Oasis. Two classic Mickeys are on the honeycomb on the right as you face the rear wall. Find the bee inside a hexagon at the upper center of the honeycomb. One Hidden Mickey is in the hexagon adjacent to the bee at the upper right, and a second Hidden Mickey is one hexagon away to the lower left of the bee. A third classic Mickey hides on the left honeycomb, three hexagons away from the central bee, counting down and to the right. Collections of spots in other hexagons on the honeycombs may also resemble the classic Mickey shape, but these three images are the best proportioned.

– The Tree of Life

Hint 125: On the front of *The Tree of Life*, facing the Oasis and about one-third the distance up the tree trunk from the bottom, is a classic Mickey made of green moss.

You'll find it to the left of the buffalo. (This Hidden Mickey is becoming more distorted over time.)

– Riverside Depot

Hint 126: Along the rear wall opposite the entrance door from the walkway between the Oasis and Discovery Island, three baskets come together as a classic Mickey, tilted to the left. Find the baskets on an upper shelf in a tall merchandise cabinet at the middle of the rear wall.

– Discovery Trading Company

Hint 127: At the far left room of the shop, look for the group of constellations above an inside doorway. One of the constellations (on the right side of the group and near the dolphin) has three stars with round gems in their centers that form a Hidden Mickey. It's near the upper tip of the constellation, and the dolphin's tail points to it.

Hint 128: Walk out the exit of the shop nearest *Flame Tree Barbecue*. In the pavement is a classic Hidden Mickey made of small stones. It's about 12 to 15 feet from the exit door and about one foot from the intersection of two crack lines.

– Flame Tree Barbecue Restaurant

Hint 129: In the food order area, rocks embedded in the ground form a classic Mickey at the front edge of the rock border and just to the right of the second inside post from the right wall.

Hint 130: At the outside seating area behind the food order counters, some of the grates on the ground around tree trunks have classic Mickey circles.

Oasis

– Rainforest Cafe

Hint 131: A green lizard at the Rainforest Cafe entrance sign that is inside the park has an upside-down classic Mickey in the middle of the circles on its neck.

Outside the entrance turnstiles to the park

Hint 132: When you head out of the park, turn back as you pass the ticket booths. You'll find two rock classic Mickeys, one on the right-hand lower corner of the wall of the rightmost ticket booth and the other in the wall of the leftmost ticket booth near the ground and toward the front of the booth's left side wall.

Hint 133: Outside the entrance turnstiles, near the tram loading area, the metal grates at the bases of some of the trees incorporate classic Mickeys in their design.

Chapter 6

Resort Hotel Scavenger Hunt

• • • • • • • • • • • •

Resort Hotel Scavenger Hunt

Walt Disney World's resort hotels are filled with Mickeys, hidden and otherwise. The majority are what I like to call décor Mickeys, imaginative decorations that vary among the hotels and change periodically over time. Hidden and décor Mickeys can be found along hotel hallways in the carpet, wallpaper, and lampshades. They appear in the guestrooms on covers for drinking glasses, bedspreads, pillows, day beds, furniture, lamps, lampshades, room curtains, shower curtains, wall pictures, wallpaper, carpets, soap, the outer wrapping of toilet paper rolls, and other items. The housekeeping staff sometimes creates Mickey images out of towels on the bed or elsewhere in your room for you to enjoy upon your return! Guest laundry rooms sometimes have Hidden Mickeys on the soap vending machines and in the bubbles on wall paintings, and resort laundry bins and carts show off classic and side-profile Mickeys.

In the restaurants, pancakes, waffles, butter pats, pasta, pizza, pepperoni on the pizza, and the arrangement of dishes and condiments, among other items, are sometimes Mickey-shaped. Sample menu displays in food order areas often have food items arranged to form classic Mickeys. Mugs, paper plates, and other items in the gift shops can sport Mickeys.

201

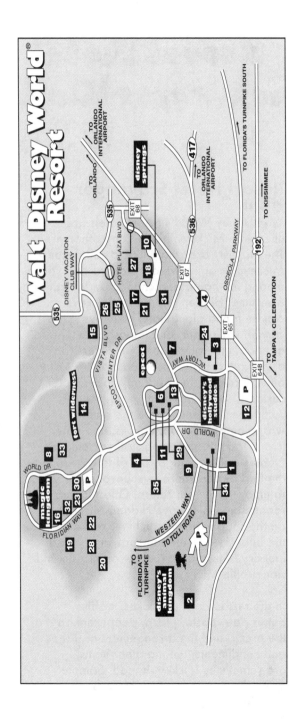

1 All-Star Resorts
2 Animal Kingdom Lodge
3 Art of Animation
4 Beach Club
5 Blizzard Beach
6 BoardWalk
7 Caribbean Beach
8 Contemporary
9 Coronado Springs
10 Disney Springs
11 Dolphin
12 ESPN Wide World of Sports Complex
13 Fantasia Gardens Mini Golf
14 Fort Wilderness
15 Golden Oak
16 Grand Floridian
17 Lake Buena Vista Golf Course
18 The Landing, in Disney Springs

19 Magnolia Golf Course
20 Oak Trail Golf Course
21 Old Key West
22 Palm Golf Course
23 Polynesian Village
24 Pop Century
25 Port Orleans – French Quarter
26 Port Orleans – Riverside
27 Saratoga Springs
28 Shades of Green
29 Swan
30 Transportation and Ticket Center
31 Typhoon Lagoon
32 Wedding Pavilion, Disney's Fairytale
33 Wilderness Lodge
34 Winter Summerland Mini Golf
35 Yacht Club
P Parking

Walt Disney World's Hidden Mickeys

Even the utilities embrace Mickey. Manhole covers and survey markers throughout Walt Disney World often have classic Mickey designs in the center.

Generally, I do not include décor Mickeys in the scavenger hunts unless they are truly unique (as many of the carpet Mickeys are) and are easily accessible to Hidden Mickey hunters at the hotels and in other WDW areas. So don't be surprised to discover dozens of Mickeys at the hotels you visit that aren't included in this scavenger hunt. They're fun to spot but you don't get points for finding them.

The best way to hunt for Hidden Mickeys at the hotels is by car. However, buses to all the WDW hotels are available from Disney Springs (the major bus depot is at the far end of the Marketplace). If you choose to bus around, be prepared for leisurely hunting. You won't be able to visit as many hotels in a given time frame as you would with a car.

Of course, driving means parking, and it's not always a slam-dunk. Guard gates stand watch at most WDW hotels. When you drive up, tell the guard that you're a Hidden Mickey freak and want to look for Hidden Mickeys at the hotel. You'll generally be greeted with a smile, an opened gate, and a wave—along with a "Good luck!" or "Go freak out!" to encourage you on your quest. In the event you aren't allowed to park, drive on to another hotel on the scavenger hunt and take transportation (bus, boat or monorail) to the one you want to explore. If you're really lucky, you may have a spouse, friend, or family member who is willing to drop you off and pick you up.

Again, be considerate of other guests and Cast Members. Ask permission to look around restaurants and avoid searching for Hidden Mickeys at meal times unless you are one of the diners. Even then be careful to stay out of the way—especially of waiters with full trays. Let others share in the fun by telling them what you are up to if they notice you looking around.

Two important notes:

1. I've arranged this hunt in a logical, efficient progression that I imagine you could follow in a car. However, you may want to hunt just one hotel or group of sister hotels at a time. That's why I list the perfect score for each resort hotel (and hotel group) in parentheses after the hotel (or group) name in the Clues section. I also list the perfect score for each of WDW's four resort areas (Animal Kingdom, Disney Springs, Epcot, and Magic Kingdom) in the Scoring section on page 234.

2. This scavenger hunt includes only those WDW resorts in which I found Hidden Mickeys. If I found no convincing (to me) Hidden Mickeys in a hotel, I didn't include it in the hunt. Keep your eyes open; you may spot one that I haven't found (yet).

★ **Bonus Points Opportunity**. During your Hidden Mickey hunt around WDW property, pay attention to the Disney buses. You may get lucky! The Disney Cruise Line bus has a Hidden Pluto on each side of the gold scrollwork on the front of the bus between the headlights. Look for a green classic Mickey on the back of many buses that are diesel. Some general Disney transport buses sometimes sport a classic Mickey on the rear of the vehicle, usually related to rear upper or lower lights. Even more subtle are faint classic Mickey images in the windows of some buses, only visible if the lighting is just right! If you spot one or more of these images, give yourself 5 bonus points for each one.

Animal Kingdom Area Resorts
(253 points)

I'll start this scavenger hunt with the seven Animal Kingdom Area resorts (Animal Kingdom Lodge, the three All-Star Resorts, Coronado Springs, Art of Animation, and Pop Century). You can start (and stop) wherever you want. Have fun!

Animal Kingdom Lodge
(113 points*)
*includes Kidani Village points

Clue 1: Look up for a classic Mickey outside near the hotel's main entrance.
2 points

Clue 2: Find a classic Mickey on a mural between the outer and inner entrance doors to the main lobby.
2 points

Clue 3: Inside the main lobby, spot a classic Mickey on a chandelier.
3 points

Clue 4: Check the logs banded to wood supports around the main lobby. Find any classic Mickeys?
2 points

Clue 5: Look for a classic Mickey on the rock formation next to the short bridge on the right side of the main lobby (as you face it on entering).
4 points

Clue 6: Search the Kudu Trail at the rear of the lobby for a classic Mickey on a post.
4 points

Clue 7: Try to spot a green Hidden Mickey in side profile outside the rear doors of the main lobby. He's on the vine-covered column, on your right as you exit, and he's

looking into the lobby.
5 points

Clue 8: On the trail to Arusha Rock Overlook, outside the rear exit from the main lobby, explore the decorative reliefs on the rock wall for a giraffe sporting a classic Mickey.
3 points

Clue 9: Spot another classic Mickey along the walkway in Arusha Rock Overlook.
4 points

Clue 10: Search for a classic Mickey on the rock wall as you descend the stairs from the right side of the main lobby to Boma restaurant.
4 points

Clue 11: Examine the chairs inside Boma.
2 points

Clue 12: Inside Jiko restaurant, check out the ceiling above the large oven exhausts.
2 points

Clue 13: From inside Jiko, spot a classic Mickey out the window.
5 points

Clue 14: From the path alongside the walkway to the pool's water slide, find a classic Mickey impression low on a rock.
4 points

Clue 15: Farther along this walkway, around the back of the swimming pool, look for a light-colored classic Mickey cut into the rock wall.
4 points

Clue 16: From a fence at the flamingo overlook, study the rock wall for a classic Mickey.
4 points

★ Walk back to *The Mara* and then turn

and walk toward the pool.

Clue 17: On your way, look down for a classic Mickey.
5 points

Clue 18: Search the wall outside in the back of The Mara eatery seating area for a classic Mickey.
4 points

★ Now find two classic Mickeys inside The Mara food area.

Clue 19: One is on the left upper wall.
3 points

Clue 20: The other is on the right upper wall.
3 points

– *Back inside the Lodge* (12 points)

Clue 21: Spot a classic Mickey in the elevator to the Fitness Center.
2 points

Clue 22: Walk around to spot some classic Mickeys in the carpet below the fifth floor as well as either on or above the fifth floor.
4 points for two or more different classic Mickeys

Clue 23: Search for Mickey near the main Zebra Trail on the third floor.
2 points

Clue 24: Go to the second floor of the Zebra Trail for a Hidden Mickey near the elevators to Simba's Cubhouse.
4 points

– Walk to *Kidani Village*. (32 points)

Clue 25: Look for Mickey on a clock.
4 points

Clue 26: Search high for Mickey in the

lobby.
5 points

Clue 27: Spot him as you approach Sanaa restaurant.
4 points

Clue 28: Locate Mickey on a wall inside Sanaa.
3 points

Clue 29: Study Sanaa's dining tables.
3 points

Clue 30: Now leave the restaurant and find Mickey on a rock near the exit door to the outside walkway.
4 points

Clue 31: Stroll the hallways for carpet Mickeys.
4 points for two or more

Clue 32: Check out the cement walkway from the main lobby to the Samawati Springs Pool for a classic Mickey traced in the cement.
5 points

Disney's All-Star Resorts (18 points)

★ *All-Star Sports Resort* (6 points)

Clue 33: Go to the main building gift shop and find classic Mickeys in the carpet.
2 points for all

Clue 34: Look for classic Mickeys on a wall in the food court.
2 points

Clue 35: If you know what I (the author of this book) look like, I'm a spectator at a hockey game in the food court.
5 bonus points

Clue 36: Find the classic Mickey in the cement outdoors behind and to the right of the registration building. (Psst! It's near the Mickey Mouse statue.)
2 points

★ *All-Star Music Resort* (8 points)

Clue 37: Scan the Intermission Food Court order area for a Hidden Mickey.
3 points

Clue 38: Examine the Jazz Inn courtyard to spot classic Mickey ears.
3 points

Clue 39: Take a look at the boots in the Country Fair area.
2 points

★ *All-Star Movies Resort* (4 points)

Clue 40: Find a classic Mickey in a display window of the gift shop.
3 points

Clue 41: Check out Andy's Room in the resort's "Toy Story" section.
1 point

Coronado Springs Resort (38 points*)

*includes Dig Site points

Clue 42: Take a good look at the large wooden doors at the front entrance to the main lobby.
3 points

Clue 43: Search in the registration area for a spotlight Mickey.
4 bonus points

Clue 44: Look around for a statue of a bird with a Hidden Mickey.
3 points

Clue 45: Now study the wooden doors at the exit labeled El Centro.
3 points

Clue 46: Admire the walls of Rix Lounge for a Mickey image.
2 points

Clue 47: Walk to the hallway outside the Veracruz Exhibit Hall in the Convention Center and look around for two classic Mickeys.
4 points for spotting both

Clue 48: Examine the cement near the Marina rental gazebo.
4 points

– Around the *Dig Site* (19 points)

Clue 49: Spot a classic Mickey at the Dig Site swimming pool on a wall facing the lake.
3 points

Clue 50: Now find a classic Mickey on a wall facing the Dig Site pool.
3 points

Clue 51: Look for a whitish classic Mickey on a stone block on the Mayan pyramid at the Dig Site.
4 points

Clue 52: Spot Mickey near the Dig Site restrooms.
3 points

Clue 53: Locate a classic Mickey made of rocks in the sidewalk near Ranchos Building 6A.
4 points

Clue 54: Check the bus stop signs around the periphery of the resort.
2 points for one or more

Art of Animation Resort (36

points)

Clue 55: Look around just inside the entrance doors for furniture Mickeys.
3 points for all

Clue 56: In the food court seating area, study the light covers for Lightning McQueen.
4 points

Clue 57: Search for Mickey on the bottom of another light cover in the food court seating area.
5 points

Clue 58: Walk behind The Big Blue Pool and find Mickey inside the blue coral reef kids' play area.
5 points

Clue 59: Now face Animation Hall and head to the sidewalk to your right that borders the fence around The Big Blue Pool. Spot a Hidden Mickey on a fish.
5 points

Clue 60: Explore the Boneyard outdoors in the resort's Lion King section for a Hidden Mickey.
5 points

Clue 61: In The Little Mermaid section, locate a Hidden Mickey near a clam.
4 points

Clue 62: Check the hallway carpets of the various sections.
5 points for three or more

Pop Century Resort (48 points)

Clue 63: Search for a fishbowl with a Hidden Mickey near the check-in area.
4 points

Clue 64: Find two classic Mickeys behind

the registration counter.
5 points for both

Clue 65: Look low for Hidden Mickeys at the Everything Pop Food Court.
4 points for two or more

Clue 66: Now raise your eyes up for a Mickey in the lights. (Note: It's not always there!)
5 bonus points

Clue 67: Locate Hidden Mickeys on walls in the food court.
4 points for four or more

Clue 68: In the gift shop adjoining the Everything Pop Food Court, find Hidden Mickeys on the merchandise stands.
2 points

Clue 69: Also in the gift shop, search for two classic Mickeys on the wall.
4 points for both

Clue 70: Step into a guest elevator for a Hidden Mickey.
3 points

Clue 71: Spot a classic Mickey on a wall near the Computer Pool.
4 points

Clue 72: Now look near the Computer Pool for two Hidden Mickeys that could help you type.
2 points for both

Clue 73: Marvel at a Hidden Mickey on a wall behind Mowgli on the '60s building.
5 points

Clue 74: Find Hidden Mickeys in laundry rooms near the Hippy Dippy Pool and the Bowling Pool.
4 points for four

Clue 75: Search for Mickey's name near

213

the Bowling Pool (and, just for fun, a reference to "Disneyland" nearby).
4 points

Clue 76: Look around for a Hidden Mickey near the bus stop out front of the Pop Century lobby.
3 points

Disney Springs Area Resorts

(146 points)

The Disney Springs area resorts with Hidden Mickeys are the Caribbean Beach, Old Key West, the Port Orleans Resorts, and Saratoga Springs Resort & Spa.

Caribbean Beach Resort (24 points)

Clue 77: Examine a group of logs in the ground between Martinique Buildings 24 and 25 for a classic Hidden Mickey.
4 points

Clue 78: Spot a classic Mickey on the lighthouse behind Old Port Royale.
2 points

Clue 79: Search for a classic Mickey in the children's water play area near the main (Old Port Royale) pool.
4 points

Clue 80: Study the rockwork of the main pool for a faint classic Mickey. (Psst! Look under a cannon.)
5 points

Clue 81: Walk around just outside the main pool to marvel at this Mickey image.
5 points

Clue 82: In Shutters restaurant, find a classic Mickey in a painting.
4 points

Old Key West Resort (23 points)

Clue 83: Check the fences inside Conch Flats General Store.
2 points

Clue 84: Take a close look at the fence railings in the registration area.
2 points

Clue 85: At the pool, spot a Mickey with a big mouth.
3 points

Clue 86: Find a Hidden Mickey near the steps to the water slide.
4 points

Clue 87: Notice the design of certain railings on the guest buildings outside.
2 points

★ Search for classic Mickeys formed by three-shell imprints in the cement on the paths leading from parking spaces to Building 36.

Clue 88: Search the pavement on the right side of the first path for imprints.
5 points

Clue 89: On the second path, explore the corner of the sidewalk after the first right turn.
5 points
(Note: More of these amazing Mickeys may be scattered around Old Key West Resort.)

Port Orleans Resort – French Quarter
(5 points)

Clue 90: Find a classic Mickey in the registration area.
3 points

Clue 91: Look up for a classic Mickey in the food court area.
2 points

Port Orleans Resort – Riverside
(16 points)

Clue 92: Look for classic Mickeys in the latticework of the registration area.
2 points

Clue 93: Also in the registration area, find more classic Mickeys near the giant fans.
2 points

Clue 94: Now spot Hidden Mickeys on the fans themselves.
3 points

★ Cross the river and visit Parterre Place.

Clue 95: Find some Mickeys outside the Parterre Place building.
4 points for all

Clue 96: Amble along the sidewalk next to the river and stop in front of Acadian House. Squint your eyes to locate a Hidden Mickey on the sidewalk.
5 points

Saratoga Springs Resort & Spa
(78 points)

Clue 97: Locate Mickey in the registration lobby.
2 points

Clue 98: Behind The Artist's Palette shop, look around for Mickey on a door handle.
5 points

Clue 99: Notice classic Mickeys on a jacket near The Turf Club Bar and Grill.
2 points

Chapter 6: Resort Hotel Scavenger Hunt

Clue 100: Spot Mickey on a gate.
3 points

Clue 101: Find more Mickey images inside on a wall.
2 points for one or more

Clue 102: Look around inside The Turf Club for a classic Mickey on a wall.
3 points

Clue 103: Check out a statue outside the main lobby for three pairs of Hidden Mickeys. (Note: This statue also sports a décor Mickey.)
10 points for finding all six

Clue 104: Search for two Hidden Mickeys near stairs outside The Artist's Palette.
5 points for spotting both

Clue 105: In the children's play area of the pool, find a large classic Hidden Mickey.
5 points

Clue 106: Locate three Hidden Mickeys near the zero grade pool entrance.
5 points for all three

Clue 107: Look for Hidden Mickeys on the outside wall and the downstairs entrance door of the spa.
4 points for spotting both

Clue 108: Admire the guest buildings for small Mickeys.
2 points for one or more

Clue 109: Search for a Hidden Mickey on an outdoor wall, near the check-in point.
5 points

Clue 110: Now find a similar Hidden Mickey on a wall in the Congress Park section near the Disney Springs lagoon.
5 points

Clue 111: Check for a Hidden Mickey

inside the Aquatic Play Area at The Paddock Villas pool.
4 points

Clue 112: Look around for Hidden Mickeys on outdoor wall lights.
4 points for one or more

Clue 113: Find classic Mickeys in the various Villa courtyards.
2 points for one or more

Clue 114: Smile at Hidden Mickeys on a gazebo at the Carousel Villas.
2 points

Clue 115: Locate Mickey in a gate near the Grandstand Pool.
3 points

Clue 116: Search near the Backstretch Bar for Mickey.
5 points

Epcot Area Resorts (133 points)

You'll find Hidden Mickeys in Disney's BoardWalk, Beach Club, and Yacht Club Resorts, as well as the WDW Dolphin Hotel. To explore them, park at one and walk around Crescent Lake to the others. Smile and tell the guards that you're searching for Hidden Mickeys.

BoardWalk Resort (43 points)

Clue 117: Spot two classic Mickeys on a horse in the main lobby.
3 points for both

Clue 118: Search for a classic Mickey on a lobby wall.
4 points

Clue 119: Squint to spot some classic

Mickeys above an elephant.
4 points for one or more

Clue 120: Look for Mickey near the Villa elevators.
4 points for one or more

Clue 121: Wander around the guestroom and elevator hallways in both the BoardWalk Inn and the BoardWalk Villas.
8 points for four or more different Mickey images

Clue 122: Find Mickey (and his hands!) at an outside bar.
2 points

Clue 123: Study a BoardWalk surrey bike for a Hidden Mickey.
3 points

Clue 124: Admire the decor inside AbracadaBar to discover a Hidden Walt Disney with a rabbit.
4 points

Clue 125: Search inside AbracadaBar for a Hidden Mickey on a playing card.
4 points

Clue 126: Walk into the waiting lobby for Trattoria al Forno Restaurant. Scan the walls of the lobby for a tiny Hidden Mickey.
5 points

Clue 127: Step inside Ample Hills Creamery (and enjoy some ice cream if you wish) to find two Mickey images.
2 points for both

Beach Club Resort (67 points)

Clue 128: Look around just inside the entrance to Cape May Cafe for Mickey on a plate.
4 points

Walt Disney World's Hidden Mickeys

Clue 129: Search for Mickey Mouse along the inside walkway in front of the Cape May Cafe.
3 points

Clue 130: Walk along the hallway behind Cape May Cafe and find Mickey in a painting.
4 points

Clue 131: Search for Mickey in the tile floor in the hallway across the main lobby from Cape May Cafe. (Psst! Look near the luggage room door.)
4 points

★ Walk to the *Beach Club Solarium* to find more Hidden Mickeys. (Psst! Check the walls.)

Clue 132: Spot some car tires with Mickey's full face.
3 points

Clue 133: Now look for classic Mickeys in the same general area.
2 points

Clue 134: Gaze at Mickey's face in the sky.
3 points

Clue 135: Search for Mickey on the sand.
4 points

Clue 136: Now find classic Mickeys in the water.
2 points

Clue 137: Do you see other classic Mickeys floating in the air?
2 points

Clue 138: Squint for a Hidden Mickey atop a building.
5 points

Clue 139: Look low for Mickey in the

Marketplace shop.
2 points

Clue 140: Still inside the Marketplace shop, wander near the shop entrance from the elevators to come across a Hidden Mickey.
3 points

Clue 141: Walk to a guestroom hallway to find classic Mickeys under your feet.
2 points for one or more

Clue 142: Look for Mickey in an elevator near the Beach Pool (aka the Quiet Pool).
3 points

Clue 143: Study the area near the entrance to the Beach Club Villas for a classic Mickey.
4 points

Clue 144: Enter the Breezeway in the Beach Club Villas and locate three different Hidden Mickey images.
5 points for all three

Clue 145: Walk toward the nearby restrooms inside and find Mickey in a painting.
5 points

Clue 146: Wander into the Beaches & Cream Soda Shop to spot a tasty Hidden Mickey on the wall.
4 points

Clue 147: Now watch hamburger preparation on the Beaches & Cream grill for a classic Mickey.
3 points

Yacht Club Resort (20 points)

Clue 148: Study the globe in the main lobby.
5 points

Clue 149: Look for a cabinet in the

221

main lobby with character names on the drawers.
4 points

Clue 150: Check out the lobby carpet.
2 points

Clue 151: Search other resort carpets for Mickeys.
4 points for two or more

Clue 152: In the Yachtsman Steakhouse, look for the photograph of (now deceased) Minnie Moo, a cow born with a black classic Mickey on her side. (You may have to ask a Cast Member where the photo is located. It's sometimes not on public display.)
5 points

WDW Dolphin Hotel (3 points)

Clue 153: Walk into the main lobby and look for classic Mickeys.
3 points

Magic Kingdom Area Resorts
(328 points)

This area is home to seven resorts as well as Disney's Fairytale Wedding Pavilion. The resorts include Disney's Fort Wilderness, Wilderness Lodge and Villas, Shades of Green, and the three monorail resorts (Polynesian Village, Grand Floridian, and Contemporary), so-called because they are all connected to one another and the Magic Kingdom by monorail.

Tip: To explore Fort Wilderness and Wilderness Lodge, take a boat from the Magic Kingdom or from the Contemporary Resort to their respective marinas, or hop on a Disney bus or into your car for transportation to their front entrances.

Fort Wilderness Resort (24 points)

If you drive to Fort Wilderness, swing by the entrance to the *Golden Oak* commmunity at the intersection of Vista Boulevard and Bonnet Creek Parkway (not far from Port Orleans Resort – Riverside) to spot another Hidden Mickey.

Clue 154: Look for a Hidden Mickey on a sign.
3 bonus points

At Fort Wilderness, you'll need to ride an internal bus between the Hidden Mickeys at the rear near the lake (where your hunt begins) and the Hidden Mickeys near the front parking area.

Clue 155: Stroll into the Tri-Circle-D Ranch Horse Barn and admire Hidden Mickeys in a display.
3 points

Clue 156: While you're in the Horse Barn, search for Hidden Mickeys near the horse stalls.
3 points

Clue 157: Visit the Blacksmith (near the Horse Barn) and find a Hidden Mickey.
3 points

Clue 158: Check out Trail's End Restaurant inside for a classic Mickey.
3 points

Clue 159: Stop by the Meadow Depot area and search near the Bike Barn for a Hidden Mickey.
3 points

Clue 160: Go to the Trail Ride Check-In building near the front parking area to find two Hidden Mickeys.
3 points for both

Clue 161: Stroll over to the Fort Wilderness registration building ("Reception Outpost") at the far side of the front parking area and look for Mickey.
3 points

Clue 162: Admire a trash can for a Hidden Mickey!
3 points

Wilderness Lodge (141 points*)

*includes Cub's Den and Wilderness Lodge Villas points

Clue 163: Check out the signs on the right side of the entrance drive.
2 points

Clue 164: Search out a classic Mickey on the guard gate kiosk.
3 points

Clue 165: Near the car unloading area, look up for a classic Mickey etched in a support pole above a black metal band.
4 points

Clue 166: Now search for a classic Mickey etched in another support pole and partially hidden under a black metal band.
4 points

Clue 167: Glance down for a tiny classic Mickey traced in the cement on a black stripe.
5 points

Clue 168: Look up again for a classic Mickey etched on a side support pole.
4 points

Clue 169: Find a classic Mickey on a large key in the registration area.
1 point

Clue 170: Look overhead for Mickey driving a bus.

Chapter 6: Resort Hotel Scavenger Hunt

2 points

Clue 171: Find a classic Mickey on the rock of the main lobby fireplace.
5 points

Clue 172: Peek at a fireplace inside the Whispering Canyon Cafe for a classic Mickey. (Ask a Cast Member to let you into the rear of the cafe.)
4 points

Clue 173: Search around the bubbling spring in the lobby for a classic Mickey.
4 points

Clue 174: Look for a classic Mickey on a wall map at the entrance stairs to the Territory Lounge.
3 points

Clue 175: Now go inside and spot a classic Mickey on a ceiling mural above the bar.
4 points

Clue 176: Inside the Artist Point restaurant, spot a classic Mickey in a large mural above the entrance to the rear left dining area.
4 points

Clue 177: Now scan another mural for a classic Mickey near the restaurant's ceiling. (Psst! Turn back toward the entrance.)
5 points

Clue 178: Next scan the walls of the restaurant for Winnie the Pooh.
3 points

Clue 179: Search inside the Roaring Fork snack bar for a Hidden Mickey in a display case.
3 points

Clue 180: Find a classic Mickey in one or more lights near the elevators close to the snack bar.

Walt Disney World's Hidden Mickeys

3 points

Clue 181: Glance at the hallway walls for small Hidden Mickeys.
3 points

Clue 182: Look down in the hallways for more.
2 points

Clue 183: Locate a classic Mickey near Room 6100.
3 points

Clue 184: Explore one floor down for a classic Mickey near Room 5066.
3 points

Clue 185: Find another classic near Room 4035.
3 points

Clue 186: Search for a classic Mickey in the rock outside at Fire Rock Geyser.
4 points

Clue 187: Find stairs outside an exit door from the main building (on the side toward the Boat and Bike Rental) and look up for a classic Mickey.
4 points

Clue 188: Locate a rope Hidden Mickey near the Boat and Bike Rental cabin.
4 points

– *In the Cub's Den* (8 points)

(Tip: Visit in the afternoon if possible. It's less crowded then and the Cast Members are more likely to let you in. Tell them you're searching for Hidden Mickeys.)

Clue 189: Spot a plush Mickey doll in a mural.
2 points

Clue 190: Look higher for a side-profile

Mickey.
3 points

Clue 191: Find a classic Mickey in the same mural.
3 points

– *Wilderness Lodge Villas* (44 points)

Clue 192: Just inside the main entrance to the Villas, stop before you get to the elevators on your left. Check out the rock pillar to your right for a Hidden Mickey.
5 points

Clue 193: Search for four classic Mickeys near the elevators. (Psst! Look behind some fabric for one of the four.)
5 points for all finding all four

Clue 194: Look around the rock pillars near the Villas lobby for a classic Mickey in the rock.
5 points

Clue 195: Smile back at Mickey hiding in a hole in a beam in the lobby.
5 points

Clue 196: Locate a side profile of Mickey on a wall near the lobby.
4 points

Clue 197: Admire a classic Mickey inside the small telephone alcove near the lobby.
5 points

Clue 198: Spot Mickeys around a painting in a room near the lobby.
3 points

Clue 199: Find Mickey in the rock in the Carolwood Pacific Railroad Room near the lobby.
5 points

Clue 200: Look up to spot Mickey in the hallways of the Wilderness Lodge Villas.

2 points

Clue 201: Search for Mickey on a hallway wall near Room 1507.
5 points

Magic Kingdom Monorail Resorts
(154 points*)

*includes Disney's Fairytale Wedding Pavilion points

To find the Hidden Mickeys in these resorts and the nearby Fairytale Wedding Pavilion, park at the Polynesian Village or the Grand Floridian and ride the monorail to the other two resorts and past the Wedding Pavilion. Or if you prefer, walk or drive to the Wedding Pavilion. (Note: Polynesian Village has the bigger parking lot.)

★ *Polynesian Village Resort* (35 points)

Clue 202: On the lower level, look for a classic Mickey on the floor near the main entrance.
4 points

Clue 203: Find Mickey overhead in the lobby.
4 points

Clue 204: Spot three Hidden Mickeys in the Tiki Boutique store.
4 points for finding all three

Clue 205: Study the bamboo-ring wall decorations by the corner staircase.
3 points

★ Find a Hidden Mickey in the Moana Mercantile shop.

Clue 206: Look along a wall.
3 points

Clue 207: Walk by the Kona Cafe and find a classic Mickey.
2 points

Clue 208: At the Kona Island coffee bar, search for a small classic Mickey.
5 points

Clue 209: Look down for Hidden Mickeys in hallways and elevators.
3 points for spotting them in both places

Clue 210: Wander to the marina area and admire a Sea Raycer for a Hidden Mickey.
2 points

Clue 211: Stroll along the lagoon walkway toward Disney's Wedding Pavilion and spot small, white Hidden Mickeys near your feet.
5 points for one or more

★ *Disney's Fairytale Wedding Pavilion*
(3 points)

Clue 212: As your monorail car passes by the pavilion buildings, observe the weather vane.
3 points

(Note: A Hidden Mickey may be lurking inside, but the Wedding Pavilion isn't open to the general public.)

★ *Grand Floridian Resort & Spa* (57 points)
Clue 213: Take a good look at the weather vanes on the roofs.
3 points for one or more

Clue 214: Check the large trolley carts outside the hotel.
1 point

Clue 215: Study the lobby carpet.
2 points

Clue 216: Look at the floor tile for a classic

Walt Disney World's Hidden Mickeys

Mickey.
2 points

Clue 217: While you're at it, check the tile for the Fab Five.
5 points for five characters

Clue 218: Look near 1900 Park Fare restaurant for a Mickey hat.
3 points

Clue 219: Also near 1900 Park Fare, find Mickey and Minnie below your feet.
2 points for both

Clue 220: Now look for other Disney movie characters, as well as Mickey and Minnie, in the floor encircling the main lobby and in front of the Grand Floridian Café.
5 points for five or more characters

Clue 221: Search a wall map for a Hidden Mickey.
4 points

Clue 222: Spot Mickey on the outside of the ornate lobby elevator by the stairs.
4 points

Clue 223: Look up high for Mickey on the ceiling above the main lobby.
4 points

Clue 224: Check out the classic Mickey in front of the M. Mouse Mercantile shop.
1 point

Clue 225: Find Hidden Mickeys in the hallway walls.
2 points for one or more

Clue 226: Now look down for others in the hallways.
2 points

Clue 227: Locate a Hidden Mickey while walking outside toward the Grand Floridian

Villas.
3 points

Clue 228: Study the area around the main pool near the Villas for a Hidden Mickey in rock.
5 points

Clue 229: Find Mickey and other characters in the lobbies of the outer buildings.
4 points for four or more

Clue 230: Stroll into Gasparilla Island Grill and search for Mickey.
3 points

Clue 231: Walk into the Grand Floridian Convention Center's main entrance and look around for Mickey.
2 points

★ *Contemporary Resort* (59 points*)
   *includes some Bay Lake Tower points

Clue 232: From the window of the California Grill restaurant, on the top floor, spot a stretched out Mickey watchband on the ground in front of the hotel.
4 points

Clue 233: Go to the sixth floor and walk in the direction of the Transportation and Ticket Center to an outside balcony to spot this amazing Hidden Mickey.
5 points
Caution: Be sure to prop the hallway door open, as it may lock upon closing.

Tip: This Mickey can also be seen from the resort and express monorails.

Clue 234: Look for Mickey's profile inside Chef Mickey's restaurant. (You'll also encounter many décor—not Hidden—Mickey images inside the restaurant.)
1 point

Walt Disney World's Hidden Mickeys

Clue 235: Don't miss Mickey's ears at the rear of Chef Mickey's!
3 points

Clue 236: Find Mickey low on a wall near the Contempo Café.
3 points

Clue 237: Now study this mural higher up for a classic Mickey in a basket.
4 points

Clue 238: Look high for a classic Mickey on an animal in the next mural to the right.
4 points

Clue 239: Search around for a stick-figure Mickey near the shops.
3 points

Clue 240: Look for classic Mickeys in The Game Station Arcade.
3 points for all

Clue 241: Walk to the Market shop for a Hidden Mickey right at the entrance.
3 points

Clue 242: Ride up the monorail escalator to spot a classic Mickey on the wall. (Enjoy the five-legged goat while you're up there!)
4 points

Clue 243: Find a classic Mickey silhouette in the bricks behind the main hotel. (Psst! It's near Mickey Mouse himself.)
2 points

Clue 244: Scan the marina dock for a Hidden Mickey.
3 points

Clue 245: Stare at the nautical flags on the glass front of the Sand Bar. Can you guess what they spell?
3 points

Clue 246: Locate a classic Hidden Mickey

in The Sand Bar.
3 points

Clue 247: Spot Mickey in the tile at the exit from the Garden Building to the parking lot.
5 points

Clue 248: Look up for Mickey at the hotel entrance.
2 points

— *Bay Lake Tower* (4 points)

Clue 249: Walk to Bay Lake Tower and locate Mickey from the outside. (Psst! Look high!)
4 points

Shades of Green Resort (9 points)
(Only folks with military connections are allowed into this resort.)

Clue 250: Search for four classic Mickeys in the lobby.
5 points for finding all four

Clue 251: Find a large classic Mickey outside (or on a map of the resort).
4 points

It's time to tally your score.

A perfect score for this scavenger hunt is 860. You may have done even better if you earned bonus points at Coronado Springs registration desk, in the All-Star Sports and/or Pop Century food court(s), by finding the Hidden Mickey in the entrance sign to the Golden Oak community, and/or by spotting Hidden Characters on the WDW buses.

Total Points for Hotel Hunt =

```
┌─────────────────┐
│                 │
│                 │
│                 │
└─────────────────┘
```

How'd you do?

Give yourself Gold if you scored at least 80% of the points available for the places you've searched, Bronze if you scored at least 40%.

Here is a point breakdown by area and resort or resort group, so that you can compare your score with the perfect score for the areas you've covered. You'll find the total points for each section in parentheses.

Animal Kingdom Area (253)
    Animal Kingdom Lodge (113)
        - Kidani Village (32)
    Disney's All-Star Resorts (18)
        All-Star Sports Resort (6)
        All-Star Music Resort (8)
        All-Star Movies Resort (4)
    Coronado Springs Resort (38)
        - Dig Site (19)
    Art of Animation Resort (36)
    Pop Century Resort (48)

Disney Springs Area (146)
    Caribbean Beach Resort (24)
    Old Key West Resort (23)
    Port Orleans Resort–French Quarter (5)
    Port Orleans Resort–Riverside (16)
    Saratoga Springs Resort & Spa (78)

Epcot Area (133)
    BoardWalk Resort (43)
    Beach Club Resort (67)
    Yacht Club Resort (20)
    WDW Dolphin Hotel (3)

Magic Kingdom Area (328)
    Fort Wilderness Resort (24)

234

Chapter 6: Resort Hotel Scavenger Hunt

Animal Kingdom Area Resorts

Animal Kingdom Lodge

Hint 1: Outside, above the lower roof, the second tall figure to the left of the car baggage drop-off area has a classic Mickey in its mouth.

Hint 2: On the right wall mural between the outer and inner entrance doors to the main lobby, an orange and brown creature sports a classic Mickey in a circle on its mid back.

Hint 3: Inside the main lobby, you can find a classic Mickey near the bottom of the second chandelier on the right (as you face in from the front entrance). The Hidden Mickey is near the bottom of one of the

Hint 4: Around the main lobby, classic Mickeys are formed by logs banded to wood supports. One of the best is the second support on the right (as you enter the lobby from the front doors). It's on the second level, on the side away from the main lobby entrance.

Hint 5: On the right side of the main lobby (as you face in from the front entrance), a short bridge crosses a rockbound pool of water. A classic Mickey is visible on the rock from the side of the bridge nearest the lobby. It's toward the rear on the right side. To spot it, look for the first recess in the rock from the right edge of the pool. Mickey is at the back of this recess, above the water line.

Hint 6: Go down the staircase at the rear of the lobby. Turn left and walk down the Kudu Trail hallway. In the first small lobby, near the elevator, a classic Mickey is on the top end of a piece of wood that's roped to two giant "log" supports. Mickey is above the second rope binding, near the ceiling.

Hint 7: Outside the rear doors of the main lobby, a green Mickey in side profile hides in the decorative vines to the right as you exit. He is about two-thirds of the way up the side of the vine-covered column, above the middle horizontal brace, at the top of an open space in the vines. He's looking into the lobby.

Hint 8: Outside the rear exit from the main lobby, on the left side of the trail to Arusha Rock Overlook, check the rock wall for a decorative relief of a group of giraffes. You'll find a classic Mickey among the spots on the middle of the large giraffe in the center, above its inner front leg.

Hint 9: Along the walkway in Arusha Rock Overlook, a rock sports a classic Mickey.

Look for it where the trail first turns left between rock walls. It's on the right side in the first small alcove, about six feet up from the path and under a large overhanging rock.

Hint 10: Toward the bottom of the staircase that winds from the right side of the main lobby to Boma restaurant, there's a classic Mickey on the rock wall.

Hint 11: Inside Boma, you'll see classic Mickeys on some of the chairs with tall metal backs.

Hint 12: Inside Jiko restaurant, a classic Mickey is formed on the ceiling above the two large orange oven exhausts and the white column behind them.

Hint 13: From the entrance to Jiko, walk to the third table on your left, next to the glass windows. Outside in the shallow pool area, a classic Mickey is sculpted on the first rock island from the left that has a pillar jutting out of it.

Hint 14: Outside the exit from the restaurants, a large rock on the left side of the path behind the water slide has a classic Mickey impressed on its lower half near the ground. The rock is about three-quarters of the way along the walkway to the water slide. A small light pole juts out of the top of this rock.

Hint 15: A light-colored classic Mickey is cut into a rock wall behind the swimming pool. The wall forms the back of the pool's water slide. The Mickey is several feet above the walkway, below a gazebo that marks the starting point for the water slide.

Hint 16: Walk behind the pool to the bird and flamingo overlook. From the rightmost "Bird Spotter Guide" on the fence along the main trail, look to your right to the opposite fence. About two-thirds of the distance along this fence from the main trail, a pinkish classic Mickey with a white right ear is about one foot down from the top of the rock.

Hint 17: A Mickey image is etched in the cement outside of The Mara restaurant. Go to the walkway leading to the pool, which is directly opposite the rear exit door from the restaurant. Near the end of this short walkway, and on the left side as you stroll toward the pool, you'll find the Hidden Mickey.

Hint 18: A classic stone Mickey is on the rear of the short wall behind The Mara seating area. It's about three feet up from the ground, behind an emergency phone and a tall brown pole.

Hint 19: In the food area of The Mara, a classic Mickey is on the upper left wall in the third leaf from the left tree (in the mural of falling leaves).

Hint 20: Also in the food area, a classic Mickey hides in a leaf in the middle of the upper right mural of falling leaves.

Hint 21: As you enter the elevator to the Fitness Center, you can spot a classic Mickey on the lower left panel (as you face the rear of the elevator).

Hint 22: Many small classic Mickeys can be found in the carpet in the hallways in front of guestrooms. Classic Mickey images in the carpets below the fifth floor differ from those on and above the fifth floor.

Hint 23: On the third floor, at the end of the first short hall to the right of the main Zebra Trail hallway, an upside-down classic Mickey is formed by three plates on a wall.

Hint 24: On the second floor of the Zebra Trail, near a hat display and the elevators to Simba's Cubhouse, a classic Mickey is etched at the bottom end of a piece of wood that's roped to two giant "log" supports. Mickey is below the upper rope binding. (Note: these images change or disappear from time to time.)

– *Kidani Village*

Hint 25: A classic Mickey is at the 6:30 position on a large decorative gold clock on a table just inside the entrance to the lobby.

Hint 26: A white classic Mickey is on a ladybug on the middle level of the closest chandelier to the front lobby entrance.

Hint 27: At the entrance to Sanaa restaurant downstairs, a classic Mickey made of dark brown baskets is on the far left of the wall behind the check-in desk. It's tilted slightly to the left.

Hint 28: Inside Sanaa, a classic Mickey is above a booth on a white wall. It is to the left as you enter.

Hint 29: Classic Mickeys hide in the woodwork in the middle of Sanaa's dining tables.

Hint 30: Outside Sanaa, a classic Mickey is etched on the rockwork at the bottom rear of the lobby stairs.

Hint 31: A variety of small classic Mickeys can be found in the carpet in the hallways in front of guestrooms.

Hint 32: A classic Mickey is lightly traced in cement in the walkway from the Kidani Village main lobby to the Samawati Springs Pool. It's near the curb and about 25-30 feet before the parking directions sign.

(Other Hidden Mickeys are in the Samawati Springs Pool area, but sometimes

241

only Kidani Village guests are allowed to
enter there.)

Disney's All-Star Resorts

★ *All-Star Sports Resort*

Hint 33: In the main building gift shop,
classic Mickeys are part of the carpet.
Each is composed of a baseball with two
circles for ears.

Hint 34: Midway along the left wall of
the food court seating area, one painting
shows Mickey after he's hit in the head
with a basketball. Some of the "stars" he
sees are yellow classic Mickeys.

Hint 35: In the food court, an image of me
(Hidden Mickey Guy, Steve Barrett) is on
the last design pane near the rear exit from
the food court seating area. I'm sitting in
the stands behind hockey player Minnie
Mouse, and you can find me on both sides
of the pane. I'm holding a yellow *Hidden
Mickeys* book with a magnifying glass on
the cover, and a tiny classic Mickey is on
my shirt! Needless to say, I'm incredibly
honored by this!

Hint 36: Outside, behind and to the right
of the registration building, and past the
buildings with surfboards, a large Mickey
statue stands directly over a classic Mickey
(white head and black ears) in the cement.

★ *All-Star Music Resort*

Hint 37: A painting of an animal orchestra,
conducted by Mickey Mouse, is on the
right wall as you enter the Intermission
Food Court. In the painting are three black
classic Mickey notes, each on a different
music sheet.

Hint 38: In the Jazz Inn courtyard, classic
Mickey ears top the cymbal stands. Each is
a winged nut that holds a cymbal in place.

(These nuts come and go.)

Hint 39: In the Country Fair area, you'll find classic Mickeys on the front and back of the huge boots.

★ *All-Star Movies Resort*

Hint 40: On a mural in an outside display window in front of the gift shop next to the lobby, a small black classic Mickey hides at the lower right of the mural. It's on the front of an orange book with the title "Future Plans."

Hint 41: The large checkers in Andy's Room in the "Toy Story" section sport classic Mickeys.

Coronado Springs Resort

Hint 42: At the front entrance to the main lobby, a medallion in the upper left rectangle of the left large, open wooden door is a three-dimensional relief of Mickey's face.

Hint 43: On the far wall opposite the main entrance to the registration area, three spotlights sometimes create a classic Mickey image. The light circles change size from time to time.

Hint 44: At the far end of the registration lobby, a statue of an eagle stands on the left side. Circles on an emblem on its chest form a classic Hidden Mickey.

Hint 45: A three-dimensional Mickey face is on the large right wooden door (as you face the doors) at the exit labeled "El Centro."

Hint 46: Subtle circles form classic Mickeys in the ornate design of the outside black glass walls of Rix Lounge. They're on the walls that face the Pepper Market.

Hint 47: In the hallway outside the Veracruz Exhibit Hall in the Convention Center, a black classic Mickey pattern repeats along the sides of some of the ceiling chandeliers. Nearby, a similar Mickey pattern can be spotted on rectangular light covers that are flush with the ceiling.

Hint 48: A classic Mickey is chipped into the cement next to the lamppost nearest the Marina rental gazebo.

Hint 49: At the Dig Site swimming pool's main entrance (closest to the lake), a classic Mickey hides on a wall to your right. To spot it, check out the upper middle part of the wall facing the lake before you enter the Dig Site.

Hint 50: After you enter the Dig Site, examine the wall to your left (as you enter) that faces the pool. A classic Mickey is on the upper left side.

Hint 51: Also at the Dig Site, you'll find a whitish, somewhat distorted classic Mickey near the very top of the Mayan pyramid, on the side facing the pool. It's on the second stone block from the left, fourth row from the top.

Hint 52: To the left of the restrooms at the Dig Site, a circular stone tablet with relief images is hanging on the wall. A somewhat distorted sideways classic Mickey hides at the lower right.

Hint 53: A section of the walkway in front of Ranchos Building 6A is made of circular flat gray rocks. Some of these rocks form classic Mickeys. You'll find one of them near the far end of the rock section. It's on the right side as you approach the Ranchos buildings.

Hint 54: Mickey Mouse (side profile) is sitting in a bus on some of the bus stop signs located around the periphery of the resort (such as at Bus Stops No. 2, No. 3, and No. 4).

Art of Animation Resort

Hint 55: In the registration lobby of Animation Hall, classic Mickeys are woven in the upholstery of benches located along the wall opposite the check-in area.

Hint 56: In the Landscape of Flavors food court seating area, an image of Lightning McQueen is in the clouds on the side of a large circular light fixture hanging from the ceiling.

Hint 57: In the same seating area, the painting on the bottom of another large circular light fixture includes a faint full-body image of Mickey Mouse. Look for Mickey near the bright light at the center of the overhead fixture. The image is in what appears to be a framed photo that is sitting on a shelf above some books.

Hint 58: Behind The Big Blue Pool is a play area for kids formed by a blue coral reef rising from the ground. Walk to the left of the slide exit and duck your head as you enter a small passageway through the coral. Halfway along the passageway, about three-quarters of the way up on the right wall, depressions in the rock form a classic Mickey.

Hint 59: Face Animation Hall and walk on the sidewalk next to Finding Nemo Building #5. This sidewalk is to your right and follows the fence encircling the Big Blue Pool. As you walk, look for a green fish perched in the grass near the fence. You'll find the fish after you pass the end of the Finding Nemo Guest Room Building on your right. A decent sideways classic Hidden Mickey is on each side of the fish, below each eye and near both corners of the mouth.

245

Hint 60: Outdoors in the resort's Lion King section, there is a cave in the Boneyard play area. Walk under the elephant ribs to enter the cave on the right side and then keep your eyes peeled. About halfway through the cave, depressions in the rock form a classic Mickey on the right wall.

Hint 61: In The Little Mermaid section, three orange spots on green seaweed under a clam design form a classic Hidden Mickey. You can find this image repeated in several of the clam designs along the inner perimeter of the guest room buildings facing the pool.

Hint 62: A variety of classic Mickeys hide in the hallway carpets of the resort's various sections. Each carpet design is consistent with the décor of the specific section, so these carpet Hidden Mickeys vary, too.

Pop Century Resort

Hint 63: In a small TV room near the check-in area, classic Mickey bubbles rise under a fish in a fishbowl painted on the wall.

Hint 64: In a photograph on the wall behind the middle of the long registration counter, two Hidden Mickeys formed of craters and shadows lie on the moon. Look at the lower right of the television screen and below the word "moon" for a small sideways classic Mickey and above the same word for a large upright classic Mickey.

Hint 65: Several classic Mickeys are hiding on the tile floor of the food court order area. One is in the center of the order and pay area. Another is in front of the middle cash register.

Hint 66: A tiny black classic Mickey is inside one or more round lights suspended from the ceiling in the food court order area. (Note: These images change or even disappear at times.)

Hint 67: Inside the food court seating area, classic Mickeys made of circles can be found on the undulating purple, brown, blue, and green divider walls.

Hint 68: In the shop near the food court, classic Mickey holes are in the poles that hold merchandise racks.

Hint 69: Inside the gift shop, near the exit to the bus stop, check the wall behind the cash registers to spot round gift boxes that form a classic Mickey. The image appears twice in faux package-locker windows. One image is in the second window from the top of the second column of windows from the right side. The other is in the third window from the left along the top row.

Hint 70: Poster ads for pizza delivery are inside the guest building elevators. Check out the upside-down classic Hidden Mickeys formed by pepperoni pizza toppings on each slice.

Hint 71: Behind Roger Rabbit, in a mural on one of the '80s buildings near the Computer Pool, a classic Mickey hides at the top of a bush beside a building. The bush's topmost leaf is just above Mickey's head and ears, and one hand of a traffic signal points to Mickey!

Hint 72: Two black classic Mickeys are on the keyboard of the huge computer near the Computer Pool. Both are on the lower row of keys. One is on the second key from the left and the other is on the second key from the right. (More obvious decorative classic Mickeys are in the computer monitor's screensaver.)

Hint 73: Look sharp for a faint classic Mickey in green paint on an outside wall of the '60s building, behind the Mowgli figure and just past the Hippy Dippy Pool. It's on the left side of the wall with green plants, between two complete vertical leaves, near the wall's left border.

Hint 74: In the guest laundry rooms near both the Hippy Dippy Pool and the Bowling Pool, bubbles form two sideways classic Mickeys. You'll find them in the same places in both laundry rooms. One is on the lower right front of the soap vending machine and the other is at the upper right.

Hint 75: "Mickey Mouse Club March" is choice "C2" on the giant jukebox near the Bowling Pool. ("I've Got a Date at Disneyland" is choice "F10.")

Hint 76: Outside the main lobby, classic Mickeys are at the ends of the guardrails near the bus stops.

Disney Springs Area Resorts

Caribbean Beach Resort

Hint 77: A group of three logs stuck in the ground forms a classic Mickey. Find the image in a border of logs along the lakeside promenade and between Martinique Buildings 24 and 25. The Hidden Mickey is next to a recessed drain that faces and is adjacent to the lakeside promenade. To find it, turn right from the sidewalk between Buildings 24 and 25 onto the lakeside promenade.

Hint 78: Behind Old Port Royale, a classic Mickey appears in the "Barefoot Bay Boat Yard" sign on the side of the lighthouse near the bike racks.

Hint 79: In the child's water play area near the main pool, a classic Mickey is on the helm near the wheel of the pirate ship.

Hint 80: At the main swimming pool, a tan classic Mickey is on the rockwork of the small slide's wall. To spot it, stand at the back of the pool and look under the left cannon. Mickey is on a long rock in the second row of rocks from the bottom. This great Mickey image has almost faded away.

Hint 81: Where the sidewalk from Trinidad North meets the sidewalk outside the main (Old Port Royale) pool, they are joined by a short sidewalk that takes you to the right toward the main resort parking area. As you face the parking area from this intersection, look down at the lower right corner of the first white cement section of the short sidewalk. A small classic Mickey is etched in the pavement not far from a green lamppost.

Hint 82: In Shutters restaurant, a cloud classic Mickey hides in a painting on the left wall of the room close to the rear exit door.

Old Key West Resort

Hint 83: Throughout Conch Flats General Store, the design in the fence woodwork includes classic Mickeys.

Hint 84: Classic Mickeys are worked into the design of the fence railings behind the check-in counter in the registration area.

Hint 85: At the main pool (behind the registration building), the water slide (hidden in the rock) opens into the pool through the head of a classic Mickey.

Hint 86: At the upper right of the entrance to the steps to the water slide, a classic Mickey is impressed in the white rock, above a space in the wall.

Hint 87: You'll see classic Mickeys in the outdoor railings around the guest buildings.

Hints 88 and 89: Classic Mickeys formed by three shell imprints in the cement can be found on the two paths leading from parking spaces to Building 36. On the first path, you'll find the Hidden Mickey just after the first right turn on the right side. On the second path, the three shell imprints are in the corner of the sidewalk, after the first right turn and just before the next left turn.

Port Orleans Resort – French Quarter

Hint 90: On the third painting from the left behind the registration counter, an upside-down classic Mickey is on a man's crown.

Hint 91: Upside-down classic Mickeys made of blue and white gemstones adorn the top of a crown hanging from the ceiling on the right side of the food court seating area.

Port Orleans Resort – Riverside

Hint 92: Above the registration area, classic Mickeys are repeated in the wooden latticework circling the central lobby.

Hint 93: In the registration area, classic Mickeys decorate the sides of the brackets that hold the giant fans hanging from the ceiling above the center of the lobby.

Hint 94: Classic Mickeys are at the base of the strapping on the big ceiling fans.

Hint 95: Small classic Mickeys are in the upper level side rails at Parterre Place.

Hint 96: A subtle classic Hidden Mickey is in the sidewalk in front of the Acadian House Building. Walk across Ol' Man Island and around the right side of the pool, then cross the first bridge on the right over the waterway and turn left onto the sidewalk.

Just before you reach the white benches in front of Acadian House (Rooms 8001-8432), spot a lighter coloration in the stone walkway that forms a Hidden Mickey. The image is difficult to spot, and it may fade over time.

Saratoga Springs Resort & Spa

Hint 97: In the main registration lobby, red swirls in the center carpet form a series of classic Hidden Mickeys.

Hint 98: Halfway down the hallway behind The Artist's Palette shop (turn right as you enter the shop from the main lobby), a full-body impression of Mickey Mouse swinging a golf club is on a handle on the left door.

Hint 99: In the hallway leading to The Turf Club Bar and Grill, the jacket in a display on the left wall sports black classic Mickeys.

Hint 100: Just before entering the lounge area in front of The Turf Club, notice the small, ornate gate to your right, near The Turf Club menu posted on the brick wall. Examine the right half of the gate. Three small blue circles in the left middle area form a classic Mickey image tilted sideways to the left. (This image is not proportioned perfectly, but many guests and Cast Members consider it a Hidden Mickey.) Other circles on the gate also resemble classic Mickeys.

Hint 101: On a wall inside the lounge in front of The Turf Club, Mickey and other Disney characters decorate billiard balls. They are in the first display to the left as you enter from the hallway.

Hint 102: Just inside the dining area of The Turf Club, three circles on equestrian

251

equipment in the upper right section of a wall display form an upside-down classic Mickey. The display is on the left wall (as you enter).

Hint 103: On a statue of a horse and rider outside the main lobby, the rings attaching the bridle to the reins and bit on both sides of the horse's mouth form classic Mickeys. Tiny classic Mickeys are also hidden in the roses on both sides of the horse's winner's blanket. You'll find them in the middle of the blanket in about the third or fourth row down. Finally, large blue classic Mickeys decorate the back and front of the jockey's jersey. (In addition, a blanket on the horse includes a yellow décor Mickey.)

Hint 104: As you walk away from The Artist's Palette, look for depressions in the left rock wall at the top of the stairs to the High Rock Spring Pool. One classic Mickey is in the middle of the top horizontal rock of the wall, and a second classic Mickey is on the lower horizontal rock near the handrail post.

Hint 105: Behind Donald Duck in the children's water play area at High Rock Spring Pool, a classic Mickey, about six feet tall and tilted to the left, is made of three depressions in the rock wall behind the waterfall. As you face the rock wall, the Hidden Mickey is at the left side. It's easier to see when the waterfall is turned off.

Hint 106: At the left side of the High Rock Spring Pool (as you face it from the main building), impressions in the rock wall that borders the zero grade entrance to the pool form three classic Mickeys. Three large circles on the middle of the rock face form an upright classic Mickey, while three smaller circles at the right middle tilt to make a sideways classic Mickey. Behind the layered stone wall, three more circles on the end of the gray rock form another upright classic Mickey.

Hint 107: Small classic Mickeys adorn the spa signs on the wall outside and on the glass door at the downstairs spa entrance.

Hint 108: Some balcony railings on the guest buildings have classic Mickey holes.

Hint 109: In the resort's Springs section (Villas 4101 to 4436), across from the check-in parking lot, a large faint classic Mickey is on an outdoor red wall.

Hint 110: In the resort's Congress Park section (Villas 1501 to 1836), near the lagoon over which you can see Disney Springs, another large faint classic Mickey is on an outdoor red wall. I stood near this red wall and could spot the Rainforest Cafe across the lagoon.

Hint 111: A classic Mickey is inside the Aquatic Play Area at The Paddock pool. This Hidden Mickey is formed by three stones in the middle front of a pillar that is on your right after you pass through the entrance gate.

Hint 112: Classic Mickeys can be found in the upper corners of some of the outside lights on the guest buildings, such as on the exterior of the enclosed stairways.

Hint 113: Classic Mickeys are at the bottom of obelisks in the various Villa courtyards.

Hint 114: Classic Hidden Mickey holes are in the corners of the decorative design work along the ceiling perimeter of the carousel-themed gazebo at the Carousel Villas.

Hint 115: Partial classic Mickeys hide in the left side of the gate to the Grandstand Pool and on the back gate next to the restrooms.

253

Hint 116: At the Grandstand Pool's Backstretch Pool Bar, a classic Mickey hides at the top of the green trees painted on the lower front wall below the bar counter.

Epcot Area Resorts

BoardWalk Resort

Hint 117: In the main lobby, a horse on the outer ring of the small carousel has brown spots that form two classic Mickeys, one on the neck and one on the thigh.

Hint 118: In the middle painting on the wall above the middle registration counter in the main lobby, a classic Mickey is formed by the second small group of trees from the right.

Hint 119: Along a side wall inside the lobby, tiny classic Mickey holes are at the very tops of the red latticework designs on all sides of the canopied seat (called a "howdah") atop the elephant.

Hint 120: On the first to the fifth floors of the BoardWalk Villas, a classic Mickey sits atop light fixtures alongside the elevators.

Hint 121: Classic Mickeys hide in the carpet in front of some elevators and also appear in the lobby carpets and the guestroom hallway carpets in both the BoardWalk Inn and BoardWalk Villas. (Note: The images in these areas change or disappear from time to time.)

Hint 122: Walk outside behind the BoardWalk Villas to the Leaping Horse Libations pool bar to spot a classic Mickey at the top of the wall clock behind the bar counter. Mickey's hands tell you the time.

Hint 123: Three circles make a classic Hidden Mickey in each of the small round headlights on the BoardWalk surrey bikes.

Hint 124: Look in the room to your right as you enter AbracadaBar from the outside promenade. A photo of Walt is in the right lower corner of a huge display case next to an exit door at the opposite side of the room. Walt is pulling a rabbit out of a hat!

Hint 125: Inside AbracadaBar, a club suit in a framed Ace of Clubs is altered to form a classic Mickey. This frame hangs in the hallway leading to the restrooms, on the right wall. It is next to the magical mirror.

Hint 126: The words "Trattoria al Forno" are etched in the wall behind the check-in counter for the restaurant. A tiny classic Mickey is impressed in the lower right leg of the first "A" in "Trattoria."

Hint 127: Two Mickey images are in the long, rear wall mural inside Ample Hills Creamery. In the middle section of the mural, you'll find a red Mickey balloon and Mickey's ears on the Earffel (or Earful) Tower, a previous landmark at Disney's Hollywood Studios.

Beach Club Resort

Hint 128: A classic Mickey is on a blue plate inside Cape May Cafe. The plate is perched on a small shelf on the right wall just past the check-in podium at the restaurant's entrance. Mickey is on the inside of the plate and has a red circle for the "head" and two black circles for the "ears."

Hint 129: Along the inside walkway in front of the Cape May Cafe, a full length Mickey Mouse is standing in a sandcastle. It's the sculpture farthest to the left, on the wall facing the pool. (This image disappears at times.)

Hint 130: A gold upside-down classic

Walt Disney World's Hidden Mickeys

Mickey hides in an old painting of Florida and its landmarks that hangs in a hallway near the back entrance to Cape May Cafe. Look to the lower left of the painting at the gazebo below the words "Cape May Point." The Hidden Mickey is above the steps to the right in the gazebo's facade.

Hint 131: In the Beach Club lobby, on the left as you walk toward the Marketplace shop, a white classic Mickey surrounded by a white circle is inlaid in a floor tile. Look for it under a light fixture and in front of the luggage room door.

Hint 132: Enter the Solarium from the Beach Club main lobby. The first painting on the wall to your left has Mickey's face on spare tires on the backs of the yellow car (left side) and the blue car (right side).

Hint 133: Classic Mickey hood ornaments adorn the blue and red cars on the right of this painting.

Hint 134: In the second painting on the left wall, you can see Mickey's face looking out at you from the clouds at the upper right.

Hint 135: In this second painting, a lady on the beach is sitting on a Mickey Mouse towel.

Hint 136: The cruise ship smokestacks in this second painting have classic Mickey decals.

Hint 137: Mickey balloons are on the right side of the third painting to your left.

Hint 138: Also on the right side of this third painting is a tiny white classic Mickey atop the front post of a small building with a brown roof.

Hint 139: Sand dollars form classic Mickeys in the carpet of the Marketplace shop.

Chapter 6: Resort Hotel Scavenger Hunt

Hint 140: A small gold classic Mickey is on the right lower corner of a picture frame in the Marketplace shop. This painting hangs on the wall next to the entrance to the Marketplace shop from the elevators.

Hint 141: The guestroom hallways have carpet segments with classic Mickeys.

Hint 142: Check the elevator that's near both the Beach Pool (aka the Quiet Pool) and Room 1571 for an ad for the Beaches & Cream Soda Shop. Onion rings in the ad form a classic Mickey.

Hint 143: Under the Ariel statue in front of the entrance to the Beach Club Villas, seashells are embedded in the ground. One group of three shells forms a classic Mickey.

Hint 144: In The Breezeway at the Beach Club Villas, three different Mickey images hide in a painting on the left wall (as you enter The Breezeway from the front doors):
  - Classic Mickeys are on a fence in the lower part of the painting.
  - A full-body shadow of Mickey Mouse is in a bottom-floor hotel window in the middle of the painting.
  - A subtle dark smiling Mickey face drawn in the sand lies to the right of the two people standing closest to the water.

Hint 145: Near the restrooms off the lobby inside the entrance doors to the Beach Club Villas, a colorful picture entitled "Cape May" is on the left wall in the short hallway to the left of the Breezeway. Look at the top border and you'll spot a train just to the left of center. A classic Mickey is formed by the coal in the car behind the engine.

Hint 146: Onion rings form a classic Mickey in one of the food images decorating the Beaches & Cream Soda Shop. The image is on the left wall as you enter, on the second panel back from the rear wall.

Hint 147: You can spot classic Mickey holes in the hamburger press used at the Beaches & Cream Soda Shop to hold the burgers on the hot griddle.

Yacht Club Resort

Hint 148: On the globe in the main lobby, a blue classic Mickey is at the bottom near a sea monster, under the sea monster's head and below the island of Madagascar.

Hint 149: In a seating area in the main lobby, the names of Mickey, Minnie, Donald, Daisy, Goofy, and Huey are on small labels on the drawers of a corner cabinet. (This cabinet is moved around at times to different parts of the lobby.)

Hint 150: Near the main lobby seating area, dark classic Mickeys are in the rug.

Hint 151: Various other classic Mickey images can be found in other carpets around the resort, especially near elevators and in the guest hallways.

Hint 152: A photo of (now deceased) Minnie Moo, a cow born with a black classic Mickey on her side, often hangs in the Yachtsman Steakhouse. Examine the left wall just past the entrance podium. Minnie Moo once resided at Fort Wilderness.

WDW Dolphin Hotel

Hint 153: Walk toward the piano in the main lobby and observe the backs of the brown chairs nearby. Several classic Mickeys are formed by wooden circles on the chair backs.

Magic Kingdom Area

Resorts

Fort Wilderness Resort

Hint 154: On the sign at the entrance to the *Golden Oak* commmunity on Vista Boulevard near the Fort Wilderness Resort, a classic Mickey is hidden in the tree of Golden Oak's logo.

Hint 155: In the room to the right as you enter the Tri-Circle-D Ranch Horse Barn, classic Mickeys decorate the horse bridle gear hanging in a display.

Hint 156: Inside the Tri-Circle-D Ranch Horse Barn, horse stalls are identified by numbers, which are posted on Mickey-shaped labels above the stall gates.

Hint 157: A classic Mickey brand is on the left side of the Blacksmith sign near the Horse Barn.

Hint 158: Inside Trail's End Restaurant, a classic Mickey is formed by frying pans hanging from hooks on the wall behind the food serving station.

Hint 159: Two white classic Mickeys are on a rock across the walkway in front of the Bike Barn.

Hint 160: At the front parking lot, two Hidden Mickeys are on the Tri-Circle-D Ranch sign on the small Trail Ride Check-In building. They are in the middle of the scrollwork at both sides of the sign.

Hint 161: Inside the Fort Wilderness registration building ("Reception Outpost") at the far side of the main parking lot, a plush Mickey Mouse stands in a metal jug at the far left of a shelf directly over the registration counter.

Hint 162: A small classic Hidden Mickey,

tilted to the right, is at the lower middle of the logo on the trash cans. It's under the "C" in "Campground."

Wilderness Lodge

Hint 163: On the right side of the entrance drive to the hotel, a full length Mickey Mouse is walking on top of the "Bear Crossing" sign.

Hint 164: A classic Mickey is on the slanted end of the first horizontal log beam of the guard gate kiosk as your car approaches the entrance gate.

Hint 165: As you approach the center steps from the parking lot, you'll see that the roof of the covered unloading area in front of the entrance is supported by huge wooden logs, banded together (four to a set) by black metal strips. The right rear pole of the first set to the right (as you face the entrance) has a classic Mickey etched in the wood above the upper black metal band. This Mickey faces the parking lot.

Hint 166: In the set of support poles on the left after you walk up the center steps from the parking lot, the pole in the corner closest to you and the hotel entrance has a classic Mickey etched in the wood. This Mickey is partially covered by the upper black metal band; only his head and part of his right ear are visible. This Mickey faces the steps.

Hint 167: In the cement of the car entrance drive-through, the black stripe nearest the center steps from the parking lot hides a tiny classic Mickey. From the red rectangle in the cement, follow the right (as you face the hotel entrance) diagonal crack to the black stripe. The tiny classic Mickey is traced in the cement about six inches to the right of the intersection of the crack and the stripe.

Hint 168: As you face the hotel entrance, the left rear support pole of the far left set of poles closest to the parking lot has a classic Mickey etched in the wood. It's above the lateral crossbeam on the lower part of the pole.

Hint 169: A classic Mickey hides on the left side of a large key in a wall display behind the registration counter. Look near the entrance to the Mercantile shop.

Hint 170: A sign that says "Walt Disney World Transportation" hangs from the ceiling near the Mercantile shop. Mickey (in side profile) is driving the bus at the top of the sign.

Hint 171: In the lobby, you'll find a classic Mickey on the rock in the corner at the upper right of the fireplace. Search at the level of and near the lower round wooden horizontal beam that juts toward the lobby.

Hint 172: The outer grillwork of a fireplace in the rear room of the Whispering Canyon Cafe is adorned with decorative cutouts. Bend down low and look for a classic Mickey on the bottom row. It is the third cutout from the left corner.

Hint 173: A small classic Mickey lies on the floor at the left front corner (as you face the rear of the lobby) of the rectangle of dark hardwood slats that surround the bubbling source of the water spring. The "head" is formed by a circle in the wood with small indentations in the wood for "ears." You may need to lift the corner of the rug to spot it.

Hint 174: At the entrance stairs to the Territory Lounge, a classic Mickey decorates a pot in the right lower section of a wall map.

Hint 175: Inside the Territory Lounge, a classic Mickey rests on the rear of a beige mule in a ceiling mural. Look above the center of the bar.

Hint 176: Inside the Artist Point restaurant, examine the large mural above the entrance to the rear left dining area. You can spot a classic Mickey in the upper part of the lowest tree on the right if you look between the third and fourth lights (counting from the left) illuminating the mural. The Hidden Mickey is tilted to the right.

Hint 177: Turn left toward the Artist Point entrance and study the large mural near the ceiling and between the two front sections of the restaurant. On the clothing at the lower back of the leftmost of four horsemen is a light brown classic Mickey, tilted slightly to the right.

Hint 178: Inside the rear left dining area, the top middle part of a dark cloud in a painting on the left wall is shaped like a side profile of Winnie the Pooh. He's looking to the right.

Hint 179: A display case on an inside wall facing the entrance to the Roaring Fork snack bar contains three chestnuts arranged to form a classic Mickey.

Hint 180: You'll find classic Mickey images on a few of the wall-light covers, most often as a sideways image at the lower center of the light cover. Some of these covers are near the elevators just past Roaring Fork snack area. One or more can be found elsewhere around the hotel.

Hint 181: The wallpaper in the guest hallways on most floors (for example, near the elevators) includes classic Mickeys in the design.

Hint 182: Segments of the guest hallway carpets contain blue classic Mickeys.

Hint 183: A classic Mickey is etched near the bottom of a flat vertical wooden post around the corner from Room 6100 and near a green EXIT sign.

Hint 184: Near Room 5066, a classic Mickey is etched on a flat vertical wooden post about five and a half feet from the floor. It's across from an ice machine.

Hint 185: A classic Mickey is etched on a vertical wooden post about six feet up from the floor across from Room 4035.

Hint 186: Outside, from the walkway next to Fire Rock Geyser, scan the shallow stream running down from the small pool by the geyser. You'll find a slightly distorted classic Mickey with white rocks for ears in the rock of the streambed about a third of the way up to the geyser.

Hint 187: Walk toward the Teton Boat and Bike Rental cabin and locate stairs to an exit door in the corner of the main building. A classic Mickey is impressed in a vertical wooden beam at the left side of the exit door (as you face the door) across from the fourth-floor balcony. Mickey is on the right side of the beam, just below the log that juts out to the right.

Hint 188: At the marina, to the left of the Boat and Bike Rental cabin, the Cast Members usually maintain a classic Hidden Mickey made of coiled rope. Look for it on the front of a display boat that sits on the marina pier. (Note: The Disney Navy decorates the front of some of the Sea Raycer display boats with classic Mickey coils of rope. You can often spot this Hidden Mickey at the marinas of various WDW Resorts.)

– *In the Cub's Den*

Hint 189: A plush Mickey doll sits in the rightmost teepee in the mural on the right

Hint 190: In this same mural, a side-profile shadow of Mickey (standing and looking right) falls on the side of a mountain to the right of the center of the mural and above the tree line.

Hint 191: On the far left of this mural, about midway up and left of the mountains, you can spot a classic Mickey.

– Wilderness Lodge Villas

Hint 192: Turn left toward the elevators after you enter the Villas' main entrance. On the rock pillar to your right as you walk toward the elevators, an almost upside-down classic Hidden Mickey is etched in a square, dark gray rock. Find it on the second rock from the floor, about two and one-half feet up.

Hint 193: Near the lobby elevators to the left of the entrance to the Villas, four classic Mickeys hide on the wall. One is to the right of the elevators near the lower left corner of a picture frame. Two more are part of the wall decoration between the elevators, and a fourth can be found to the left of the leftmost elevator. This last Mickey is hiding behind the red tapestry.

Hint 194: A classic Mickey made of depressions in the rock is tilted to the right on the last stone pillar to your left as you walk to the lobby from the elevators. You can spot this image just before you step into the lobby. It is about three feet from the floor, on the corner (facing the entrance) of the second horizontal rock from the floor.

Hint 195: Mickey Mouse is peeking out of a hole on the outer side of the first overhead beam to your right as you enter the lobby of the Wilderness Lodge Villas. The beam is jutting out into the lobby and has a rattlesnake on top.

Hint 196: A side profile of Mickey Mouse is on the upper part of a wall, between two moons, near the lobby of the Wilderness Lodge Villas (and to the right as you face the lobby).

Hint 197: Looking out from inside the small telephone alcove near the lobby, a sideways (to the right) classic Hidden Mickey is impressed in the rock on the right near the floor.

Hint 198: Examine the art hanging in the first room to the right after you pass through the Villas' lobby entrance doors. A painting that's hanging on the room's right wall has a frame with classic Mickeys in the corners.

Hint 199: Walk to your right (as you face the Villas lobby) to the Carolwood Pacific Railroad Room. On the left side of the fireplace, a classic Mickey - tilted right - is embedded in the stonework at about the height of the fireplace mantel.

Hint 200: High along the hallways of the Villas, you'll find classic Mickey corner brackets.

Hint 201: To the left of the entrance doors to the Villas, in a hallway on the left past the elevators, a dark classic Mickey appears on the baseboard near the hall carpet. It's down the hallway on your right, about eight to ten feet before you reach Room 1507.

Magic Kingdom Monorail Resorts

★ *Polynesian Village Resort*

Hint 202: On the lower level, just inside the main lobby entrance, there's a classic

Walt Disney World's Hidden Mickeys

Mickey design in the flagstone tiles of the lobby floor.

Hint 203: Overhead in the lobby, some rope knots securing the round lights resemble Hidden Mickeys.

Hint 204: Inside the BouTiki store on the first floor and near the various entrances, three wooden statues holding merchandise are adorned with classic Mickeys. Two of the Mickeys are blue and white while the third is red.

Hint 205: Along the right rear corner staircase from the lobby, bamboo wall decorations are composed of rings. Seen end on, some of the lower bamboo rings in the decoration on the right side form classic Mickeys.

Hint 206: Inside Moana Mercantile Shop upstairs, a classic Mickey is formed of blue and green balls hanging in knotted ropes high along the middle of the rear wall, above the merchandise shelves.

Hint 207: The carpeting on the floor of the Kona Cafe includes many flowers. Some of the flowers contain classic Mickeys of different colors. You can see these carpet images from the railing outside the cafe.

Hint 208: At the Kona Island coffee bar, in front of the Kona Cafe, small purple tiles on top of the mosaic tile counter form a classic Mickey. You'll spot it to the left of the glass case.

Hint 209: The carpet in some of the hallways and elevators sports classic Mickeys.

Hint 210: On the display Sea Racer boat outside by the marina, three dials at the left side of the dashboard form a classic Mickey. (You can see other Sea Racers with this dashboard classic Hidden Mickey on display at other Walt Disney World Resorts.)

Hint 211: Four sets of tiny, white classic Mickeys in pairs lie along the lagoon walkway, about halfway between the Polynesian Village Resort and Disney's Fairytale Wedding Pavilion. Look for them in the area where you see a wooden wall a few feet to the side of the walkway and opposite the lagoon. The Hidden Mickey pairs appear every few feet along the length of the wall. One is on the walkway itself and the other on the curb just above it. I hope they last!

★ *Disney's Fairytale Wedding Pavilion*

Hint 212: The weather vane on top of the building closest to the monorail has a full-length side profile of Mickey Mouse.

★ *Grand Floridian Resort & Spa*

Hint 213: Weather vanes on various roofs at the front of the resort sport classic Mickeys.

Hint 214: The large trolley carts outside the hotel have classic Mickeys in the woodwork around the luggage storage areas at the back of the carts.

Hint 215: In the main lobby, gold classic Mickeys are in the carpet.

Hint 216: Green classic Mickeys are in the corners of the marble tile designs on the floors of the first and second levels of the main building.

Hint 217: You'll find the Fab Five Disney characters (Mickey, Minnie, Pluto, Donald, and Goofy) in the tile floor near the main lobby's front entrance—and directly above in the tile on the second floor entrance from the monorail.

Hint 218: Along the entrance hall to 1900

267

Park Fare restaurant, a Mickey-hat image is at the left lower corner of the left lower picture in a group of carousel pictures on the wall.

Hint 219: Minnie is here with Mickey (green full-body images) on the tile floor of the foyer in front of the dining area of the 1900 Park Fare restaurant.

Hint 220: Other Disney movie characters are in the tile floor encircling the main lobby and in front of the Grand Floridian Cafe. They include Tinker Bell, Cinderella and Prince Charming, Peter Pan and friends, Mrs. Potts and Chip, and of course Mickey and Minnie.

Hint 221: Wall maps of the Grand Floridian Resort are on the first and second floors, toward the front of the building. A small sideways classic Mickey is formed by bushes at the upper right of the Sago Cay building, located at the left middle of the map.

Hint 222: Ornate ironwork encloses the elevator out in the lobby, and the decorative sections between the floors host multiple classic Mickeys. You'll find four classic Mickeys in each ironwork panel at the intersection of the diagonal spokes and the large circle. The ears are oriented toward the center. (Tip: Stand inside the main lobby elevator for the best view of these classic Mickeys.)

Hint 223: A classic Mickey design is at the bottom of each of the four tall blue flowers in the stained-glass dome above the main lobby of the Grand Floridian.

Hint 224: On the second floor, a classic Mickey hides on the top of a pole on the M. Mouse Mercantile sign in front of the shop.

Hint 225: Most guestroom hallways have classic Hidden Mickeys in the wallpaper.

Chapter 6: Resort Hotel Scavenger Hunt

Hint 226: Classic Mickeys are also in the guest hallway carpets.

Hint 227: Along the covered walkways outside the Grand Floridian Villas, look up for classic Hidden Mickeys in the latticework design. They occur only at certain points along the walkways.

Hint 228: A classic Mickey is two-thirds of the way up the huge rock wall at the side of the main pool near the Grand Floridian Villas. The Hidden Mickey, made of circular depressions in the rock, is behind the waterfall and is sometimes difficult to make out if the water flow is heavy and obscures the image.

Hint 229: In the lobbies of the outer guest buildings, the carpets have Hidden Mickeys as well as a Hidden Minnie Mouse, Donald Duck, Goofy, and Pluto.

Hint 230: Inside Gasparilla Island Grill, classic Mickeys are in the metalwork above the individual lights on the ceiling light fixtures.

Hint 231: Step into the main entrance area of the Grand Floridian Convention Center and look up for a hot air Mickey balloon painted on the ceiling.

★ *Contemporary Resort*

Hint 232: From the window of the California Grill restaurant on the hotel's top floor, you can see a stretched out Mickey watchband on the ground in front of the building. It's among the conical-shaped trees. (You can see part of this watchband from the monorail.)

Hint 233: *(Caution: Prop the hallway door open before you step out onto the balcony to look for Mickey.)*

From the sixth floor outdoor balcony closest

to the front of the hotel, look left to see Mickey sitting on the edge of a roof below! This Mickey can also be spotted from either monorail just outside the hotel (the opening nearest the Transportation and Ticket Center). If you're on the resort monorail, you have to bend down to view Mickey through the lower part of the window (to the left of forward motion) and below the express monorail track next to you. On the express monorail, look to the right of forward motion.

Hint 234: Inside Chef Mickey's restaurant, a large side-profile Mickey decorates both sides of the large black, white, and red tile divider.

Hint 235: Mickey ears are atop posts at the rear of Chef Mickey's restaurant.

Hint 236: On the lower part of the wall mural facing Contempo Café, the fourth girl from the right corner of the wall has a classic Mickey on her dress.

Hint 237: At the upper middle of this wall mural facing Contempo Café, a girl in a blue and white dress is carrying orange and light purple round fruits in a basket on her head. In the right side of the basket, a light purple "head" and two smaller orange "ears" form a classic Mickey tilted to the left.

Hint 238: High on the wall mural facing Bay Lake, a black classic Mickey is on an owl perched on a girl's head. It's on the red right wing (as you face the mural).

Hint 239: On the fourth floor, a stick-figure Mickey is in an artwork display on the side of the Bayview Gifts store facing the monorail.

Hint 240: On the fourth floor, classic Mickeys are in the carpet inside The Game Station Arcade.

Chapter 6: Resort Hotel Scavenger Hunt

Hint 241: Large but faint classic Mickeys are in the carpet in the Market shop. You can spot one just inside the entrance to the shop.

Hint 242: On the wall mural facing the monorail, an upside-down classic Mickey has a blue circle for a "head" and yellow circles for "ears." It's at the top of a tree that is positioned to the lower left of the five-legged goat.

Hint 243: Behind the main hotel, a classic Mickey silhouette can be found in the bricks under the metal Mickey Mouse sculpture. (The sculpture itself is a decorative Mickey, not a Hidden Mickey.)

Hint 244: At the marina, a classic Mickey is on the dashboard of the display speedboat on the dock. It's made of the faint white circles surrounding the dials.

Hint 245: Also at the marina by the pool, the marine alphabet letter flags on the glass front of the Sand Bar spell "MICKEY."

Hint 246: Inside the Sand Bar, near the middle of the upper left wall border, one of the semaphore figures is wearing Mickey ears.

Hint 247: At the exit from the Garden Building to the parking lot (facing the monorail), a huge classic Mickey is traced in the tile under the exit canopy between the benchs.

Hint 248: Subtle, large white classic Mickeys are frosted into glass partitions that support the curved roof covering the vehicle drive-though entrance area to the hotel.

– *Bay Lake Tower*

Hint 249: Classic Mickeys are at the top of both elevator towers at the sides of the hotel. (Ceiling lights hang from these Mickey-shaped metal plates.) You can spot one of them from the monorail and either or both from the ground.

Shades of Green Resort

Hint 250: In the lobby, a Mickey statue stands in front of a framed picture of a blue sky with puffy clouds. Three classic Mickeys are in the clouds and another, made of fireworks, decorates the statue Mickey's right ear.

Hint 251: The Millpond pool is shaped as a classic Mickey. You can visit this pool outside or spot it on a resort map posted on hallway walls.

Chapter 7

Hither, Thither & Yon Scavenger Hunt

• • • • • • • • • • • •

A car is the most efficient method for hunting the following areas. I've planned the hunt taking time of day and location into consideration. However, some backtracking will help keep you ahead of the crowds. Don't forget to be courteous to the shoppers, diners, golfers, swimmers, other guests and Cast Members you encounter during your hunt. (Note: Because you may want to hunt only one area at a time, I've listed the perfect score for each area in parentheses after its name in the Clues section.)

★ **Bonus Points Opportunity.** As I advised in Chapter Six, pay attention to the Disney buses during your Hidden Mickey hunt around WDW property. You may get lucky! The Disney Cruise Line bus has a Hidden Pluto on each side of the gold scrollwork on the front of the bus between the headlights. Look for a green classic Mickey on the back of many buses that are diesel. Some general Disney transport buses sometimes sport a classic Mickey on the rear of the vehicle, usually related to rear upper or lower lights. Even more subtle are the faint classic Mickey images in the windows of some buses, only visible when the lighting is just right! If you spot one or more of these images, give yourself 5 bonus points for each one you find.

273

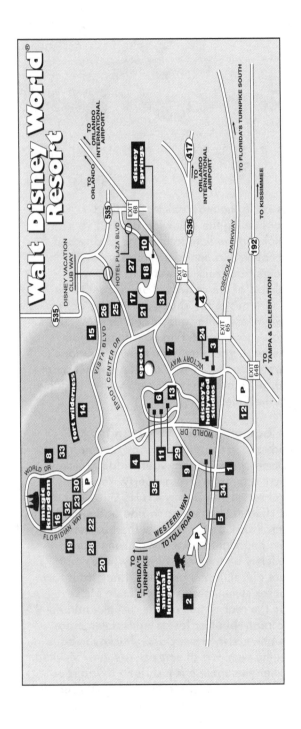

1 All-Star Resorts
2 Animal Kingdom Lodge
3 Art of Animation
4 Beach Club
5 Blizzard Beach
6 BoardWalk
7 Caribbean Beach
8 Contemporary
9 Coronado Springs
10 Disney Springs
11 Dolphin
12 ESPN Wide World of Sports Complex
13 Fantasia Gardens Mini Golf
14 Fort Wilderness
15 Golden Oak
16 Grand Floridian
17 Lake Buena Vista Golf Course
18 The Landing, in Disney Springs

19 Magnolia Golf Course
20 Oak Trail Golf Course
21 Old Key West
22 Palm Golf Course
23 Polynesian Village
24 Pop Century
25 Port Orleans – French Quarter
26 Port Orleans – Riverside
27 Saratoga Springs
28 Shades of Green
29 Swan
30 Transportation and Ticket Center
31 Typhoon Lagoon
32 Wedding Pavilion, Disney's Fairytale
33 Wilderness Lodge
34 Winter Summerland Mini Golf
35 Yacht Club
P Parking

275

Magnolia Golf Course (5 points)

Clue 1: If you're a golfer, look around you for a classic Mickey sand trap.
5 points

Vista Boulevard (3 points)

Clue 2: Drive east along Vista Boulevard away from Fort Wilderness and stay alert for a classic Mickey on a sign to your left.
3 points

ESPN Wide World of Sports (10 points)

Clue 3: Search hard for a three-dimensional Mickey Mouse head near the high central ceiling of The Milk House (the Field House). He's on an upper rafter opposite the main entrance.
5 points

Clue 4: Now head for the softball fields and check out the pitcher's mounds for possible bonus points.
5 bonus points for one or more

Clue 5: Stroll around the Sports Fields to locate a Hidden Mickey on the discus field.
5 points

WDW Water Parks (51 points)

★ *Blizzard Beach* (15 points)

Clue 6: Take a close look at the Beach Haus store's right rear wall near the dressing rooms.
3 points

Clue 7: Inside the Beach Haus, spot Hidden Mickeys near the merchandise.
2 points

276

Clue 8: Hop on the *Chairlift* to spot a classic Mickey formed by three round rocks on the ground near one of the support poles for the ride.
5 points
Tip: The Singles line for the *Chairlift* is usually shorter than the Standby line.

Clue 9: Go to the rear of the park (by tube or on foot) to find a classic Mickey with a sorcerer's hat that's formed by three stones topped by a small triangular rock. (Psst! He's near the center of the side of a stone bridge that crosses over *Cross Country Creek*.)
5 points

★ *En Route to Typhoon Lagoon* (4 points)

Clue 10: On your way to Typhoon Lagoon from Blizzard Beach, spot Mickey on the Disney Vacation Club white tower, which will appear on your left at the intersection of Buena Vista Drive and Bonnet Creek Parkway.
4 points

★ *Typhoon Lagoon* (32 points)

Clue 11: Check out a Tip Board for a Hidden Mickey. (Note: These images come and go.)
3 bonus points

Clue 12: At the front of the surfing lagoon, scan inside the Board Room for a Hidden Mickey.
3 points

Clue 13: Look around the *Crush 'n' Gusher* elevator for a Hidden Mickey.
4 points

Clue 14: Search for Mickey on a bridge over *Castaway Creek*, near *Shark Reef*.
4 points

Clue 15: Marvel at Mickey if you snorkel

with the sharks in *Shark Reef*.
5 points

Clue 16: Don't pass by Mickey on the steps up to the *Storm Slides*.
4 points

Clue 17: Climb the trail up to *Humunga Kowabunga* and locate a classic Mickey along the way.
4 points

Clue 18: Spot the Main Mouse hiding under a cannon along *Castaway Creek* at the rear of the park.
4 points

Clue 19: Squint for Mickey in the wall of a cave at *Ketchakiddee Creek*.
4 points

The Landing in Disney Springs (11 points)

★ *Raglan Road Irish Pub and Restaurant* (3 points)

Clue 20: Locate a Hidden Mickey near the stage.
3 points

★ *Morimoto Asia Restaurant* (3 points)

Clue 21: Check out the walls (outside and inside) for Hidden Mickeys.
3 points

★ *Chef Art Smith's Homecomin'* (5 points)

Clue 22: Study a mural on an outside wall of the restaurant for a Hidden Mickey.
5 points

Disney Springs West Side (36 points)

278

Chapter 7: Hither & Thither Scavenger Hunt

★ *Cirque du Soleil* (8 points)

Clue 23: Look down for a Hidden Mickey in the sidewalk near Parking Lot Q.
5 points

Clue 24: Head for the outside restrooms (they're under the main entrance staircase to the theater) and examine the floor in either one (men's or women's). See a small classic Mickey?
3 points for either (or both)

★ *House of Blues* (3 points)

Clue 25: Search for a classic Mickey on the ceiling.
3 points

★ *Splitsville Luxury Lanes* (12 points)

Clue 26: Admire the mural inside on the lower level for Hidden Mickeys.
5 points for three different kinds of Mickey images

Clue 27: Find Mickey on a huge orange on the upper level.
3 points

Clue 28: Search the orange trees on the upper level.
4 points

★ *Wolfgang Puck Cafe* (5 points)

Clue 29: Study the mosaic tile pyramid behind the reception counter to find a classic Hidden Mickey.
5 points

★ *Disney's Candy Cauldron* (4 points)

Clue 30: Go inside to find a classic Mickey marking on a stone.
4 points

★ *Starbucks* (4 points)

Clue 31: Locate a Hidden Mickey on a wall in the seating area. (Tip: You may need to wait a few minutes for it to appear!)
4 points

Disney Springs Marketplace (213 points)

★ *Entrance to the Marketplace* (8 points)

Clue 32: Find Hidden Mickeys at the bus stop area near the main entrance.
5 points for five or more

Clue 33: Check out the signs over the entrances.
1 point for one or more

Clue 34: Study the green benches for Hidden Mickeys at the entrance and elsewhere around Disney Springs Marketplace.
2 points

★ *Disney's Wonderful World of Memories* (3 points)

Clue 35: Search for Mickey outside the store.
3 points

★ *Disney's Days of Christmas* (15 points)

Clue 36: Step inside and search for a Mickey made of rocks.
3 points

Clue 37: Find at least one classic Mickey on each of three large trees.
4 points total for one or more on each tree

Clue 38: Study the walls and carpet for classic Hidden Mickeys.
3 points for two or more

Clue 39: Take a good look at the ceiling in

the rear room of the shop.
2 points

Clue 40: Admire an outside window of the store for subtle Hidden Mickeys.
3 points

★ *Goofy's Candy Company* (10 points)

Clue 41: Search for a Goofy shadow in the store.
4 points

Clue 42: Find Goofy and other characters on the wall.
4 points for three or more characters

Clue 43: Find Mickey in a store window.
2 points

★ *Rainforest Cafe* (4 points)

Clue 44: Look for Hidden Mickeys on the outdoor signs.
4 points for both

★ *Sassagoula River Cruise ferry* (5 points)

Clue 45: If you have time, take the *Sassagoula River Cruise* ferryboat to Port Orleans – French Quarter, disembark, and then ride the next boat back to Disney Springs Marketplace. During both your crossings, study the Treehouse Villas for Hidden Mickeys.
5 points for one or more

★ *Marketplace Carousel* (5 points)

Clue 46: Study the decorative inner and outer panels on the Carousel for four classic Mickeys.
5 points for spotting all four

★ *Once Upon a Toy* (38 points)

Note: This store sports numerous Mickeys and other Disney characters in the décor in

Walt Disney World's Hidden Mickeys
addition to the Hidden Mickeys below.

Clue 47: Examine the interactive fountain near the store.
(Note: Two Hidden Mickeys are there all the time, a third appears only when the water is on.)
4 points for two, 5 points for spotting all three

Clue 48: Find a faint classic Mickey in the cement outside.
5 points

Clue 49: Outside the main entrance, look for classic Mickeys with tires for ears.
2 points for one or more

★ Now enter the store and keep your eyes open.

Clue 50: Gaze up for classic Mickeys.
2 points for one or more

Clue 51: Check out the tops of merchandise stands. (Only some sport Hidden Mickeys.)
1 point for one or more

Clue 52: Now examine the bottoms of these stands.
1 point for one or more

Clue 53: Search for a classic Mickey on large and small sandals in the middle of the first room.
3 points for both

Clue 54: In the first room, find a tiny Mickey near Mrs. Potato Head. (Note: Three other more obvious décor Mickey images are on or near her body.)
4 points

Clue 55: Examine the mural behind the service desk in the same room.
2 points for two or more images

Clue 56: Look at the upper beams of the

wooden merchandise displays.
1 point for one or more

Clue 57: Now observe the bolts on those displays.
1 point for one or more

Clue 58: Study the floor for a Mickey.
3 points

Clue 59: Find a classic Hidden Mickey cloud in a central room.
3 points

Clue 60: Look for a Mickey shadow in a central room.
3 points

Clue 61: Locate some Hidden Mickey lollipops.
2 points for one or more

★ *Disney's Pin Traders* (10 points)

Clue 62: Before you enter the store, glance around outside for a big classic Mickey below your feet.
2 points

Clue 63: Spot a Hidden Mickey on a Mickey statue inside the store.
3 points

Clue 64: Find three Hidden Mickeys on Donald's statue.
5 points for all three

★ *Tren-D* (31 points)

Clue 65: Look around for classic Mickeys on the tops and sides of various merchandise tables in the store.
3 points for two or more

Clue 66: Check out Mickey in wallpaper.
2 points

Clue 67: Find Mickey on a mannequin.

Walt Disney World's Hidden Mickeys
4 points

Clue 68: Look for a Mickey ring on Minnie Mouse, a Mickey watch on another Minnie, and a gold Hidden Mickey on a third Minnie.
5 points for all three

Clue 69: Spot a blue Hidden Mickey on the wall inside the store.
5 points

Clue 70: Search for a small Hidden Mickey on a door.
4 points

Clue 71: Smile at the initials of two Disney characters on a countertop!
5 points

Clue 72: Locate Mickey circles on a countertop.
3 points

★ *Marketplace Co-Op* (15 points)

Clue 73: Find a classic Mickey in the Disney Vacation Club (DVC) display near Marketplace Co-Op.
2 points

Clue 74: Check out the signs inside Marketplace Co-Op for a red Hidden Mickey.
2 points

Clue 75: Search for a Hidden Mickey inside D-Tech on Demand.
3 points

Clue 76: Examine a display outside the Disney TAG shop for Hidden Mickeys.
5 points for three Hidden Mickeys

Clue 77: Find classic Mickeys in the Caricature Booth nearby.
3 points for one or more

Chapter 7: Hither & Thither Scavenger Hunt

★ *Ghirardelli Ice Cream & Chocolate Shop*
(4 points)

Clue 78: Locate Mickey on a wall inside.
4 points

★ *Near the lake* (3 points)

Clue 79: Do you see any chairs with Hidden Mickeys outside the Ghirardelli Shop?
2 points

Clue 80: Spot Mickeys in the fence around the lake.
1 point

★ *World of Disney* (52 points)

Clue 81: Look up for Mickeys on the store sign.
1 point

Clue 82: Find light brown Mickeys outside the store.
2 points

Clue 83: Look for classic Mickeys in some of the clothing racks.
2 points

Clue 84: Find a classic Mickey emblem on the Chinese Theater in a mural in the high-ceilinged central room.
4 points

Clue 85: In the same room, find an upside-down classic Mickey on the Pocahontas airship.
4 points

★ Now find the two classic Mickeys below on the Tweedle Dee and Tweedle Dum mural in the same room.

Clue 86: Look for a flag.
2 points

Walt Disney World's Hidden Mickeys

Clue 87: Check out an apron.
2 points

Clue 88: Study the mannequins in this room.
4 points

Clue 89: Stare up high for classic Mickeys.
2 points for four

Clue 90: Spot classic Mickeys on paintings in the central Genie Room.
2 points

Clue 91: In the same room, take a close look at the "antique" maps decorating the walls. (Psst! Think character profiles.)
5 points for three or more

Clue 92: In the Women's Apparel room at the back right of the store, find a side-profile Hidden Mickey above your head.
4 points

Clue 93: In the Women's Apparel room, keep gazing high for a classic Mickey.
3 points

Clue 94: In the Princess Room, locate an orange flower classic Mickey on a wall.
3 points

Clue 95: Search for a tiny Hidden Mickey on a metal disk on the sides of some merchandise stands.
3 points

Clue 96: Look for Mickey on top of and underneath merchandise bins.
3 points for both

Clue 97: Now find him on a wall near the restrooms.
3 points

Clue 98: Outside the store, in an entrance area to the Marketplace, look around for a classic Mickey. (Psst! Examine the pots.)

3 points

★ *T-REX* (10 points)

Clue 99: Find a Hidden Mickey just outside the main entrance.
5 points

Clue 100: Admire a classic Mickey in the bar area.
5 points

WDW Casting Center (3 points)

Clue 101: Drive to the Casting Center building, across Buena Vista Drive from Disney Springs Marketplace, to locate more classic Mickeys. (These Hidden Mickeys can also be spotted from Interstate 4.)
3 points

Miniature Golf Courses (25 points)

You can find these Hidden Mickeys while you play the courses. Or you may be able to walk the courses without playing if it's not crowded, due to rain or luck. (Tell the attendants that you're hunting Hidden Mickeys and ask if you can take a look around.)

★ *Fantasia Gardens* (4 points)

Clue 102: Check the tee-off areas.
1 point

Clue 103: Take a good look at the 12th hole on the Gardens Course.
3 points

★ *Winter Summerland* (21 points)

Clue 104: Can you point to a Hidden Mickey at the check-in area?

287

Walt Disney World's Hidden Mickeys
3 points

Clue 105: Find Mickey on the third hole.
3 points

★ Now head straight for the 16th holes.

Clue 106: Spot Goofy on the 16th hole of the Winter Course.
3 points

Clue 107: Now check around the same hole for a Mickey Mouse gingerbread cookie.
2 points

Clue 108: Find Mickey and Minnie on the 16th hole of the Summer Course. (Psst! This Hidden Mickey is also visible from the 16th and 17th holes of the Winter Course.)
3 points for both

Clue 109: Wait for Mickey on the 17th hole of the Winter Course.
1 point

Clue 110: Study the Christmas tree on the 17th hole of the Summer Course for Hidden Mickeys.
3 points for three Hidden Mickeys

Clue 111: Look around for Mickey near the 18th tee for the Summer Course.
3 points

Near Epcot (5 points)

Clue 112: You can only admire this huge classic Mickey made of solar panels from above with a Google Earth search. It sits near Disney's Yacht Club Resort.
5 points

Near Celebration, Florida (4 points)

Okay, I admit it, this Mickey isn't hidden.

288

Just the opposite, in fact. But it is unique. So I decided to include it anyway. You'll find a huge classic Mickey near Celebration, Florida, on the west side of Interstate 4.

Clue 113: Look for it as you get close to Exit 62.
4 points

Near the Magic Kingdom (5 points)

Clue 114: You can only see this classic Mickey made of tree groves from the air or on an image from a Google Earth search. It's a few miles northwest of the Magic Kingdom. Good luck!
5 points

Total Points for Hither, Thither & Yon Hunt =

How'd you do?

A perfect score for this hunt is 371. You may have done even better if you earned bonus points in ESPN Wide World of Sports, Typhoon Lagoon, and/or by spotting Hidden Characters on the Disney buses.

You'll find a breakdown by area below, so that you can tally your score for only those places you've covered. Give yourself Gold if you scored at least 80% of available points, Bronze if you scored at least 40%.

Magnolia Golf Course (5)

Vista Boulevard (3)
ESPN Wide World of Sports (10)

WDW Water Parks (51)
    Blizzard Beach (15)
    En route to Typhoon Lagoon (4)
    Typhoon Lagoon (32)

Disney Springs West Side (36)
    Cirque du Soleil (8)
    House of Blues (3)
    Splitsville Luxury Lanes (12)
    Wolfgang Puck Cafe (5)
    Disney's Candy Cauldron (4)
    Starbucks (4)

Disney Springs Marketplace (213)
    Entrance to the Marketplace (8)
    Disney's Wonderful World of Memories (3)
    Disney's Days of Christmas (15)
    Goofy's Candy Co. (10)
    Rainforest Cafe (4)
    Sassagoula River Cruise ferry (5)
    Marketplace Carousel (5)
    Once Upon a Toy (38)
    Disney's Pin Traders (10)
    Tren-D (31)
    Marketplace Co-Op (15)
    Ghirardelli Ice Cream & Chocolate Shop (4)
    Near the lake (3)
    World of Disney (52)
    T-REX (10)

The Landing in Disney Springs (11)
    Raglan Road Irish Pub and Restaurant (3)
    Morimoto Asia Restaurant (3)
    Chef Art Smith's Homecomin' (5)

WDW Casting Center (3)

Miniature Golf Courses (25)
    Fantasia Gardens (4)
    Winter Summerland (21)

Chapter 7: Hither & Thither Scavenger Hunt

Near Epcot (5)

Near Celebration, Florida (4)

Near Magic Kingdom (5)

Magnolia Golf Course

Hint 1: A sand trap at the sixth green is shaped like a classic Mickey.

Vista Boulevard

Hint 2: If you drive east from Fort Wilderness along Vista Boulevard, you can spot a sign for the Golden Oak community on your left. A classic Mickey is hidden in the tree of Golden Oak's logo.

ESPN Wide World of Sports

Hint 3: A three-dimensional Mickey Mouse looks out over the court from near the high central ceiling in The Milk House (the Field House). He's on an upper rafter above the sign, "The Milk House," in front of a yellow triangular wall partition that is opposite the main entrance. I spotted him to the upper left of the lower seats of section 104.

Hint 4: On some days, you may spot classic Mickey circles around the pitcher's mounds on the nearby softball fields.

Hint 5: Walk past Champion Baseball Stadium, the Field House, and several multipurpose sports fields to the Track and Field Complex way in the back. A clever classic Mickey forms the base of the discus-throwing launch pad. (Tip: You can get a better vantage point for viewing this Mickey image by climbing up into the nearby bleachers.)

WDW Water Parks

– Blizzard Beach

Hint 6: Find a lighting fixture on the wall at the right rear of the Beach Haus store near the dressing rooms. There's a painting on the cover in which a small classic Mickey is formed by rocks at the lower center of an outdoor mountain scene.

Hint 7: As in many WDW shops, one or more of the merchandise stands has classic Mickey-shaped holes on its center pole.

Hint 8: From the *Chairlift* ride that takes you to the Mount Gushmore water slides, look to the ground on the second level of the mountain just past support pole #4 (counting from the beginning of the lift) and below the right side of your chairlift to spot a classic Mickey made of three round rocks. (Depending on the foliage, sometimes you can spot part of this rock Hidden Mickey from the left edge of the Observation Deck at the top of Mount Gushmore.)

Hint 9: At the rear of the park, a classic Mickey is formed by three stones jutting out from near the top edge of a stone bridge crossing *Cross Country Creek*. It is on the side of the bridge, near the center. A small triangular rock over this Hidden Mickey gives it the appearance of wearing a sorcerer's hat.

Tip: You can see this Mickey from the water or dry land. It is visible from the floating tubes as you approach the bridge by water. On land, you can see it through the trees (past the "Runoff Rapids Tube Pickup" area) either from just past the *Runoff Rapids* "Red Slope" entrance sign or from several points on the walkway on the other side of the bridge.

– *En Route to Typhoon Lagoon*

Hint 10: Classic Mickey holes are in the railing around the white Disney Vacation Club (DVC) tower that stands to the left of Buena Vista Drive at its intersection with Bonnet Creek Parkway.

– *Typhoon Lagoon*

Hint 11: Tip Boards with wait times written in chalk are situated around Typhoon Lagoon. If there is zero wait time for an attraction, the zero is drawn in the shape of a classic Mickey. (These images come and go.)

Hint 12: The Board Room is a shack on a small deck at the front of the surfing lagoon. On the right wall inside the Board Room is a painting of an alligator holding a surfboard. In the middle of the sand dune behind the alligator, impressions in the sand come together as a classic Mickey.

Hint 13: At *Crush 'n' Gusher*, on the upper floor near the elevator, paint circles on the cement form a classic Mickey.

Hint 14: Mickey ears are at the bottom of a vertical strut in the railing of a bridge. You can see the ears if you enter *Castaway Creek* at Shark Landing (near *Shark Reef*) and look behind you as you float under the first bridge. The ears are toward the right side of the bridge. You can also usually see the ears if you walk downstream on either side of the creek and look back at the bridge.

Hint 15: As you snorkel along in *Shark Reef*, you can often see a classic Mickey resting on the bottom of the swim route. Recently, the Mickey was located on the right side, about halfway along the route after the island.

Hint 16: About halfway up the wooden steps to the *Storm Slides*, and past the stranded motorboat on the right side of the path, Mickey ears are on the left side of a walkway slat.

Hint 17: Near the end of the long trail up to *Humunga Kowabunga*, three of the last short logs in the ground under the rope fence to the left of the walkway form an upside-down classic Mickey when viewed from above. (Note: You may spot other groups of short logs in the ground along walkways that resemble classic Mickeys.)

Hint 18: You'll find a classic Mickey formed by cannonballs along *Castaway Creek*. He's on your left by the second cannon past the waterfall if you're drifting in the creek. If you're walking on the nearby trail, you'll see him just past *Forgotten Grotto* in the rear of the park as you walk alongside the drifters. (Sometimes this cannonball image is moved around in this area.)

Hint 19: In the walk-through cave at the rear of *Ketchakiddee Creek*, there is a classic Mickey impression in the rock. It's on the back wall of the cave, about one and a half feet up from the ground, and near the drain at the right side of the cave as you enter the cave from the water.

The Landing in Disney Springs

– Raglan Road Irish Pub and Restaurant

Hint 20: A girl with Mickey ears is at a table at the left middle of a painting on the wall behind the stage.

– Morimoto Asia Restaurant

Hint 21: In the metal designs on the exterior walls of Morimoto Asia Restaurant, Hidden Mickeys are randomly mixed in with other Japanese symbols. They light up at night! Also, as you enter the restaurant, study the walls to your left. Three dark circles are painted high on a wall behind the right side of the drink bar. This classic Hidden Mickey is repeated in other places on the inside walls.

– Chef Art Smith's Homecomin' Restaurant

Hint 22: On a rear outside wall of the restaurant is a "Jasper Family Farms" mural with a bucking horse. A faint dark marking on the horse's rear left thigh is shaped like a classic Mickey. This mural is best viewed from a nearby bridge.

Disney Springs West Side

– Cirque du Soleil

Hint 23: A classic Mickey is etched in the sidewalk near *Cirque du Soleil*, on the second slab back from Parking Lot Q, just past a manhole cover and near the grass.

Hint 24: Under the main entrance staircase to the show are restrooms for men and women. You'll find tiles laid to approximate a small classic Mickey on the floor of each restroom, in a corner just inside the entrance doors. These circles don't touch, but the design is convincing to my eyes.

– House of Blues

Hint 25: Walk through the front door and

down the right side aisle. A classic Mickey is on the ceiling past the first server's station.

– Splitsville Luxury Lanes

Hint 26: In the right wall mural inside the main entrance on the lower level, you can see the Mickey Earful Tower, balloons with Mickey ears, and classic Mickey holes in a red bowling ball.

Hint 27: On the upper level near the escalator, holes form a classic Mickey in a huge "orange" in the left wall mural.

Hint 28: A few classic Mickeys are formed by groups of oranges in the trees in the upper level left mural.

– Wolfgang Puck Cafe

Hint 29: Behind the reception counter, about two-thirds of the way up the mosaic pyramid, a white tile and two smaller black tiles form a classic Mickey.

– Disney's Candy Cauldron

Hint 30: Inside the store, on the upper wall above the candy display, a dark marking on a stone near the ceiling forms a classic Hidden Mickey.

– Starbucks

Hint 31: On a wall inside the seating area, an interactive electronic screen periodically allows you to draw inside white picture frames. Classic Mickeys are in the corners of a frame at the top middle of the screen.

Disney Springs Marketplace

– Entrance to the Marketplace

Hint 32: Coca-Cola vending machines stand near Bus Stops 2, 3, and 4 in the

Chapter 7: Hither & Thither Scavenger Hunt

Disney Springs Marketplace bus stop area. In colorful paintings on these machines, one full-body Mickey is pouring water and several classic Mickeys can be found on signs, a tower, and an awning.

Hint 33: Signs over the entrances to the Marketplace sport classic Mickeys at their sides.

Hint 34: Green benches with classic Mickey emblems on the top and sides are scattered around the Marketplace and the interactive fountain.

– Disney's Wonderful World of Memories

Hint 35: The sign on the store contains a full-figure Hidden Mickey on the page of a book.

– Disney's Days of Christmas

Hint 36: A large dark brown circular rock and two smaller rocks for "ears" form a classic Mickey on the middle side of the "chimney" inside the store. You'll see Dalmatians on the mantelpiece around this chimney.

Hint 37: Inside the shop, three large trees surrounded by merchandise have classic Mickeys carved in their bark near the tops of their trunks. The trees are not Christmas trees, and each of the three has one or two Mickey carvings.

Hint 38: Various sections of wallpaper and carpet often hide classic Mickeys.

Hint 39: In the rear room of the shop, classic Mickeys hide in the scrollwork on the ceiling.

Hint 40: At the corners of the store's far right outside windows that look toward the Marketplace Carousel, subtle classic Hidden Mickeys are in snowflakes.

Walt Disney World's Hidden Mickeys
– Goofy's Candy Co.

Hint 41: A shadow of Goofy is on the upper back wall of the store, behind the large Krispy Treats display.

Hint 42: Goofy, Mickey Mouse, Pluto, and other characters hide in the light brown mural on the upper wall around the store.

Hint 43: Classic Mickey circles are part of the design in the middle of the side window that faces the lagoon.

– Rainforest Cafe

Hint 44: A green lizard on the large sign outside Rainforest Cafe has an upside-down classic Mickey in the middle of the circles on its neck. On the smaller sign at the left of the cafe entrance, the lizard's mid-neck classic Mickey is tilted sideways to the left.

– Sassagoula River Cruise ferry

Hint 45: From the Marketplace boat dock, take the ferryboat to Port Orleans – French Quarter and then back to Disney Springs Marketplace. Both ways, spot small white classic Mickeys in some of the Treehouse Villas' windows.

– Marketplace Carousel

Hint 46: At least four classic Mickeys are hiding on the inner and outer decorative panels on the Carousel near Disney's Days of Christmas store. (You may find more than four Mickey images, but these are the ones I like best.)
   - A blue classic Mickey is on the sign under Minnie Mouse.
   - Two light green classic Mickeys, tilted slightly to the right, hide on the dragon's nose. (For the best view of the dragon, check out an inner panel on the ceiling above the riders.)
   - Two tiny classic Mickeys hide on the

pink window awnings on the right side of the panel that shows part of a store from a distance. You'll see blue umbrellas on the left side of this panel.

- Pink classic Mickeys formed of roses hide in the upper part of the panels in the center of the Carousel.

– *Once Upon a Toy*

Hint 47: In the interactive flat fountain near the Once Upon a Toy store, water-tube heads are shaped like classic Mickeys, recessed lights in the cement are arranged in a classic Mickey shape, and the fountain water collects into a huge classic Mickey on the cement!

Hint 48: Outside the store, you'll find several faint classic Mickey hats in the cement near the side entrance.

Hint 49: Outside the store's main entrance, classic Mickeys are formed by truck tires (the "ears") atop Lincoln Logs.

Hint 50: Classic Mickey pincers or clamps (holding toys) circulate on a track that hangs from the ceiling in the room with Mr. Potato Head.

Hint 51: Tinker Toys on top of merchandise stands around the store form classic Mickeys.

Hint 52: At the bottom of these merchandise stands, you'll find classic Mickey supports.

Hint 53: Two black classic Mickeys are on blue sandals on one of the Mr. Potato Heads in the first room just inside the store's main entrance. Also notice black classic Mickeys at the sides of the small sandal accessories in the bins.

Hint 54: In the center of this Mr. Potato Head display in the first room, a tiny white classic Mickey adorns the clasp of Mrs. Potato Head's handbag. (Note: She's holding decorative Mickey balloons, wearing Mickey sunglasses, and has a Mickey sticker on her shoe.)

Hint 55: In this same room, the mural behind a service desk includes a classic Mickey balloon, several pairs of Mickey ears, and a Mickey ice cream bar.

Hint 56: The centers of the upper beams on wooden merchandise displays sport classic Mickey shapes.

Hint 57: On the same merchandise displays, large wing nuts on some of the bolts form Mickey ears.

Hint 58: Across the first and second rooms (as you enter from the front main entrance), large letters in Scrabble tiles on the floor spell "MICKEY."

Hint 59: In a central room of the store, a classic Mickey cloud appears in a window in a mural behind the service desk.

Hint 60: In the same room, a partial classic Mickey shadow is at the top of a wall mural. It's to the left of the classic Mickey cloud and above a checkout counter.

Hint 61: In the rear room, lollipops are arranged to form classic Mickeys on the outside of a merchandise stand.

– *Disney's Pin Traders*

Hint 62: A large, white classic Mickey lies in the walkway between Lefty's "The Left Hand Store" and Disney's Pin Traders store.

Hint 63: On the large statue of Mickey and Minnie, Mickey wears a classic Mickey pin on his tie.

Hint 64: On Donald's statue, a red, white, and blue classic Mickey pin is on the upper right side of Donald's duffel bag. You'll find a second classic Mickey, a red one, at the front of Donald's purple suitcase, on the inside of one of the black Mickey-shaped pins spilling out of the suitcase.

– Tren-D

Hint 65: Look for Hidden (and decorative) classic Mickeys on the merchandise tables in the store. You can find decent Hidden Mickeys on the tops and sides of various tables.

Hint 66: Classic Mickeys are repeated in sections of framed wallpaper artwork inside the store.

Hint 67: A tiny black classic Mickey is on a female mannequin's cheek, under the left eye.

Hint 68: Minnie Mouse is painted on several columns inside the store in a variety of costumes and poses. In three of these paintings, she sports accessories adorned with Hidden Mickeys. In one, she wears an upside-down classic (Hidden) Mickey ring and clothing with purple decorative classic Mickeys. In another, she wears a Mickey watch and enjoys a decorative Mickey lollipop. In a third painting, Minnie's necklace has a small, gold classic Mickey pendant that stands out against her green outfit. (Other Mickey images in paintings of Minnie are decorative, not Hidden.)

Hint 69: A blue paint-splash classic Mickey is high on the wall inside the store near the entrance from the Marketplace Co-Op. If you enter the store from the main promenade, the image is on the upper wall to the right.

Hint 70: A yellow side profile of Mickey Mouse is at the top - maybe it's the clasp? -

of Minnie's handbag. Minnie is painted on a "Cast Members Only" door at the rear of the store.

Hint 71: On the check-out countertop to the right as you enter from the outside promenade, smile at a reference to Mickey and Minnie. On the side closest to the main entrance, and near the angle of the countertop, "M M + M M" is carved into the counter.

Hint 72: Near the end of the left side of the check-out countertop, circle impressions form a classic Mickey. (The circles are all the same size, but this image is accepted by guests and Cast Members as a Hidden Mickey.)

– Marketplace Co-Op

Hint 73: Outside the entrance to the Marketplace Co-Op, you'll find a classic Mickey repeated in the white picket fence bordering the Disney Vacation Club display.

Hint 74: Along the main inside corridor of Marketplace Co-Op, a red classic Mickey is at the bottom of the overhead sign for "The Trophy Room."

Hint 75: Inside the D-Tech on Demand shop, classic Hidden Mickeys are in the "circuit board" background design of the work station touch screens.

Hint 76: In a display of faux airplane seats outside the Disney TAG shop, watch clouds float by the "windows." You'll be greeted by several different Hidden Mickeys: a cloud classic Mickey, holes in the clouds that make Mickey, and a side profile Hidden Mickey minus one ear.

Hint 77: Classic Mickeys hide in the clouds in the background of several paintings on the rear wall of the Caricature Booth near

– Ghirardelli Ice Cream
& Chocolate Shop

Hint 78: A dark side-profile image of Mickey looking to the left appears as a shadow in a painting on a rear wall of the shop (to the left as you enter). Look for a streetcar in the painting. The shadow is in the streetcar's second window from the left.

– Near the lake

Hint 79: Green chairs with classic Mickeys on top are scattered around outside in the Marketplace and near the Ghirardelli shop.

Hint 80: Several sections of the green fence around the lake have repeating classic Mickeys near the top of the railing.

– World of Disney

Hint 81: Blue classic Mickeys are on the far sides of the World of Disney entrance signs.

Hint 82: Light brown classic Mickeys can be found near the tops of the columns outside the store.

Hint 83: Classic Mickey holes are drilled in some of the metal posts that support the clothing racks.

Hint 84: In the high-ceilinged central room, behind the three little pigs floating overhead, a wall mural has a classic Mickey emblem above the doors of the Chinese Theater.

Hint 85: In the same room, the Pocahontas airship has an upside-down classic Mickey at the very bottom of the rear vertical tail fin, near where the tail fin connects to the body of the airship.

Hint 86: In the same room, you'll find a classic Mickey on a flag in the background of the Tweedle Dee and Tweedle Dum wall mural.

Hint 87: That mural also includes a classic Mickey on Tweedle Dee's apron.

Hint 88: In the same room of the store, some of the female mannequins have classic Mickey freckles under their eyes.

Hint 89: In this same room, four black classic Mickeys are high on a wall under air vents near the ceiling.

Hint 90: On the walls in the central Genie Room, blue classic Mickeys can be spotted in the compass paintings.

Hint 91: Also on the Genie Room walls, antique-looking maps on wood panels painted to look like tapestries have land masses that resemble the side profiles of Mickey Mouse, Winnie the Pooh, Goofy, and possibly Donald Duck. (Donald is a bit of a stretch.)

Hint 92: Just past the Villain Room is the Women's Apparel room at the right rear of the store. Glance up at the ceiling and find the moon surrounded by clouds, which resemble Mickey's "ears" and "nose" and seem to form a side-profile view of Mickey.

Hint 93: On a ceiling panel at the middle rear of the Women's Apparel room, a black classic Mickey spot is on Jessie's pants, on her lower right leg.

Hint 94: Glass window paintings are behind a check-out counter in the Princess Room. At the bottom of the second to the leftmost painting, look for a classic Mickey made of orange flowers, tilted slightly to the left.

Hint 95: A round metal emblem is used to cover holes or the ends of rods on the sides of some of the merchandise stands in the store. Tiny classic Mickeys are at the sides of the "World of Disney" banner on the emblem.

Hint 96: Display bins that hold merchandise in some of the rooms have classic Mickey-shaped feet and a band of classic Mickeys around the top. (Mickey bins like these can sometimes be found in other Disney stores as well.)

Hint 97: Near the restrooms at the far end of the store, a picture frame on the wall is lined with small classic Mickeys.

Hint 98: Near the World of Disney store, in an entrance to Disney Springs, there is a fountain surrounded by colorful flowers in clay pots. The fountain is composed of pots and bowls of varying sizes and shapes arranged so that water flows from one to another. A decorative topiary Mickey pours water into the topmost pot. Lower down, three clay pots form a classic Mickey when viewed from above.

– *T-REX*

Hint 99: A classic Mickey is formed by a clearing in the dirt (or sawdust) in the covered truck bed at the rear of the truck parked outside and to the right of the restaurant entrance.

Hint 100: Just inside the entrance and over the bar, a pink classic Mickey hides on the body of an octopus across from a green praying mantis.

WDW Casting Center

Hint 101: Classic Mickey holes can be seen in the upper outside walls of the Casting Center building. (These Hidden Mickeys can also be spotted from Interstate 4.)

WDW Miniature Golf Courses

– *Fantasia Gardens*

Hint 102: The tee-off areas on both courses are marked with classic Mickeys.

Hint 103: On the Gardens Course, the green at the 12th hole is shaped like a classic Mickey.

– *Winter Summerland*

Hint 104: Several classic Mickey ornaments hang in the decorations over both sides of the check-in area.

Hint 105: On the third hole of the Winter Course, candy canes, milk, and gingerbread men pop out of "Defrosty" (the cooler). One is a gingerbread cookie featuring Mickey ears.

Hint 106: On the 16th hole of the Winter Course, you'll find a Goofy nutcracker on the left side of the mantelpiece.

Hint 107: A Mickey Mouse gingerbread cookie pokes out from a stocking hanging on the right side of the same mantelpiece.

Hint 108: On the left side of the 16th hole of the Summer Course, Mickey and Minnie are sitting in a sleigh on the mantelpiece, along with Pluto. Since the 16th holes of both courses are close together, this mantelpiece is also visible from the 16th and 17th holes of the Winter Course.

Hint 109: Mickey pops out of the present on the 17th hole of the Winter Course when you putt the ball under the gift box. This Mickey is big, but he is hiding most of the time!

Hint 110: At least three classic Mickey ornaments hang on the Christmas tree at the 17th hole of the Summer Course.

Hint 111: A red classic-Mickey Christmas ornament hangs from a rafter above your right shoulder as you face the 18th tee of the Summer Course.

Near Epcot

Hint 112: Solar panels at the solar panel farm near Epcot are arranged as a huge classic Mickey. Not visible from the ground, you can admire the image from Google Earth, satellite maps, Geocaching maps, etc.

Near Celebration, Florida

Hint 113: On the west side of Interstate 4, south of exit 62 near Celebration, you'll find a huge classic Mickey atop an electrical transmission line pole.

Near the Magic Kingdom

Hint 114: A few miles northwest of the Magic Kingdom, a huge green classic Mickey made of groves of trees can only be seen from the air (or on a Google Earth image). The Hidden Mickey is in a field just off Highway 27 and near the 192 merge.

Chapter 8

Other Mickey Appearances

· · · · · · · · · · · ·

These Hidden Mickeys won't earn you any points, but you're bound to enjoy them if you're in the right place at the right time to see them.

★ Look for holiday Hidden Mickeys if you're at WDW during the Christmas season or any major holiday. For example, the "Osborne Family Spectacle of Dancing Lights" along the Streets of America in Disney's Hollywood Studios includes many hiding Mickeys.

★ Other "Hidden" Mickeys—décor and deliberate—appear with some regularity throughout WDW. Notice the Mickster on popcorn buckets, WDW brochures, maps and flags, Cast Member name tags, guestroom keys, pay telephones and phone books, menus, and restaurant and store receipts. The restaurants sometimes offer classic Mickey butter and margarine pats, pancakes and waffles, pizzas and pasta, as well as Mickeys on napkins and food trays. They also arrange dishes and condiments to form classic Mickeys, and some condiment containers are shaped like Mickey. You might notice classic Mickey holes in the backs of some high chairs.

The Mickey hat and ears on top of the "Earful Tower" are obvious to every visitor in the vicinity of Disney's Hollywood Studios. Many road signs on WDW Resort property sport Mickey ears and classic Mickey images, and WDW vehicles and monorails have Mickey Mouse images and insignia.

Cleaning personnel will often spray the ground, windows, furniture, and other items with three circles of cleaning solution (a classic Mickey) before the final cleansing. Or they may leave three wet Mickey Mouse circles or other Disney character images on the pavement after mopping! Mickey even decorates manhole covers, survey markers, and utility covers in the ground, as you've had a chance to find out for yourself on some of the scavenger hunts. In the evenings, you may encounter Mickey spotlight images on the pavement or on outside walls near WDW attractions.

Enjoy all these Mickeys as you explore WDW. And if you want to take some home with you, rest assured that you can always find "Hidden" Mickeys on souvenir mugs, merchandise bags and boxes, T-shirts, and Christmas tree ornaments sold in the Disney World shops. So even when you're far away from WDW, you can continue to enjoy Hidden Mickeys.

Note: There are usually some especially good Hidden Mickeys on souvenir mugs—tiny and hard to spot. The designs change every couple of years, and every time they come up with a new design, the Hidden Mickeys change.

Chapter 9

My Favorite Hidden Mickeys

• • • • • • • • • •

In this book, I've described over 1,100 Hidden Mickeys at Walt Disney World. I enjoy every one of them, but the following are extra special to me. They're special because of their uniqueness, their deep camouflage (which makes them especially hard to find), or the "Eureka!" response they elicit when I spot them—or any combination of the above. Here then are my Top Ten Hidden Mickeys and, not far behind, Ten Honorable Mentions. I apologize to you if your favorite Hidden Mickey is not (yet) on the lists below.

My Top Ten

1. Once-a-Year Mickey. *Under the Sea ~ Journey of The Little Mermaid*, Fantasyland, Magic Kingdom. Each year around noon on Mickey Mouse's birthday (November 18), sunlight shines through holes in the rock to form a classic Mickey on the wall of the inside entrance queue. Stay alert because Mickey might show up here at other times of the year! (Chap. 2, Clue 95)

2. Fern Mickey. The Garden Grill restaurant, The Land, Epcot. This Mickey hides behind a fern in the big mural inside the restaurant. When I outline this Mickey (a Cast Member often helps me by handing me a broom to reach it and then highlighting it with a flashlight), I have witnessed folks in the restaurant smile and shout, "I see him! Look, there's Mickey!" (Chap. 3, Clue 102)

3. Cloud Mickey. *Splash Mountain,* Frontierland, Magic Kingdom. This wonderful image of Mickey has reappeared! He looks so relaxed, floating in the clouds and contemplating the night sky. (Chap. 2, Clue 44)

4. Jafar Rock. *Gorilla Falls Exploration Trail,* Africa, Disney's Animal Kingdom. This three-dimensional head of Jafar is one of the most remarkable sculpted characters you'll see anywhere on Disney property. (Chap. 5, Clue 47)

5. Steamboat Willie Mickey. *Under the Sea ~ Journey of The Little Mermaid,* Fantasyland, Magic Kingdom. The Imagineers sculpted Mickey in his Steamboat Willie persona on a series of large rocks at the exit of the attraction. It's a tour de force in the world of Hidden Mickeys! (Chap. 2, Clue 103)

6. Roof Mickey. Near the Contemporary Resort. Sitting on the edge of the roof of a backstage building next to the Contemporary Resort, this playful Mickey welcomes you to the Magic Kingdom. When you're on the monorail, show this Mickey to fellow travelers so they can join in the fun! (Chap. 6, Clue 233)

7. Mickey in cement. Near *Astro Orbiter,* Tomorrowland, Magic Kingdom. A classic Mickey, lightly traced in cement, is growing more faint with time. Hard to find, but worth the effort! (Chap. 2, Clue 148)

8. Beam Mickey. Wilderness Lodge Villas. Mickey peeks out of a hole in an overhead beam in the Villas lobby. Outstanding effect! Most folks don't even know he's up there, hiding! (Chap. 6, Clue 195)

9. Grim Reaper Mickey. *Haunted Mansion,* Liberty Square, Magic Kingdom. A classic, this wonderful Mickey image has survived refurbishments and seems even better and spookier than ever! (Chap. 2, Clue 83)

314

10. Purple Tile Mickey. Polynesian Village Resort. A classic Mickey in tile hides on the counter of the Kona Island coffee bar. This one's a real winner, especially when you point it out to folks who've never seen it. It's hiding in plain sight! (Chap. 6, Clue 208)

Ten Honorable Mentions

1. Silhouette Mickey. *Splash Mountain*, Frontierland, Magic Kingdom. Keep your eyes peeled for this fleeting image of Mickey's head and ears that appears for just a second. Don't blink! (Chap. 2, Clue 40)

2. 3-D Volcano Mickey. *Toy Story Mania!*, Pixar Place, Disney's Hollywood Studios. While you're racking up points in the game, stay alert for this Hidden Mickey behind the target balloons. A convincing 3-D effect! (Chap. 4, Clue 2)

3. Sorcerer Mickey. At the rear of Blizzard Beach, Sorcerer Mickey is formed by stones jutting out from a bridge over *Cross Country Creek*. Very clever! (Chap. 7, Clue 9)

4. Globe Mickey. Yacht Club Resort. The lobby greeter will gladly give you hints if you have trouble spotting this great classic Mickey. It's faint and well-hidden! (Chap. 6, Clue 148)

5. Aquarium Rock Mickey. *The Seas with Nemo & Friends*, Future World, Epcot. At the bottom of the aquarium lies one (or more) classic Mickeys formed of rocks. Cast Members (and guest divers) do a great job of maintaining these images. (Chap. 3, Clue 109)

6. Moniker Mickey. Sunset Boulevard, Disney's Hollywood Studios. Stamped in the cement sidewalk are references to the year Mickey was "born," 1928, and his first name, "Mortimer." A cool homage to the Main Mouse! (Chap. 4, Clue 107)

7. Vine Mickey. Animal Kingdom Lodge. This green side-profile Mickey hides on the vine-covered column outside the rear lobby doors. Well-camouflaged and hard to find, but fun to spot. (Chap. 6, Clue 7)

8. Mickey in the Street. Main Street, U.S.A., Magic Kingdom. A properly proportioned classic Mickey is impressed in the side street, and countless folks walk over it, unaware. Don't tread on Mickey! (Chap. 2, Clue 188)

9. Bioluminescent Mickey. *Avatar Flight of Passage,* Pandora - The World of Avatar, Disney's Animal Kingdom. Appearing several times along the entrance queue and once on the ride, this unearthly classic Mickey invites us to experience a lush, foreign world that amazes our senses. (Chap. 5, Clues 1-3)

10. Tree grove Mickey. Near the Magic Kingdom. Check out this huge classic Mickey on Google Earth or from the air if you're flying over. It's a perfect Mickey shape, and you can't appreciate it from the ground. (Chap. 7, Clue 114)

Chapter 10

Don't Stop Now!

• • • • • • • • • • • • •

Hidden Mickey mania is contagious. The benign pastime of searching out Hidden Mickeys has escalated into a bona fide vacation mission for many Walt Disney World fans. I'm proud to include myself among them. Searching for images of the Main Mouse can enhance a solo trip to the parks or a vacation for the entire family. Little ones delight in spotting and greeting Mickey Mouse characters in the parks and restaurants. As children grow, the Hidden Mickey game is a natural evolution of their fondness for the Mouse.

Join the search! With alert eyes and mind, you can spot Hidden Mickey classics and new Hidden Mickeys just waiting to be found. Even beginners have happened upon a new, unreported Hidden Mickey or two. As new attractions open and older ones get refurbished, new Hidden Mickeys await discovery.

It may be just my imagination but I swear that every time I visit Walt Disney World, I spot a Hidden Mickey up in the clouds, watching over his domain! Do you think the Imagineers might actually have some influence on the atmosphere over Walt Disney World?

The Disney entertainment phenomenon is unique in many ways, and Hidden Mickey mania is one manifestation of Disney's universal appeal. Join in the fun! Maybe I'll see you at Walt Disney World, marveling (like me) at these Hidden Gems. They're waiting patiently for you to discover them.

Acknowledgements

No Hidden Mickey hunter works alone. While I've discovered many of the Hidden Mickeys in this book on my own—and personally verified every single one of them—finding Hidden Mickeys is an ongoing group effort. I am indebted to the following dedicated Hidden Mickey lovers for alerting me to a number of Hidden Mickeys I might otherwise have missed. Thanks to each and every one of you for putting me on the track of one or more of these WDW treasures and, in some cases, also helping me verify them. Extra special thanks to Sharon Dale for spotting over 240 Hidden Mickeys and to Jesse Kline for finding over 100 of these elusive gems!

Names in bold have spotted 10 or more. You can find each person's contribution(s) by visiting my website, www.HiddenMickeyGuy.com.

Candi A., Maxine A., Nancy A., Frank Abbamonte, Scott Abney, Alex Abrahamzon, Debbie Acres, Jonah Adams, Kaitlyn Rae Adams, Ron Adams, Sarah Adams, The Adornettos, **Nancy Ahlsen**, Michael Akers, Lindsey Albrecht, Sabaheta Alek-Finkelman, James Algatt, Katie Allen, Matt Allgaier, Anthony Almeyda, Jordan Altug, Brianna Alvarez, Eric and Danielle Ambielli, Cathy Ames, John Ames, Jonah Amundsen, Mariah Amundsen, Amy Amyot, Alex Anderson, Chelsea Anderson, Michelle Anderson, Robert Anderson, AJ Angeline, Robert Anschuetz, Sarah Anzjon, Kristin Archibald, Elena Argaluza, Jason and Tammy and Lily Armstrong, Stanley Arnold, Jennifer Ashley, Mark and Dean Ashwaite, Michelle Astuti, Tacey Atkinson, **Attractions Magazine**, Chloe Augustine, Barb B., Dan B., Devon B., Ian B., Jason B., Jessica B., Andrew Babb, Ryan Bachman, Priscilla Baer, Sarah Bagwell, Tony and Matthew and Caroline and Stephanie

Banzer, Salina Barbosa, Angie Barclay and kids, Mark Barnes, Sarah Barnes and son, Daniel Barrach, Mario Barrozo, Steven Madison Barrett, Vickie Barrett, Chris Barry, Diana Barry, Diane Barry, Samantha Barry, Anthony Bartiromo, Nicholas Bartoli, Johnny Bartolomeo, Fred Bastien, **James Baublitz**, Sarah Baywell, Penny and Jeff Beam, Eric Beaulieu, Adam Beauregard, Mike Beckerman, Brittany and Craig Bedelyon, Jonathan Beer, The Beesinger Family, Leila Beikmohamadi, **April Beisser**, Heather Beland, **Annmarie and David and Josh and Rick Benavidez**, Rich Benneau, Lauren Benson, Steve and Colleen and Michaela and Amanda Benson, The Benson Family, Richard Bent, Clark Benton, Jeffrey Berg, Patti Berg, Bryan and Stacy and Jenna and Barry Berger, Jason Berrang, Terry Berringer, David Berry, **David and Celia Berset**, Jenny Bess, Kristen Bevacqua, Tom Binder, Andy Birkett, Murray Bishop, Roberta Blackburn, Mark Blackie, **Erin Blackwell**, Trevor Blair, Louis Blanco, Isabel and Jeff Blank, **Nancy Blevins**, Fred Block, Laurie and Rebecca Bloodworth, The Bodmann Family, Jennifer Bogdan, **Tyler and Brandie Bolton**, Rich Bonneau, Michael Bonnett, Jr., Kevin Booton, Storie Borgman, Katie Borland, Craig Boudreaux, Ed Bouligny, Alicia Bourne, Wendy Bowen, The Bowles Family, Holly Bowling, Elizabeth Bowman, Alex Bowman, Nicole Bowman, Donna Brackin, Alan Brainard, Shane Braisdell, Brent Brandon, Tina Brannen, Leyla Brborich, Todd Breakey, David Breede, Matthew Brennan, J. Bridge, Christine Bristow, Patrick Broaddus, Ryan Brock, Colin Brooks, **Larry E. and Tanya Brooks**, Stuart Brooks, Daniel Brookwell, Stephen Brookwell, Chrissy Brown, Jaye Brown, Jeff Brown, Karen Brown and daughter, Peter Brown, Roberta Brown, The Brown Family, Emily Brubaker, John and Susan P. Bruederle, Paul Brune and family, Gabriella and Thierry and Matthieu

Bruxelle, Erica Bryant, The Buaas Family, Cheryl Buchanan, Matt Buchanan and son, Justin Bucks, Earl Burbridge, Nancy Burke, Lisa Burleson, Todd Busby, Jon Bushee, Brett Butcher, Ruth Butler and daughter, Giovanni C., Shari C., Kimberly Cabral, Villa Cadlle, Bret Caldwell, **Peter Caldwell**, Kerri Callahan, Sarah Callanan, Abigail Campbell, Anne Campbell, David Campbell, Lisa Campbell, Rob and Annabel Campbell, Michael-Lindsay-Alex and Hailey Campe, Craig Canady, Jason Cannons, Todd Carballo, Stan Carder, Chris Carlson, Cedric Caron, Deborah Carpenter, Gary Carr, James Carraher, K. A. Carter, Kacey Cassette, Robbie Castro, Jade and Dominic Cavalco, Alexis Cavileer, Mary Anne Ceci, Christina Cella, Kelly Challand, Austin Chanu, J. Chappa, Julie Chappa, Chloe Charette, Jim Cheslin, Catherine Chiarello, Nikki Christensen, Dana Christos, Alyssa Ciaccio, Vito Ciaccio, Andrew Ciampi, Michael Ciampi, Samantha Ciampi, Anne-Marie L. Clanton and family, Jay Andy Clark, Matt Clarke, Matthew Clemons, Malcolm Cleveland, John Clover, Lizzie Cochran, Alexa Cohen, Serena Anne Cohen, Zach Cohen, Rob Coile and daughter, Elizabeth Coler, John Coliton, Kent Collins, **Mary Jo Collins**, Michael Collins, William and Colleen Colmenares, Jason Colpitts, Eleanor Coltman, Greg Conlin, Joey Connors, Jeffrey Contompasis, Lindsay Contreras, Timmy Coogan, Ian Cordle, Cheryl Costello, Colleen Costello, Calvin Cotanche, Bill Cote, Sherrie Cotton, Angela Coutavas, Sara Cox, Karen Crabtree, David Craig, George Crippen, Rob Croskery, Lydia and Michael Cross, Catherine Crouch, Gary Cruise, Halley Crum, Denise and Tyler and Ashley Cruz, Kasie Culp, Erica Culver, Nancy Curl, Brian Currier, Traci Curth, Aiden D., Curtis D., Katie D., Nick D., Tyler Daganzo, Marie and Bruce Daigneault, Alicia Dakins, **Sharon and Chloe Dale**, John Anthony D'Alotto, Christina Darce and brother, Jim

320

Darling, Christopher Dash, Alex Davessar, David Davies, Shannon DeAraujo, Anthony Dearman, Bob Decker, Keenan DeFrisco, Amy Degenstein, Dwayne Degler, Michele DeGrace, Pam De Guzman and daughter, Bethany and Christine DeLaurentis, Robert Delgado, Sarah Del Grande, Dottie Del Signore, Mike Demopoulos, Jacob DePriest, Michael DeRose, Stephen DeSanto, Marcel Despres, Rich DeTeresa, Wanda Deveau, **Tim and Karen Devine**, Dania Dewese, Sondra Dewey, James Dezern, The DiBenedetto Family, Cara Di Cicco, Jennifer Dickey, Mary DiEuliis, The Digon Family, Doug Dillard, James and Jennifer DiMaggio, Suzannah DiMarzio, Max Dinan, Sam Dinan, Mark Dingman, Mario DiPlacido, Alexander Disney, Calvin Dolsay, Gina Dorkins, Marcus Dorothy, Michael Doucette, Jim Doyle, Sarah Dozert, Kelsey Draves, Dave Drumheller, Dave Drylie, Laura Dubberly, Jim Dufek, Angelica Dufer, James Duggan, Joey Duggan, Tom Durr, Abby Dwyer, Alex Dwyer, Ian Dwyer, Robert E., Jamillia Ear, John Early, Joy and Abigail Eats, Jason Ebels, Linda Eckwerth, Susan Edgington, The Familie Edmondson, Erik Edstrom, Seth Edward, Nicholas Elardo, M. Eldred, Amber Ellis, Karen Ellis, John Emmert, Eric England, Lillie England, Ben English, David and Elizabeth Epley, Kelly and Kimberly Erickson, Michael Ethridge, Nick Exley, Larissa F., Eric Fabian, Alyson Fair, Nick Falco, Adam Fanjoy, Ken Fanti, Ashley Fayett, Ronald and Gianna Fazio, Joshua and Krystina Fears, Gracie and Jamie Fenton, Alan and Craig Fergus, Ronald Ferraco, Kathy Fetters, Dom Fiandra, Kenney Fichter, Jim Finley, John Finley, Elaine Finnigan, Ashley Rae Fischer, Dennis Flath, Michelle Flege, Kendra Fleming, Chelsey Flood, Sharon Flood, Jessica Flowers, Anthony Flynn, Dave Flynn, Stephanie Foley, Taylor Fong, Carlos Font, Melissa and Jacob Forbes, Mario Forcellati, Eldon J. Forcey, Chet Ford, Terry Foreacre, Joseph Fortenbaugh, Mark

Fowle, Joe Franceschino, Sr. and Joe and Diane Franceschino, Jessica and Brent Fraser, Debbie Frazier, Eden Frazier, Matt Freeman, Connie Freese, Jordyn Freiermuth, T.J. Frey, Eli Fried, Devon Friedman, Rachel Friedman, Ryan and Fairen Frisinger, Chip Froelich, Jake Fruci, Anna and April and Anthony Fuchs, Diane Furtado, Shane G., Eric Gagnon, Jackie Gailey, Michelle Gala, **Jason Gall**, Jack Gallaher, Dave Gallant, Chrystine Gallegos, Justine Gamale, Traci Garber, Traci Gardellis, Brad Garfinkel, Marilyn Garfinkel, Scott Garland, Gunnar Garner, Tony Garon, Melissa Garrigus, Kristen Gartrell, Terry and Julia Garvey, Ryan Gatewood, Christy Gattis, Adam Geaneas, Anthony Gentile, Rick Giancarlo, Pauline Gibson, Kaela and Ryan and Jake Gilbert, Ethan Giles, Owen Gilley, Alana Girard, **James Girard,** Ryan Glynn, **Tyler Glynn**, Chase Goeser, Mark Goldhaber, Nathan Goley, Jeremiah Good, Ty Goode, Andrew Goodwill, Jack Goodwill, June Goodwill, William Goodwill, Vanessa Gordon, Trevor Goren, James and Edward Goring, Alyssa Gormish, Ryan Goukler, The Graebner Children, Josh Graham, Michele Gramm, Jeff and Joyce Grant, Todd Grasley, Tim Grassey, Dani Gray, Jim Greenhouse, Mark Greenwald, Rick Gregg, Adam Gregorich, Bill Griffin, George Griffin, Robert Grohman, Werner Grundlingh, Louis C. Guidry, Lorri Gumanow, Amanda Gunn, Elizabeth Gutman, Ryan Gutzat, Chris and Cindy H., Christine H., Cindy H., Rick Haas, Daniel Hadden, Evan Hade, The Hade Family, Brandi Hall, Byron Hall, Gracie and Dana Hall, Lydia Hall, Melanie Hall, Michael Halverson, Mike Hamilton, Shannon Hamilton, Theresa Hamway, James Hansen, Jake Hardin, Elsa Harding, Donna Hardter, Ray Harkness, Ed Harriger, Stephen Harris, Alan Harrison, Beth Harrison, **Stephanie Harrison**, Brian Harshberger, Grant Hart and brother, David Hartzell, Bernice Hasher, Laura and

Ross Haston, Bryan Hauser, Mike Hawkins, Abbi Hawthorne, Debbie Hayden, Colin Healy, Sean Heard, Ryan Hecht, Mary Heidenberg, Kurt Heinecke, Haley Heintz, Claudia and Ralph Hemsley, Carrie Henderson, Sean Hendrix, Brian Henry, Denise Hernandez, Liz Hernandez, Otto Hernandez, Louise Herrick, **Iris and Zachary Herron**, Amanda Hertel, Jennifer Hess, Ricky Hett, Tobias Heyn, Meredith Hiatt, Beth Higginbotham, Aaron Hill, Jamie Lee Hindes, Jim Hines, Joan Hinkle, Mark Hitt, Jay Hobson, Matt Hochberg, Rick Hoefinghoff, Ed Hoffman, Paul Hoffman, Denise Hoffmann, sdmt Hogan, Chip Holland, Vivian Holland, Matt Holley, Michael Hollingsworth, Joyce Holroyd, Melanie Holtsman, Jamie Holz, Craig Hood, Deonna Hores, Jenny Horn, Jasmine Horning, Evelyn Horton, Noah Howard, Kim Howe, Jonathan Hoyle, Erik Hubbard, Josh Hudson, Keith Hudson, Tony Hudson, Emily and Lynette Huey, Elton Hughes, Brennan Huizinga, Amy Hunt, William Huntley, Kaitlyn Husak, Cameron Hutt, The Huwar and Fabanich Family, **Bill and Donna Iadonisi**, Dawn and Megan Ilsley, The Ilsley Family, Alex Inman, Andy Inserra, Mike Ireland, Sarah Ireland, Amanda Iseminger, James Ivers, Ashley Izzo, Andy Jackson, Graham Jackson, Mark Jackson, Scott Jackson and niece, Carley Jagel, Andy Jasinski, Mark Jeffries, Angela Jenkins, Troy Jewell, Eli and America Jimenez, Tammy Jimenez, Chris Johnson, Jessica Johnson, KJ Johnson, Kenneth Johnson, Rayanne Johnson, Trisha Johnson, Samantha and John and Brian Jonckheere, Brecken Jones, Laura Jones, The Jones Family, Tim Jones, Wendy Jones, Michael Jowett, Michelle June, Benjamin K., Julie K., Michael Kania, Gary Kaplow, Jon Karlowa, Debbie Karnes, Ray Kastner, Constance Katsafanas, Kathy Katsafanas, William Katzer, Kristin Kaylor, Dan Kearns, Brent William Kee, Aaron and Evan Keller, Gayle Keller, Jennifer Keller, Robert Keller, Declan Kelly, Devin Kelly, Jim Kelly, Steven

323

Kempa, Melanie Kemper, The Kemper Family, Deb Kendall, Jasmine Kennedy, John Kessel, Brian Keys, Heather Killough-Walden, Sam Kimport, Bonnie King, James King, Chris Kirchein, Rachel Kirk, Max Kirkpatrick, Maggie Kirkwood, Rochelle Klay, Aaron Klein, Cheryl Klein, Hilary Klein, Patty Klein, Patty and Patrick and Adam and Megan Klein, Paul and Michelle Klein, Mitchell Michini Klepac, **Jesse and Jordan Kline**, Jordan Kline, Sarah Kline, Steve Knapp, Kelsey Knee, Benjamin Knobloch, John Koerber, Deb Koma, Gloria Konsler, Rich Kordalski, Shirley Kordalski, Jack Koss, Jack and John and Christine Koss, Wendy Kraemer, Amy Krauss, Monte Kremin, Tim Kress, Chris Kretzman, Austin Kruckmeyer, Troy Kubes, Ed Kulzer, Ali and Jennifer Kurtz, Matthew Kushner, Jackie Kushnier, Katie Kushnier, Brenden L., Nathan L., Mikey Laing, **Leah Lakatosh,** Brian Lake, Joshua Lake, Paul Lalli, Kim Lamb, Anne Langlotz, Brian Lanier, Meris Larkins, **Bev and Scott and Dick Larson**, Tim Larson, Richard Lathrop, Allison Laudage, Rebecca Lawler, Julie Lawrence, Daniel Lawson, Lea Ann Lavy, Dr. E. Kye Layton, Melanie LeBlanc, Russell LeBlanc, Will LeBlanc, Joshua Lehrer, Becca Leipzig, Meghan and Chris Lemmo, Justin Lemonds, Kathryn Leonard, Lisa Leonard, Jennifer Leone, AJ Leong, Brian Leong, Linda Lesar, Angie Leslie, Jessica Levenson, **Justin Lewicki**, Billy Lewis, Bradley Lewis, Luke Licygiewicz, Taricia Lightfoot, Kyle Lighting, The Lindberg Family, Beth Lindemann, Chuck Lionberger, Jeffrey Lipack, Jenn Lisack, Elaine Litten, Louise Lloyd, Sara Lodgen, C. Loesch, Bryan Long, Christie Long, Kristen Long, J. Scott Lopes, Jamie Lopez, **Marc and Josiah Lorenzo**, Emily Lounds, Matthew Lounds, **Jeff Love**, Stephen Lovelette, John Lovett, Kent and Pam Low, Ashley Lowe, Nick Lowman, Sam Loynes, The Luckner Family, Ash Lux, Jack Lynch, Jennifer Lynch, Jim Lyon, Will Lyon, Linda Mac, Sharon Machuga (and Mei Li), Alexander Mack,

Chris Macri, Michelle MacVane, Keri Madeira, Cholle Madere, Dusty Madere, Hope Madere, Karen Madere, Mason Madere, Shane Madere, Andy Madsen, Beci Mahnken, John Majcherek, Austin Malone, Michael Manall, Salvatore Manente, Katherine Manetta, Sharla Manglass, Brent Manley, Brett Manley, Adam Manno, Kristy Mantarro, Frank Marando, Lindsay Marcus, Jeff Margheim, Alisha Markle, Michael Marla, Vanessa Marquez, John and Stephanie Marshall, Drake Martin, Jeffrey Martin, John N. Martin, Jr., Breanne Martine, Brian Martsolf, Ginny Massoni, Jake Massoni, James Massoni, Brooke Matinides, Pam May, Erin Maynard, Allison and Andy Mayo, Amy Mazzela, Greg Mazzella, Kelly McAdams, Isaiah McAllister, Aurora McBride, Kevin McCarey, Alexander McClintick, The McCully Family, Mark McCurry, Chris McDaniel, Matthew and William McDaniel, Fawn and Holden McDonald, Mark McDonald, Chris McDonnell, Dawson McFarlin, Steve McGee, Meradith McGee-Hale (and Carter), Jessica McGilvary, Sarah McGovern, Saffron McGregor, Cameron McGuire, Billy and Zoe McInerney, Andrea McKenna, Carrie McLaren, Ryan - Rachel - Samantha and Robert McMillan, **Donna McMurrey**, Allissa McNair, Michala McNair, JerriAnne and Susan McPherson, Jill Meadows, Doug Means, Mark Medley, Joseph Mehr, **Matt Mellarkey**, Andrew Melville, Amy Mentz, Brian Mentz, Tammy Metz, Sharon Meyer, Kim Michaux, **Bill and Kari Middeke**, H. Mildonian, Bill Miles, Toni-Lynn Miles, William Miles, Julie Millan, Alexis Miller, Geoff Miller, Herb Miller, Krista and Maeve Miller, Rich Miller, Todd and Jennifer and Sean Miller, Stephen and Brianna Millevoi, Patti Minden, David Mitchell, Jager Mitchell, Sandy Modesitt, Aruna Mohan, Perry Molinoff, Kelly Monaghan, Claire Monahan, Lou Mongello, Michele Moody, Jennifer Moon, Joy Mooney, David Moore,

Rick Moore, Sharon Moore, Ron Moorhouse, Marc Moran, Denise Morelli, Mickey Morgan, The Moriarty Family, Rick Morin, Patti Lel Morris, Joseph Moschinger, Phil Motto, Scott Mueller, The Muklewicz Family, Ed Muller, Christina Muller, Carla Mullin, Brodie Mumphrey, Baseer Muqri, Lori Murch, Christine Murphy, Marty Murray and son, Brenda N., L. Naizer, Lindsey Naizer, Kurt Nank, Hannah and Ed Naughton, Anthony and Kristin Neglia, Leslie Nelson, **Michael Nemeroff**, Brayson Nesbitt, Mandy Newby, Jeff Newcomb, Mary Newell, Amy Newfield, Victoria Newhuis, Benjamin and Aden Newman, Devon Newport, Debbie Newton, Kortnie Marie Nieves, Darrin Nilsson, Joe Nixon, Ashley Nolf, Dennis Nordling, Annette Nuenke, Cheryl Nutter, Andrew and Matthew Nypower, Denise O., Andrew O'Brien, Erin O'Brien, George O'Brien, Scott O'Donnell, Eileen Knight Ogle, Steve Okeefe, Jeff Oldham, David Oliver, Mitch Oliver, Giovanni Oliveras, Beth Olliges, Kim Olsen, Bob Ondercik, Bobby Ondercik, Rita Ondercik, Sheri Ondercik, Susie Ondercik, A. O'Neill, Sarah and Jim Opaleski, Lisa O'Reilly, Nicole O'Reilly, Gwen Orilio, Justin Orilio, Rodrigo and Alejandro and Rogelio Orta, Katie Ortynsky, Greg Ostravich, Joy Ousterout, The Outra Family, Denise Owen, Annette Owens, Charles Owens, Jake Owens, Annie P., Curtis P., Dom P., Josh P., Kristin P., Melissa P., Glenn and Vickie Pacheco, Bill Padonisi, Andrew Painter, Doreen Pakidis, Brad and Brittany Paliswat, Jessica Paneral, Benoit Paquin, Nancy Paris, Caleb Parry, Laura Pasquali, Tom Pasquali, Calley Pate, Bob and Maryellen Paton, Chad and Megan Paton Evans, Sam and Lucy and Kimberly Paton Vegter, Alex Patrick, Brian Patterson, Drew Patterson, Kyla and Jen Patton, Lori Payne, Denise Peczinka, Jonathan Peczinka, Tawny L. Peedin, Glenn Peeters, Natalie Pence, Liz Penland and daughter, **Maya Perez, Octavio Perez, Suzanne**

Perez, Todd Perlmutter, Matt Perkins, Caleb Perry, Jenny Perry, John Perry III, John Perry IV, Christine Peruski, Mark Petar, Sheila Peter, Kristina Peterson, Lucy Peterson, Tony and Kara Peterson, Steve Petty, Patrick Phelan, Melanie and Tessa Pickett, Martin Pierce, Victoria Pike, Ray Pilgrim, Brooke Pimental, Linda Pinto, Sara Pirraglia, Tony Pirrelli, Susan Pitts, Linda Pizzuro, Amanda Plante, Cynthia Platt and family, Brian Policano, Krista Porter, Roberta Powers, Al Prete, Karen and Grace Price, Katherine Price, Kirby Price, Nathan Price, Walt Prindle, Hayden Pronto-Hussey, Caleb Pryor, Matt Pucci, Wendy Pugh-Hummel, Todd Pushman, Erica R., Tessa R., Tim Rachuba, Deb Ragno, Richard Rando, Nicholas Ranger, Kolding Rasmussen, Chris Rathsack, Brendan Ratner, Carol Ray, Sharon Reedy, Stacy Reedy, James Reen, Derrick Rees, Amber Reeves, Davis Reeves, Len Reeves, Lynne Reilly, Johnny and Jyle Reis, Michael Remy, Kathy Riccardi, Chris Ricci, Nik Ricci, Mikey Ricco, Richie Rich, Bob Richmond, D. Richmond, Richard Rick, Chuck and Sharon Ridgely, Sarah Ridgway-Rees, Brian Rigsby, Ron Riley, Antonio Riquelme, Jose Riquelme, Rob and Kathy Risavy, Bryan Rivera, Shawn Robertson, Joy E. Robertson-Finley, Andy and Jay and Angel Robey, Joseph Robinson, Lauren Robinson, Lawrence Robinson, Lawrence Robson, S. Rodriguez, Lauren Roeser-Nordling, Geoff Rogos, Terry Rohrer, Robyn Romine, Nick Rosa, Clara Rosadas, Kimberly Rosati, Emily Rose, Jackie and Matt Roseboom, Nancy Rosenberg, Trent Routien, Teresa Rovery, Timothy Rowe, Mitch Rozetar, Kathy Rubin, Chris Rudolph, James Rudolph, Jim Rudolph, Annmarie Rumford, Shauna Rupert-Sessions, Ed Russell, Christine Russo, Steve Russo, Callie S., Heather S., Ken S., Steve S., Tom S. and Terri, Robin Sackevich, I and Y Sakurada, Andy Salerno, Ashley Saliba, Anthony Salzano, Peter Samilenko, Sheila Sanders, Tami Sanker, Christina Santoro, Hannah

Savage, Rachel Savage, Andrew Savers, Dee Dee Scarborough, Jackie Scheibis, Natalee and Lauren Schell, The Scheuher Family, John Schiaparelli, Josh Schickler, Matt Schimkus, Ashlea Schneider, Julie Schneider, **Sherrie Schoening**, Ashley Schultz, Hank Schultz, Steve Schultz, Spencer Schweinfurth, Paschal and Di Sciarra, Bethany and Michael Scibetta, Carol Scopa, Mike Scopa, Jeri Scott, Keira Scott, Liam and Michelle Scribner-MacLean, Todd Seales, Jack Seidenberg, Steve Seifert, David and Aubree Serkoch, Debbi Sessa, Trent Sexton, Khrys Sganga, Chris Shank, The Shank Family (Angela, Christopher, and Shane), Leslie Sharkey, John Sheehan, Randy Shelton, William Shelton, Yinan Shentu, Susan Shirey, Bob Shoemaker, Faith and Abby Short, Bret Shortall, Andy Shull, Bill and Kim Shultz, Stephanie Shultz, Scott Siblovin, Josh Siegel, Scott Sigouin, Deb Silhan, Tyler Silhan, Rick Simard, Stephen Simmons, Steve Simmons, James Simon, KJ Simpson, **Jimmy Sisson**, Alexander Sjursaether, Tom Skaine, Bridget Skallet, **The Skazick Family from the UK**, **Nick Skiles**, Luke Skinner, Katie Slater, Mike Sluss, Michael Smart, Byon Smiddy, Laurie Smiley and grandsons, Bonnie Smith, Elaine Smith, Neil Smith, Rebecca Smith, John Snider, Michele Snoddy, Wesley Snyder, Owen Sokoloff and son, Jack Sorensen, Benjamin Soto, Roy Souders, Zach Souders, Douglas Southworth, Kitty Spangler, Megan Spellman, Ryan Spellman, Erica Spencer, Steve Spevak, Michele Sponagle, Kailah Spratt, Morgan Stair, Megan Stallings, Todd Standley, Rich - Diane - Andrew and James Stangle, Michael and Emily Steele, Kevin Stein, Joshua Steiner, Nicholas Steinhoff, Lindsey Stephens, Sharon Stevenson, Lori Stewart, Mark Sties, Skip and Susan and Jack Stinson, Lyndsey Stoehrer, Heather Stone, **Jay Stonefield**, Ben Stowell, Branson Strawderman, Allen Stroud, The Suarez Family, Cherie Sulko, Jill Sullivan, Chris and Cathy Sutherland,

Acknowledgements

David Sutton, Dan Swain, Riley Swanson, Jeff Swearingen, Jordan and Kenya Swiss, Joey Sylvester, Kathy Szczerba, Brittani T., Jen T., Jenni Tackett, Alex Taday, Sharon Tamplain, Joe Tanzillo, Kenzie Tapia, Jared Tavernari, Jordan Taylor, Karen Taylor, Leanne Taylor, Vance Taylor, Len Testa, Samantha and Mikayla Tewksbury, Alayna Theunissen, Brian Thomas, Kimmie Thomas, Roni Thomas-Patterson, Patsy Thomasson and family, Brian Thompson, Jake Thompson, Laura Thompson, Thomas M. Thompson, Pamela Thor, Emily and Kate Thorington, Albert Thweatt, Carter Thweatt, Max Thweatt, Erin Tickno, Paige Tiffany, Susie Tilley, **Martha Tischler**, Kristy and Scott and Jim and Kim Todd, Debra Tolsma and Alex, Holly Tomashek, Frank Tonra, Frank Tonra Jr., Frank Tonra III, Keith Tonra, Mallory Tonra, The Tonras, Kevin Toomey, Donald Torr, Whitney Townsend, Lauren and Steven Tracy, Kendra Trahan, **Scott Trask**, Nathan Trent, Jessica Trentacosta, Marcel Troost, Beverley Tuck, Brandon Tucker, Ashley Kennedy Turner, Glenn Turner, Matthew and Emma Turrisi, Derek Tyler, Charles Tyner, Thomas Tyner, Terry Ulrich, Luke Urso, Melissa Uzzilia, Nicole V, Stephen Valente, Sandra Valgardson, Shivani Varma, Adrian Vasquez, Helen Vaterlaws-Whiteside, Max-Emanuel Vingerhoets, Aninka van Staden, Frank van Wijk, Mason Vaughan, Chris Vaughn, **Wayne and Angie Vaughn**, Tairyn Velie, Tracy Vesel, Jim Vignola, The Vitrano Family, Jared Voegele, Fred Vosecky, Christpher and Alisha Vozella, Joshua W., Kym W., Deven Wagenhoffer, Maureen Wahtera, Caio Wakamatsu, Harry Walker, Jeanne Walker, Lucille Walker, Amanda Wallace, Michael Walsh, The Walsh Family, Grace Walter, Christine Wang, Matthew Wang, Jonathan Ward, Rachel Ward, Sharon Ward, Kathy Warner, Sean-Paul Warnick, Michael Waters, Christopher Watson, Matthew Watson, Mary Weaver, The Weaver Family, Andy Webb, Austin Weber, Dena

Weber, Eric Weber, Rebecca Webster, Scott Weideman, Fred Weiner, Joshua Weiss, Cheri Weitkamp, Max Weitkamp, The Welch Family, Brett Weldon, Carrie Welf, Matt Wells, Jed Werner, Robert Wescovich, Michelle Wesolowski, Dustine West, James West, John Weyrich, Matthew Whalen, Craig Wheeler, John Wheeler, Kate Whiddon, Shona Whiddon, Jennah and Noah Whitcomb, **Alena White**, Jared White, Jeff Whitlock, Katarina Whitmarsh, Sharon Whitney, Patricia Whitson, Dylan Whittemore, Jack Widman, Andrew Wierzbicki and sister, Victoria A. Wieting, Jim Wiggins, Becky Williams, Carla Williams, Chris Williams, Jason Williams, Kevin Williams, Scott Williams, Shannon Williams, Susan Williams, Darrel and Alexis Williamson, Ida Williamson, Garrett Willis, Johnson Willis, Deb Wills, Amory Wilson, Debbie Wilson, Jeannette Winner, Sara Witt, Darren Wittko, Brian Wojtowicz, Chrissy Wooding, Barb Wooldridge, Harry Wootan, Marli Worden, Elizabeth Worth, Brook Wozniak, Kassidy and Cody Wright, Jeanine Yamanaka, Lynn Yaw, Trevor Yeatts, Kevin Yee, Callum Young, Heather Young, Jonathon Young, Robert and Mary Jo Young, Alexandra Z., Adam Zaner, Meghann Zanotta, Eric Zech, Christianna Ziccardi, Lea Zich, Kristine Zolciak, Julie Zanolla, Catherine Zori,

AND

Aaron, Aimee, AJ, Al, Alan, Alanna, Alex, Alexis, Alison, Allie, Allison, Alpha, Alyssa, Amanda, Amber, Amelia, Amy, Andy, Anime Hockeygrrl, Ann, Anonymous, Anubis316, Areyna, Ariana, Ariel, Austin, azc, Barbara, Becky, Benjamin, Beth, Bill, Blair, Bob, Brad, Brad & Courtney, Brandon, Brandy, Brian, Brianne, Brooke, Bryan, Bryan@allaboutthemouse.com, Cailin, Caitlin, Caitlyn, Captain Mike, Carlos, Caroline, Carolyn, Casey, Cassie, Catherine, Cathreine, Caylie,

Charlene, Charles, Charlie, Charlotte, Cheryl, Chloe, Christopher, Christy, Cindy, Claire, Claudia, Cole, Colin, Colin-Kevin-Connor-Jodi-Nana and Pops, Colleen, Corey and mother-in-law, Courtney, Crispynoodle, C.T., Danielle, Darren, Dave, David, Debbie, Denise, Devon, Disney R&N, dloncub, Donna, Donna, Ear to There Tours, Eloy, Emily, Emma, Eric, Erik, Evan, Fernando, Foxx, Gage, Gen, Georgette, Gilbert, Giorgio, Giovanni, glaslady, Gracie, Graffix, Grant, Greg, Hanah, Hannah, Heidi, Hidden Kid, Hidden Mickster, Hoffman, Holden, Holly, Imercado, Jackie, jadekitty, Jake, Jake of Lake Mary, Jamie, Janelle, Jared, Jason, Jason (TrendyMagic), JB, Jean, Jeanette, JE.D, Jennah, Jennifer, Jeremy, Jessica, JG, Jim, Jodi and Nana and Pops, Joe, John, Jonathan, Jordan, Joseph, Josh, JP and son, Julie, Justin, Jyl, Kaela, Kasre, Katie, Kelly, Kelma, Ken, Kent, Keri, Kerri, Kevin, Kimberly, Kimmie, Kira, Kitzzy, Klara, Kristin, Kristy, Kyle, Laura, Laura and Joe, Lauren, Laurie, Lea, Lea Ann, Lia, Liam, Lisa, Liz, Luis, Luke, Lyinel, Lynn, Madison, Makenzie, Marc, Maria, Marissa, Mary Ann and daughter,Mason, Matt, matt@ attractionsmagazine.com, Matthew, Maureen, Max, Megan, Melanie, Melissa, Memoree, Mia, Michael, Michelle, Mike, MOEMOE55, Nao, Natalie, Nick, Nickole, Nicole, Noah, O'Malley, Patti, Peter, Quinten, Rachel, Rich, Rick, Rikki, rjf1423, Robert, Roman, Ronald, Rumbanana, Sam, Samantha, Samantha Ann, Sarah, Scott, Sean, Shannon, Sharon, Sharon from Auburn, She-Knows-CA, Sheri, Skiyalater, Snickers, Someone, Sonali, Stacey, Stacy, Stephanie, Susan, Taricia, Taylor, Thomas, Tim, Tony, Toontownkid4, Trevor, Tricia, Triffyboo, Trina, Tyler, Vicki, Vickie, Victoria, Wall-E, Wendy, Wendy and her Stepmom, Winnie, Zach, and Zachary

Index to Mickey's Hiding Places

• • • • • • • • • • • •

This Index includes only those rides, restaurants, hotels, and other places and attractions that harbor confirmed Hidden Mickeys. So, if the attraction you're looking for isn't included, Mickey isn't hiding there. Or if he is, I haven't yet spotted him.

– Steve Barrett

The following abbreviations appear in this Index:

AK	-	Disney's Animal Kingdom
DS	-	Disney Springs
E	-	Epcot
HS	-	Disney's Hollywood Studios
MK	-	Magic Kingdom
R	-	Resort venue
WP	-	Water Park

O

P

R

Walt Disney World's Hidden Mickeys